William Hadfield

Brazil and the River Plate in 1868

William Hadfield

Brazil and the River Plate in 1868

ISBN/EAN: 9783744790291

Printed in Europe, USA, Canada, Australia, Japan

Cover: Foto ©Andreas Hilbeck / pixelio.de

More available books at **www.hansebooks.com**

Dr. Gunning's House, overlooking the Valley of Macacos

BRAZIL

AND

THE RIVER PLATE

IN 1868:

BY

WILLIAM HADFIELD,

SHOWING THE PROGRESS OF THOSE COUNTRIES
SINCE HIS FORMER VISIT IN 1853.

LONDON:
BATES, HENDY AND CO., 4, OLD JEWRY, E.C.
1869.   ENT. STA. HALL.

CONTENTS.

The Voyage Out	9
The City of Monte Video	25
The City of Rio de Janeiro	31
The War in Paraguay	45
The Province of San Paulo	51
The San Paulo Railway	55
The City of San Paulo	66
San Paulo to Santos and Rio de Janeiro	83
Trip to Juiz de Fora.—The Don Pedro Segundo Railway	86
Rio de Janeiro to the River Plate, Second Trip	99
City of Buenos Ayres	103
Buenos Ayres to Colonia—Estanzuella	107
Trip on the Central Argentine Railway	112
The Western Railway of Buenos Ayres	125
Buenos Ayres—Second Notice	131
Progress of Steam Navigation on La Plata	142
Railways in the River Plate	146
Emigration to Brazil	154
Emigration to the River Plate	158
Railways in Brazil	164
Commerce of Brazil and the River Plate	173
The River Amazon	185
Telegraphic Communications	197
Religious Institutions	200
The Affluents of La Plata	203
The Republic of Paraguay	206
Brazilian Currency	217
Argentine Finances	231
The Port and Harbour of Santos	239
The Voyage Home	245
Appendix of Official and other Documents	253

PREFACE.

ERRATA.

Page 132.—For Club " El Temple " read " Del Parque."
Page 167.—Transpose in table words "Revenue" and " Working."
Page 169.—For " £150,000 " read " £15,000."

Since the year 1864, when my former work was published, a large amount of English capital has been invested in various enterprises connected with Brazil and the River Plate, and particularly for the construction of railways, the formation of banks, and the promotion of steam navigation on the great Rivers communicating with the interior. If the results have not, in several instances, proved wholly satisfactory as regards the

PREFACE.

This work makes no pretentions to literary merit, but, as its title indicates, is simply a narrative descriptive of the progress of the countries specially referred to, which, though England has long maintained intimate commercial relations with them, are still but very imperfectly known to the British public. In the Old World generations follow each other without any very perceptible alteration being observable in the characteristic surroundings, but in the New World, as America is still termed, a few years often effect changes of the most important and striking description. This is notably the case as respects Brazil and the River Plate, the growth of which has been very remarkable.

Since the year 1854, when my former work was published, a large amount of English capital has been invested in various enterprises connected with Brazil and the River Plate, and particularly for the construction of railways, the formation of banks, and the promotion of steam navigation on the great Rivers communicating with the interior. If the results have not, in several instances, proved wholly satisfactory as regards the distribution of dividends, the fact is in a considerable degree, if not entirely, owing to mismanagement of some kind or other; and I think there can be no doubt that a prosperous future yet lies before all the companies in question. On the other hand, large gains have been secured, showing that those regions present a profitable and wide field for the futher employment of our surplus capital.

The commercial tendencies of Brazil and the Platine States are most liberal, and their policy is the very opposite of that pursued under the exclusive domination of Portugal and Spain. The Empire, not long since, received the approval of all civilised nations for its decree opening up the waters of the noble Amazon to free commerce, and the unrestricted navigation of the upper riverine streams will be one of the chief advantages the victory of the allies in the present war will confer upon mankind.

The extent of territory embraced within the limits of Brazil, and what are commonly called the Platine States, cannot easily be realised by those who have never travelled out of Europe; and it is equally difficult to convey any adequate idea of their wonderful fertility and productiveness. Nature has blessed them with her choicest gifts, and, to take the highest rank amongst the nations, their sole want is increased population; and this is precisely what overcrowded Europe can very well spare. I am glad to be able to state that the respective Governments are fully impressed with the necessity of adopting comprehensive and effective measures with a view to attracting emigrants to their shores.

My intended movements during my visit were much interfered with by the cholera in the Plate and the protracted duration of hostilities in Paraguay, but I was enabled to satisfy myself of the complete realisation in 1868 of my most sanguine predictions in 1853.

BRAZIL AND THE RIVER PLATE

IN

1868.

THE VOYAGE OUT.

A BEATEN track does not present the same novelty as a fresh one, except in the case of countries in what is still termed the New World, and which are again about to be described. It was in 1853 I last visited Brazil and the River Plate, and published my observations upon them. An interval of fifteen years has wrought many changes and produced wonderful progress there, and if the Southern portion of the American Continent has not kept pace with the Northern it may be chiefly ascribed to the continued great influx of emigrant population to the latter from all parts of Europe, but consisting chiefly of the Anglo-Saxon race. From this cause, even the loss of at least a million of American citizens by the great civil war has caused no perceptible diminution in the American census, because it is constantly replenished from Europe. The African race has, however, come to the surface in a most unlooked-for manner, their shackles having been removed by a violent shock, which has, for a time at least, caused great social disturbance, and left the Southern States more or less at the mercy of the "niggers," as the blacks are generally termed. What may be the ultimate result, or how things will "settle down," is yet a problem to be solved. Meantime, slavery in Brazil remains a domestic institution, but it is doomed to inevitable extinction. The process of emancipation will be watched with much interest by all who desire to see the Brazilian Empire rise to the position it is capable of attaining. The tide of emigration to Brazil, spite of this disadvantage, has, however, fairly set in, and the subject will be treated of in its proper place. Happily, in the River Plate there exists no such hindrance to the development of free labour, for which it also presents a boundless field, and it will be the study of the writer to show how a portion, at all events, of the surplus population of Europe can be located there, to the great advantage of those who embrace the opening as well as of the country itself, whose chief and most urgent want is labour. The Paraguayan war and the terrible ravages of the cholera have been a great drawback to internal improvement in the Argentine Republic, but it is gratifying to think that the encouraging picture drawn by the writer on his first visit to the Plate has been more than realised —the motto of the Platine States should now be "*Peace and Progress.*" The "log" of an outward-bound passenger on board an ocean steamer now possesses but little interest; still, a record of the changes which have taken place in the means of transit since my last voyage, made fifteen years ago, may be worthy of notice, and will also afford information to those who contemplate a trip to Brazil or the River Plate. Success does not always attend even the best organised and most promising enterprises, but all experience had even then proved that there was ample scope for the employment of capital in promoting intercourse by means of steam with those countries that can only be reached by crossing the ocean. The South American Company, with which at that time I was connected, started under unfortunate circumstances. Ships were high in price, and rates of fuel were exorbitant by reason of the Crimean War. They lost in addition two of their steamers in a most unlooked-for manner, which sadly deranged their operations; but emphatically the two grave errors committed by the company were, first, in building more ships than they could raise capital to pay for; and, secondly, in abandoning the line after their experience had thus been paid for, and at the very moment when the traffic was becoming lucrative; for there can be no question that had they continued to run their steamers, instead of being seduced by the tempting terms of charter offered by Government, they would now have been in existence as a powerful company, paying good dividends. This was not to be however, and on the abandonment of the line, the Royal Mail Company was left without a competitor, and so enabled to realise large profits. Had this latter company read rightly the signs of the times, or met the requirements of *commerce* by despatching a steamer once a month from Liverpool, alternately with their regular mail from Southampton, they would not only have made more money, but to a considerable extent rendered themselves independent of Government subsidies. Their monopoly was exercised injuriously for the interests of the countries they were trading to, of which the French Emperor had the sagacity to take advantage, by subsidizing a company from Bordeaux, which has continued a most successful career, for it cannot be disputed that French steam navigation and the development of French commerce are almost entirely due to his Imperial Majetsy's remarkable prescience. As a natural consequence of increased facilities the passenger traffic with Brazil and the River Plate has wonderfully increased, and at times both lines are inconveniently crowded, the French one being for some reason preferred by South Americans and foreigners. Subsequently some unsuccessful attempts were made to establish other steam lines to Brazil. What was termed the Brokers' line was started from Liverpool to the River Plate, but it was not until Messrs. Lamport and Holt took the business in hand that private steam navigation was established on a firm basis from that port, and the fine fleet of the astronomical line now supersedes to a considerable extent the use of sailing ships. They have also entered into a contract with the British Government to despatch a mail steamer on the 20th of every month, the first (the Hipparchus) having left Liverpool on the 20th August last. Last on the list comes what is now generally known as "Tait's" line, on board one of the steamers of which, the City of Limerick, I am now embarked. They are fine steamers, with superior accommodation for first-class passengers at very moderate rates. A line from London, calling at Falmouth, has long been a favourite project, which Messrs. Tait have at length carried into effect with every prospect of success. They have wisely appreciated the growing requirements of population in Brazil and the River Plate, and are preparing to convey a number of third-class passengers by their steamers at a cheap rate. By confining their operations to Rio de Janeiro and the River Plate they are enabled to land goods and passengers at Monte Video and Buenos Ayres under 30 days. The importance of this line has been greatly enhanced by the contract entered into with the Belgian Government, under which the steamers are to call at Antwerp on their way out and home, the latter after landing passengers at Falmouth.*

This brief reference to the progress of steam navigation to Brazil and the River Plate will show the growth of passenger traffic during the last few years, and sufficiently indicate the great increase of commerce with these countries, not only as regards Great Britain, but also as respects continental ports, which will be more clearly illustrated in later portions of this volume; meantime, as an index to passenger traffic, it is my intention to obtain statistics from the different companies, and to present them in a table which will speak for itself. I may further remark that a steam company has been formed to run from Marseilles to the River Plate, and another between the United States and Brazil, the latter with a subsidy from these two Governments, which cannot fail to be mutually advantageous, and to promote the great object of emigration. Altogether a very large amount of capital is employed in linking this portion of the old world and the new by means of steam navigation. That it will further increase no one can doubt, particularly should the tide of emigration from Europe set in freely towards those countries, as I firmly believe will soon be the case.

And now we are moving along towards St. Vincent, —expecting to pass the island of Madeira to-morrow (24th December), five days out from Falmouth, almost entirely under steam, a breeze from the north-west, which favoured us for 24 hours after leaving Falmouth, having gradually headed us. The speed of the vessel

---

* Since writing the above, Messrs. Tait have parted with their exclusive interest in the line to a limited company, with a very influential board of direction, and of which Mr. Peter Tait is himself the chairman. No doubt this will lead to a yet more vigorous prosecution of an enterprise which has already and thus early secured so large a share of commercial patronage and support.

under steam only is 9 to 10 knots, but if we catch a good trade wind our progress southward ought to be very rapid. The City of Limerick is an excellent sea boat and all is very comfortable on board. My order of proceeding this time will still be something in the narrative form, as more adapted to the task I have set myself of recording the progress made, and the changes that have taken place since my last short visit to South America in 1853.

December 24*th*.—Passed close to the westward of Madeira, the island being enveloped in dense masses of black clouds, which poured forth their liquid streams, forming some dozen cascades of all sizes, one being conspicuous, reaching from the very top of the mountain down to the sea. No one would imagine the beauty and fertility of this island to judge from its western aspect, so different from the south-eastern side, which is well cultivated, and presents very pleasing views as you approach in that direction the Bay of Funchal. Madeira has changed very little I believe of late years, nor is it likely to do so with absurd quarantine laws in existence, which prevent vessels calling, and limits the number of visitors. The cultivation of sugar cane succeeded that of the vine, after the destruction of the latter, about the time of my former visit to the island, but to the detriment of its sanatory condition, as the refuse canes were allowed to rot, and impregnated the atmosphere offensively; otherwise, in its former glory of vines and fig trees, the island was a little garden of Hesperides. Now that real Madeira wine has become a scarce commodity connoisseurs praise it extensively, and it is to be hoped a few years will enable the island again to supply a genuine article instead of the spurious trash commonly sold under the name of **Madeira** wine. The real thing is only to be found in choice old cellars, and no doubt a glass of it is a very great treat.

Christmas Day, 1867.—Spent this day on the "deep blue sea," with a steady north-east trade blowing, which carries us swiftly along, and, if all goes well, we shall reach St. Vincent on Saturday by daylight, so as to get into the harbour and coal during the night. Nine days from Falmouth will be a very good passage. The weather has become warm, with bright sunny days and starlight nights, the days lengthening as we proceed southward. Certainly the change from an English winter is very sensibly felt, and must exercise a beneficial influence on the human frame. All traces of sea sickness have vanished from those of the passengers who were afflicted with it during the first few days, and they are now on deck, basking in the sunshine, but they will soon require the protection of awnings, as we shall then be within the tropics. Different opinions exist as to the comparative comfort of the paddle-wheel and screw. I prefer the latter, irrespective of its economy, as advantage can be taken of every favouring breeze, and except with the wind right aft, a screw steamer is steadier than a paddle wheel one. Many object to the continual thud of the screw and to the tremulous motion of the ship, but the latter is less felt in screw steamers than formerly, from the application of improved machinery and the placing of the screw well down in the water. On the other hand, the continual plunging of paddle wheels is tiresome, and they keep up a certain amount of spray which is not experienced with the screw. It is quite true that a ship is a thing "you never can be quiet in," whether propelled merely by sails, by paddle, or by screw—as everyone knows who has had experience, but this does not prevent sleep, or indulgence at times in that *dolce far niente* which is supposed to belong only to dwellers on land, under the soothing influence of an Italian sky. After all, how much we are indebted to steam, not only for comfort, but for our knowledge of distant countries. I remember several voyages made to Brazil in my early days, when 20 to 30 days were often taken to accomplish what we did yesterday in five days, —namely, passing the island of Madeira to gain the north-east trades.

St. Vincent.—Saturday evening, the 28th December, brought us safely into Porto Grande, the great coaling harbour for steamers bound to the South Atlantic, and where as many as twenty steamers a month are now coaled from the coaling establishment of Mr. Miller (also her Majesty's Consul for the Cape Verde Islands), who has at great expense built a high and low level pier, with large coal stores, a number of iron lighters and screw tugs which are employed to tow the coal barges alongside the steamers; in fact, it is impossible for anything to be more complete than the coaling arrangements here, which admit of sending off about 700 tons a day. Three vessels had to be coaled during Sunday, and two got away by night—ourselves, and a French steamer, bound from Marseilles to Brazil and the River Plate, with about 550 emigrants on board, chiefly for the River. We left, to complete her coaling the next day, the splendid new steamer the Sumatra, Captain Brown, belonging to the Pacific and Oriental Company, bound out to India, to take up her station between Bombay and Suez; she is 2,500 tons, and 500 horse power, both built by Denny Brothers, of Dumbarton. She has accommodation of the most luxurious kind for 150 first-class passengers, and is equipped in a most perfect manner. St. Vincent is her only coaling port between England and Bombay, and this was merely a matter of precaution, as she had on board sufficient to take her to India. A Russian screw corvette with a number of training cadets on board was also at anchor in the Bay when we arrived, but she sailed away southward about noon on Sunday. With the increasing demand for steam traffic to the southern hemisphere, the importance of Porto Grande as a coaling station cannot be overrated. We expected to have picked up some news from Brazil and the River Plate, but unfortunately the Royal Mail Company's steamer Seine (overdue a week) had not arrived, and various surmises were raised as to the cause of this unusual delay, which we shall only learn later on. The Brazil and River Plate Service, both by the above company and the French Messageries Imperiales, has been for many years performed with great regularity. Owing to the many steamers calling at St. Vincent, a good supply of fresh meat, fruit, eggs, &c., can now be obtained there, brought from the neighbouring islands, as St. Vincent itself continues as barren of verdure as ever. The town has extended itself somewhat, several new public buildings having been erected, including a Custom House, and some pretty cottages on the hill overlooking the harbour, for the use of Mr. Miller's numerous establishments. For the information of such of my readers as may not be conversant with the Cape Verde Islands, I reprint my remarks upon them contained in my former work already alluded to, as I shall also continue to do in other places, for a similar reason, besides the additional one of diffusing information as to countries with which we are so intimately linked by commercial and political ties. A submarine cable, connecting these Islands with Maderia and Lisbon, would be very useful, and will most probably come in time, as a link in the chain of our communications with South America and the coast of Africa. Its existence would shorten the time of receiving and transmitting news between England and Brazil very considerably, and the evils arising from such an event as the detention or loss of the Seine be greatly mitigated :—

The Cape Verds consist of seven principal islands, and were tolerably populous, but of late years have been subjected to a continuous emigration to South America and the West Indies, where, like the hardy mountaineers from Madeira, they are found most useful in tilling the soil, and in other laborious occupations; thus demonstrating the fallacy of the old notion, that laziness is the predominant element in the Spanish and Portuguese idiosyncracy. What appears to be a present disadvantage, in regard to this human flight from the Verds, may prove beneficial hereafter, when the Ilheos (as they are called) return to their homes, possessed of a little money wherewith to improve their social and moral condition. The islands produce wine, barilla, large quantities of orchilla weed, and cochineal, the cultivation of which is rapidly forming a more and more considerable item of export. Steam navigation will ere long bring them into much closer commercial contact with the world, and enhance the appreciation of their products and natural advantages. The climate is fine, though subject to occasional high temperature and frequent droughts. Despite the name Verds, suggestive of Arcadian animation, nothing can be more desolate than the appearance of the islands, as approached from the sea; bold, high rocks, against which the surge breaks violently, with mountains towering in the clouds, are general characteristics, to which those of the island of St. Vincent offer no exception. On our arrival the weather was thick, with drizzling rain, as we made Porto Grande; and only cleared up in time to enable us to see Bird Island, a most remarkable sugar-loaf rock, standing right in the entrance of the bay, after passing which we reached the anchorage ground in a few minutes. A more convenient little harbour can hardly be imagined, being nearly surrounded with hills (or mountains as they may be called), which protect it from all winds save the westward, where Bird Island stands as a huge beacon, most admirably adapted for a light-house, and on which it is to be hoped one will soon be placed. There is deep water close to the shore on most sides of the bay, that where the town is built being the shallowest; and here some wooden jetties are run out, having very extensive coal and patent fuel *depôts* close at hand where these combustibles are put into iron lighters, and sent off to the vessels. So beautifully clear is the water in the bay that you can see the bottom at a depth of from twenty to thirty feet, literally alive with fish of all kinds, but for which the people seem to care very little, either for home consumption or export, though there is no doubt that, in the latter direction, a large business might be done with profitable results.

Porto Grande must become a most important coaling station, situated as it is midway between Europe and South America, and close to the African coast. Several important steam companies have already adopted it, viz., the Royal Mail (Brazil), the General Screw, the Australian, as also the South American, and General Steam Navigation Company, whilst occasional steamers are, likewise, glad to touch at it. At the period at which I am writing, the Great Britain was the last that coaled here, on her way to Australia. In order to meet this increased demand, a proportionate degree of activity and exertion is observable on shore; and a large number of iron lighters, carrying from fifteen to forty tons each, are now in constant requisition, loaded, and ready to be taken alongside the steamers the instant they cast anchor. Unfortunately there is a very poor supply of water, the want of it having been the occasion of frequent emigration in the history of the islands; but it is understood to be attainable at a slight expense; and a small outlay conjointly made by the steam companies might not only procure a plentiful provision of this all-necessary element, but also other conveniences, essential to the comfort of passengers. There is no doubt that, as the place progresses, supplies of meat, fruit, and vegetables will be forwarded thither from the neighbouring islands, which are so productive that there is a considerable export of corn; and the cattle are numerous. Until lately fowls were only a penny a piece; and turtles abound. Hitherto there has been no regular marketable demand for such things; but one, and a large one too, is henceforth established, from the causes assigned, and will doubtless be regularly and economically supplied. The labourers here are chiefly free blacks and Kroomen, from the coast of Africa, most of whom speak English, and chatter away at a great rate, as they work in gangs, with a kind of boatswain over them, who uses a whistle to direct their toil—the movements of all the race of Ham to the days of Uncle Tom, being seemingly susceptible of regulation to musical noise of some sort or other; whether the "concord of sweet sounds," or what would appear to be such to more refined ears, does not greatly matter.

But for want of vegetation in its neighbourhood, a more picturesque little bay than Porto Grande can hardly be conceived. Towering a short distance above the town, is a kind of table mountain, some 2,500 feet high; and at the opposite side, forming the southwest entrance, is another very lofty one, remarkable as representing the colossal profile of a man lying on his back, à la Prometheus. He has his visage towards heaven, wherein there are generally soaring vultures enough to devour him up were he a trifle less tender than volcanic granite. The features are perfect, even to the eyebrows; and a very handsome profile it makes, though it does not appear that any tropical Æschylus has yet converted the material to the humblest legendary, much less epic, purpose. On the shore ground, forming the right side of the bay, looking towards the town, is a neat little monument, erected to the lamented lady of Colonel Cole, who died here on her way home from India. The spot where she lies is, from its quietude and seclusion, most meet for such a resting-place, there being a small, conical hill behind, with a cottage or two near, and a sprinkling of vegetation on the low ground between, serving to "keep her memory green" in the mind of many an ocean voyager in his halt at this half-way house between the younger and the elder world.

This little town was thrown back sadly by the epidemic which afflicted it in 1850 and decimated the population. During its continuance Mr. Miller, one of the few English residents, did so much in assisting the inhabitants as to elicit from the late Queen of Portugal the honour of a knighthood, in one of the first orders in her dominions. It requires no small degree of patience and philanthropy to aid the development of a place like this, labouring, as it does, under such great natural difficulties, and where everything has to be brought from a distance, there not being a tree or a blade of grass to be seen—nothing but dry, arid sand, or a burnt-up kind of soil. Undoubtedly, the heat is very great at times; and there are about three months of blowing, rainy weather, which is the only period when vessels might be subjected to inconvenience whilst coaling, as the southerly winds drive up a good deal of sea into the bay. There is an English Consul resident here, Mr. Rendall, who has done much to assist in bringing these islands into notice, and into comparative civilization; and, by so doing, has many times over reimbursed this country in the cost of his stipend of £400 a year, saying nothing of the services he has performed to shipping, in the ordinary discharge of his duties.

Cape Verds are a very numerous family of islands, called after a cape on the African coast (originally named Cabo Verde, or Green Cape, by the Portuguese), to which they lie contiguous, though at a considerable distance from each other in some cases. All are of volcanic formation—one, that of Fogo, or Fuego, once very celebrated as being visible, especially in the night time, at an immense distance at sea. The islands generally do not possess any very attractive points, being unlike Madeira and the Canaries in this respect, as well as in extent of population, that of the latter being four or five times more numerous than the others—say about 200,000 in one, 40,000 in the other case, though some statements make the inhabitants of the Verds considerably more. The islands are occasionally subject to shocks of earthquakes; and there was rather a strong one at Porto Grande the night before we left, supposed on board our vessel to be thunder, from the noise it made, though we were not aware until next day that a shock had been felt on shore. The chief product is salt, a valuable article for vessels trading to South America, though it is here manufactured by the somewhat primitive process of letting the sea-water into the lowlands, where the sun evaporates it. Though Porto Grande, in St. Vincent, is the great place for shipping, and as such almost the only place of interest for passengers in transit, Ribera Grande, in St. Jago, the principal island, and most southerly of the group, is the chief town, though it is at Porto Playa (often touched at by ships on the Indian voyage) that the Governor General resides, particularly in the dry season. The island second in importance, in point of size, is St. Nicholas, where are some small manufactories, in the shape of cotton-stuffs, leather, stockings, and other matters. The orchilla weed, however, is the great object of governmental interest, and its monopoly is said to yield some £60,000 per annum; the same wise policy that grasps at that interdicting the manufacture of wine, though grapes grow in profusion, and are of excellent quality for the production of a very acceptable beverage.

December 31*st*, 1867.—The last day of the old year is an event that calls for reflection and particularly at sea, when the mind is generally more open than elsewhere to receive impressions, and free to take into review the past—to enquire how the time has been spent. Few of us, probably, can answer this question satisfactorily, but at all events it is desirable to make the enquiry. There is no postman's knock at the door, no friends to see, nor any to seek us out. Our little world is the ship on which we are sailing, and those within it, the greater part of whom have been utter strangers to each other previous to embarkation. Selfishness under such circumstances finds its level, or is confined within very narrow bounds, and a common instinct draws every one together, until at the end of the voyage, when those who are only passengers part, and go each on his several mission, few in all liklihood ever to meet again in their various walks in life. Most leave friends behind, whom they look forward to rejoining, or they have friends to welcome them in the new countries to which they are speeding their way. The great ocean brings strikingly home to us the wondrous works of the Almighty Ruler of the Universe, and the littleness of man himself. Again, we are apt to forget the immensity of the ocean, which, as compared with the land, is computed at $145\tfrac{1}{2}$ million of statute miles against 51 million square statute miles of land, or a total of both of $196\tfrac{1}{2}$ millions. A little incident occurred this morning in our meeting the screw steamer Uruguay (which signalised twenty days out from the River Plate), one of the Liverpool line of steamers, making her way to St. Vincent to coal, and she will, no doubt, report us at home. Time did not afford opportunity for exchanging news, which would have been very acceptable on both sides. We also passed an American ship steering northward, being now in the track of vessels homeward bound, 10° 30' north latitude and 26° 30' east longitude; a fine steady breeze driving us, with the aid of the screw, fully eleven knots an hour.

January 4th, 1868.—We have crossed the line, gone through the variables, and are in the south-east trades. The air is cool and pleasant, and the ship making nearly twelve miles an hour, with a smooth sea and little motion—the perfection of sailing. There is a freshness about the Southern hemisphere which I have always enjoyed. Steady breezes and a clear sky, with light fleecy clouds. We passed several vessels yesterday standing to the northward, amongst them a fine Yankee screw corvette, which hoisted her number, but she was not in our signal book. Less than another week of this weather will take us into Rio de Janeiro, in somewhat over 20 days, which will be a very good passage, and we have certainly been very much favoured in having fair, moderate weather, with scarcely any rain, and no squalls. The great advantage of steam over sailing ships is not only much quicker passages, but running out of calms or variable winds, and making a straight course to the point of destination.

January 10th, 1868.—We made Cape Frio light, off Rio de Janeiro, about midnight, and came into harbour early this morning, twenty-one and a half days from Falmouth. After the usual formalities in connection with the health and custom-house departments, we steamed up to the coal island, and were soon moored alongside, ready for coaling and discharging cargo. There were fewer ships in the bay than I ever remember to have seen. Her Majesty's store-ship Egmont was lying there, and one or two other vessels of war. A splendid Spanish frigate, the Blanca, which had participated in the bombardment of Valparaiso, steamed out of harbour as we came in, but whither bound no one could say. On going on shore I found the landing place not much improved, and the custom-house formalities had increased in rigour, extending even to a charge on the small quantity of luggage required for a change whilst on shore. It is a mistake in an enlightened country like Brazil to subject passengers to such absurd regulations, which can bring in very little revenue and get the country a bad name. In other respects little or no restriction is experienced in going to or from the ship, either day or night. We found the news from the seat of war unsatisfactory as regards its progress, and, what was worse, we learned that the cholera was raging at Buenos Ayres, vessels from the River Plate being placed in quarantine on arrival at Rio; but the latter city was healthy, notwithstanding the great heat which, during the two days we remained in harbour, was most intense, the thermometer in the shade being over 90°. Working all night enabled the steamer to be ready to start again on Sunday morning, the 12th January, when we again sailed from Rio on our way to the River.

THE CITY OF MONTE VIDEO.

SEEING the accounts at Rio were not encouraging, I was advised to delay my trip southward, but as the River Plate was my ultimate destination, and my business pressing, I was desirous to reach Buenos Ayres as quickly as possible, taking Rio Janeiro on my return. So I continued on board the steamer, which left Rio on Sunday morning, the 12th January, 1868, and we came to anchor in Monte Video harbour at 1 p.m. on the 16th —a very good passage of four days and a few hours. The weather had been hot during the passage, giving us a foretaste of what we might look for here. The health inspector did not come off to us for three hours, a very annoying delay after the captain of a steamer has done his best to get quickly to his port, and to whom, as well as to his owners, hours are of consequence; but not so to officials in these countries. I believe I surmised correctly that the health officer was at dinner when we arrived, that he would take his siesta, and then come to look after us. As it was then getting past business hours, I preferred remaining cool and quiet on board the ship, but several of our passengers went on shore, and passed the night there, as it is difficult to get off after dark. The budget of news we received from the agents, who came on board after the health visit, made me wish I had taken the wise advice of Rio friends. The cholera was raging at Buenos Ayres and throughout the Argentine Republic, and appeared to be bad enough at Monte Video, in addition to which a revolution had broken out at Santa Fé against the Government, the rebels having actually got possession of Rosario, as well as some portion of the railway, whose metals they had partly torn up at one of the bridges, throwing them into the river below. It is difficult to account for this kind of wanton mischief, unless it was to show their contempt for civilized means of transit, for having reached Rosario, their policy should have been to keep the line open as a means of retreat in case of need, and then to have taken up the rails to impede troops who might be following them. I found Mr. and Mrs. Wheelwright at the Oriental Hotel, Monte Video, a new and handsome building erected since my last visit, and worthy any city in Europe, but unfortunately several of the inmates died of cholera there and it was afterwards deserted. The Oriental was full when we arrived, but we found comfortable quarters at the Gran Hotel Americano, also a large and handsome edifice lately built, nor can anything more strongly mark the advance of Monte Video than these two hotels in addition to those previously existing. The impressions conveyed in my former narrative as to the development of Monte Video were favourable, but I hardly expected to see the place grown half as large again since that time, which certainly is the case. Building of late years has taken extraordinary proportions here, and the price paid for choice spots in the city is something fabulous. Then again the streets have been all paved and flagged—roughly enough it must be confessed, but still they appear to answer the purpose for the peculiar description of traffic over them, and are a great improvement upon the sand and mud which existed before. During the few days I remained at Monte Video, everything was in a very miserable state, the mortality increasing and the telegrams from Buenos Ayres quite awful. I therefore resolved to return to Rio Janeiro, and wait a more favourable moment for prosecuting my mission. The heat was intense, and the minds of people so pre-occupied with the pestilence as to render it impossible to follow the object of my mission with any chance of success. The City of Limerick came up from Buenos Ayres on the morning of the 24th of January, and was released from quarantine in the afternoon, when Captain Peters came on shore, and his report confirmed my previous views as to returning to Rio; so at 5 p.m. I went on board with him. We got under weigh at sunset, with a fresh breeze, and, passing Flores light, were off Maldonado light about 3 p.m.—a nasty navigation, with the island of Lobos dangerously near, on which there ought also to be a light. Daylight took us to the open sea, and four and a half days' steaming brought us again into Rio harbour on the morning of Wednesday, the 5th of February, when we were put to quarantine in what is called Three Fathom Bay, where we remained until the third morning, when we were released and steamed to the coal wharf.

Precisely three months after my first arrival in Rio, I left it again to return to the River Plate, whence the pestilence had departed and things resumed more or less their usual appearance. Monte Video had, however, been the scene of a dreadful tragedy—the murder of General Flores in open day—and the subsequent terrible retribution which followed that catastrophe. A gloom hung over the country, heightened by the impending bank crisis, and it seemed as if the spirit of evil had taken possession of the place. Whatever may have been the faults or errors of General Flores, he deserved a better fate at the hands of his countrymen. In forcing himself into power he only followed in the footsteps of others who had resorted to this unconstitutional mode of proceeding. During his dictatorship the country was perfectly tranquil and highly prosperous, nor was a single life sacrificed by him, although he knew he had many secret enemies. His personal courage was undoubted and evinced in many a bloody encounter in Paraguay, where he appeared to wear a charmed life, and had he been at all prepared the assassins might have found the old man more than a match for them. Altogether, this sad event has created a feeling in Monte Video which it will take long to recover from, nor is any confidence felt in the ability of the present rulers to overcome the difficulties of their position. It is a great pity so fine a country and so fair a city should be sacrificed to objects of mere personal ambition, and be the sport of every discontented chief or partisan who chooses to set himself in array against the Government; but unfortunately this is too much the case, nor do the people themselves rise to put down such a state of anarchy.

In alluding to the new buildings erected at Monte Video I omitted the Bolsa or Exchange, which is quite an ornament to the city, with its light, highly ornamented façade. The interior is of a quadrilateral form, providing a spacious hall where the business of the place is carried on, with brokers' offices on the ground floor, the upper storey being devoted to a tribunal of commerce and other public purposes. The cost of the building is stated at about 160,000 hard dollars, or £32,000 sterling, an instance of public spirit hardly to be found elsewhere in South America.

The only thing wanting to Monte Video is business, in which respect the contrast with Buenos Ayres is very much in favour of the latter. Nevertheless, the banks have gone into considerable extravagance in the way of architecture, the Italian Bank being conspicuous by a superfluity of marble. Indeed, the facility for issuing notes has evidently led to expenditure in "bricks and mortar" to an extent that must have greatly embarrassed the managers of these institutions when called upon to meet their paper in gold.

As to the cause of the money crisis there cannot be two opinions. In the first place, Government was wrong in allowing private issues of notes, and in the second place, in interfering when it came to a question of the banks meeting their notes in gold. A "forced currency," as it was then called, was sure to lead to a depreciation in the value of the paper and only postponed the evil day. It was a curious sight to see a guard of soldiers with fixed bayonets on duty round the doors of the Italian Bank, and a crowd of people waiting outside to receive specie payment of their notes. This process had already shut up several of the banks, and there was little hope of saving the Italian Bank, although great efforts were being made by the mercantile body to do so, as from the large number of Italian tradesmen doing business with the bank serious results might attend the closing of its doors. The wisest course would have been for all the banks to have followed in the wake of Mauá and Co. and closed their doors when they found themselves unable to meet the pressure for gold. This would have brought about some remedial action on the part of Government with a view to self-preservation.

Amongst other public improvements at Monte Video is a large market, a tramway for a few miles out of the city, and the commencement of a railway intended eventually to reach Durazno, but at present only a few miles can be completed, owing to the want of capital. Unfortunately, the Government is not in a position to assist any enterprise of this kind, spite of the large amount of Brazilian gold that has been poured into the place during the war. Altogether, Monte Video has an ordeal to go through that will require time and patience on the part of those who may have to conduct its affairs.

The Bay presents its usual animated appearance as regards the collection of ships and steamers, and a large sprinkling of foreign men-of-war, whose services have been much called into requisition of late, in order to protect foreign property; but in other respects there is a total absence of vitality or of actual business.

THE CITY OF RIO DE JANEIRO.

It cannot be said in this case, as in most others, that

"'Tis distance lends enchantment to the view;"—

for the nearer you approach this far-famed city, the more sensible are you to the beauties it unfolds. Strangers are always struck with the singularly picturesque appearance of the land approaching Rio de Janeiro, but once fairly in the bay they are bewildered at its great extent, surrounded on all sides by hills and mountains of every possible form, shape, and size, most of them clothed in luxuriant verdure to the summit. No picture or representation I have seen of the Bay of Rio does justice to the splendid panorama its scenery presents. Even those who have often approached it from the sea, so far from being tired of gazing, not only recognise old familiar points, but discover some new feature in the fairy-like landscape that had before escaped their notice. It varies very much according to the light and shade,—sunrise, noonday, and sunset each possessing peculiar marks of delighting beauty. In my former description of Rio occurs the following passage:—

> The city of Rio Janeiro extends some three miles along the southwest side of the bay, and being much intersected by hills, it is difficult to get a good view of the whole range, unless from the top of one of the mountains near the city, such as the celebrated "Corcovado," which stands out like a pulpit on the plain below, and is some 2,500 feet perpendicular. The view from this pulpit on a clear day is

superb, and I should almost say unequalled in the world: the city, with its numerous divisions and suburbs below you—the bay, extending as far as the eye can reach, until lost in the plain below the Organ Mountain—the sea, studded with numerous picturesque islands, with vessels looking like white specks upon it, and seen to a great distance—all together form a most enchanting picture, and amply repay the toil of an ascent. The mountain is of granite rock, like all others in this country, but thickly wooded almost to the summit, and you come out quite suddenly on the bare point before alluded to, so much resembling a pulpit. In consequence of the tortuous formation of the streets, constructed round the base of the hills, it is difficult to get more than a bird's-eye view of the city, on ground made by encroachment on the sea; consequently, the streets are low, without drainage, and in several of the back ones the water collects and stagnates, to the great detriment of health and comfort. Rio itself is a bad copy of Lisbon—streets at right angles, a large square facing the sea, and the suburbs extending up the hills which everywhere meet your eye. In Lisbon the streets are tolerably wide, but here they have built them so miserably narrow, that scarcely even one carriage can pass through, much less pass each other; and it is evident that such vehicles were never contemplated in the original formation of these streets. The only way of getting over the difficulty is for carriages coming into the city to take one line of streets, and those leaving it another, which they do, excluding omnibuses altogether from the principal thoroughfares. Improvements in this way were what I found most backward; indeed there was a marked falling-off in such respect since I was last here, and there seems a great want of municipal government.* In many

* The Bank, Exchange, Custom House, and Arsenal (of late years greatly extended) are in the Rua Direita. Besides these, the chief public edifices and the Imperial Palace, a plain brick building; the Old Palace, on the shore, used for public offices; a public hospital, alluded to elsewhere, erected in 1841; a national library, with 800,000 printed volumes, and many valuable MSS.; and a well-supported opera house, which has supplied Europe with some very popular performers, especially in the ballet line, as witness that general favourite, Madame Celeste, who came from Rio, in 1830, with her sister Constance, another danseuse, and appeared for the first time in England at Liverpool, in the divertissement in Masaniello, Sinclair being Auber's hero. The educational establishments are, the Imperial College of Don Pedro II.; the College of St. José; Schools of Medicine and Surgery; Military and Naval Academy; and many public schools. It has also many scientific institutions; a museum rich in Ornithology, Entomology, and Mineralogy; and a fine botanic garden. Of churches there are upwards of fifty, not of much external elegance, but most sumptuously decorated in the interior.

places the pavement is execrable, and generally very bad, the difficulty having been probably increased by laying down mains for water and gas, the latter now in process of execution, and also to heavy rains having washed away many parts of the road, and otherwise caused much damage. Once this troublesome job is got through, it is to be hoped that some effective measures will be taken to put the streets and branch roads in order; otherwise they will soon be rendered impassable. Coach and coach-spring making must be thriving trades here, especially with the immense increase that has taken place in the number of carriages and omnibuses; and it is really wonderful how they stand the continual shocks they have to endure.* Government seems at last alive to the absolute necessity of doing something to improve the sanitary condition of the city, and also its internal organization, as they have lately got out some good practical English engineers, who I have no doubt will suggest an effective mode of dealing with present difficulties. If they do not adopt decisive measures the rate of mortality may be expected to augment fearfully in a dense population of 300,000 to 400,000 inhabitants, huddled together in some 15,000 houses, surrounded by impurities of every kind, not the least being the stagnant water

---

* The inhabitants of Rio Janeiro are fond of carriages, but the specimens generally seen would hardly do for Hyde Park, being chiefly old-fashioned coaches, drawn by four scraggy mules, with a black coachman on the box, and a postillion in jack-boots on the leaders, sitting well back, and with his feet stuck out beyond the mule's shoulders. The liveries are generally gorgeous enough, and there is no lack of gold lace on the cocked hats and coats; but a black slave does not enter into the spirit of the thing, and one footman will have his hat cocked athwartships, the other fore and aft; one will have shoes and stockings with his toes peeping through, the other will dispense with them altogether. But the old peer rolls on unconscious, and I dare say the whole thing is pronounced a neat turn out. The Brazilians are great snuff-takers, and always offer their box, if the visitor is a welcome guest. It is etiquette to take the offered pinch with the left hand. Rapé is the Portuguese for snuff, hence our word Rappee. They do not smoke much. The opera was good, the house very large, tolerably lighted, but not so thickly attended as it might be. The ladies look better by candle light, their great failing being in their complexions, the tint of which may be exactly described by the midshipman's simile of snuff and butter. The orchestra was good, many of the performers being blacks or mulattos, who are excellent musicians The African race seem to like music and generally have a pretty good ear Both men and women often whistle well, and I have heard the washerwomen at their work whistling polkas with great correctness. I was amused one evening on going out of the opera when it was half over: offering my ticket to a decent-looking man, he bowed, but refused it, saying that men with jackets were not allowed in the house.—*Elves.*

in the streets. No exact census has ever been taken of the population of Rio Janeiro, which is generally believed to be between the two figures above given. There is a migratory population, but the accumulation of humanity of every race and colour, contained in some of the large dwelling-houses, is something extraordinary. As before observed, nature has done much for this country, and if the natural facilities of Rio Janeiro were properly availed of, and local improvements carried out with energy and spirit, it might be rendered one of the finest and most luxuriant places within the tropics.* The opportunity is now open to them; the Government possess ample means, and it is just a question whether measures of progress are to be effectively achieved, or the city to be abandoned to its fate. The great evil attending all improvement in Brazil is an undue appreciation of native capability and a disparagement or mistrust of those whose practical experience would enable them to grapple with the difficulties that surround them—a kind of little jealousy or distrust that prevents their availing themselves of opportunities thrown in their way to carry out undertakings necessary to the well-being of the country: nor can they understand the principle on which such things are regulated in England, still less the magnitude of operations carried on there and in many other parts of Europe. Yet the time seems to be coming when these principles will be better understood here, and when the application of English capital towards the improvement of the country may be safely and legitimately brought to bear.

I quote this in order to point out the increase of population and improvements which have been carried

* The population of Rio, on the arrival of the royal family, did not amount to 50,000, but afterwards rapidly augmented; so that in 1815, when declared independent, the number had nearly doubled, and now is estimated at about 400,000 with the suburbs and the provincial capital of Nitherohy, on the opposite shore of the Bay. This increase is partly to be ascribed to the afflux of Portuguese, who have at different times left their country in consequence of the civil commotions which have disturbed its peace, as well as of English, French, Dutch, German, and Italians, who, after the opening of the port, settled here, some as merchants, others as mechanics, and have contributed largely to its wealth and importance. These accessions of Europeans have affected a great change in the character of the population, for at the commencement of the century, and for many years afterwards, the blacks and coloured persons far exceeded the whites, whereas now they are reduced to less than half the inhabitants. In the aggregate population of the empire, however, the coloured portion is still supposed to be treble the white.

out in the city since it was written, and amongst which may be enumerated :—

The paving of streets, drainage works, &c.

Lighting the city with gas.

Increased number of omnibuses, private carriages, and conveyances of all kinds.

Public gardens and ornamental squares.

Railways and tramways.

First, as regards the number of inhabitants, it is difficult to arrive at correct figures in the absence of a census, but according to the municipal authorities, the population of Rio and the suburbs (which comprise a circuit of many miles) is now about 600,000. If building be any criterion, the increase of population must be very considerable. Since the period to which I allude, the city has extended itself in every possible direction, for without actually climbing the mountains there is a limit to building ground. The new streets are wide, and many of the new buildings exhibit a beautiful style of architecture, very suitable to the climate, especially in the suburbs. The number of shops has largely increased, and they are generally nicely decorated. Some public markets have been built, such as the Gloria, Harmonia, &c. Property has also greatly risen in value, and fabulous prices have been paid for land in the city favourably situated. The paving of the streets has also been carried out most efficiently. All the leading thoroughfares in and out of the city are now well paved, and in this respect the road from the Public Gardens to Bota Fogo would compare advantageously with any in Europe, that portion passing through the Cattete being a perfect specimen of good paving. As to the drainage works, they speak for themselves to those who recollect what Rio was twenty years back, and the names of Brassey and Gotto will long be remembered as public benefactors in this part of the world. I had not time to examine these great works in detail, but shall avail of an opportunity on my return to do so. Gas has been most successfully introduced, both as regards quantity, quality, and usefulness, and it must have been an enormous saving of trouble and expense in a country where so many lights are required, and which was formerly dependent on oil lamps and candles. Not only is the city well lighted, but every suburb, miles in extent, thereby greatly adding to comfort and security. Under these circumstances it will hardly be a matter of surprise that the gas company pays a very good dividend. It has rather a curious effect on some of the country roads to see gas lamps peeping out from the thick foliage of tropical plants, as if in competition with the fire-flies dancing about.

Rio positively swarms with omnibuses, carriages, and Tilburys. The former are plain enough in appearance, but are drawn by four mules at a good speed. The carriages, which are manufactured on the spot, are generally very superior in quality, with a couple of mules or horses, and the Tilbury is a kind of cab with cover, to hold one person with the driver. The fares, considering the distances traversed, are on the whole moderate, although charges in this respect are complained of. The Public Gardens have been very much improved since I was last here, and under the shade of the trees it is very pleasant to sit and admire the beauty of the scenery presented by the surrounding hills, and the view of the bay in front, the busy city shut out, and everything in quiet repose save the rumble of carriages passing along the streets. Another public garden has been established in the square called Praça da Constituição, where there is a fine statue of the first Emperor Dom Pedro proclaiming the independence of the Empire. A still larger square, called the Campo de Santa Anna, might advantageously be converted to a similar purpose, and would form probably the most extensive area of this kind in the world, affording shade and shelter from the rays of the sun to thousands of citizens who have to cross it. At present, near the public fountains, it is occupied by laundresses, and in certain spots rubbish is thrown, but other parts are being planted, especially near the Senate House, the War Office, and those of Public Works and Foreign Affairs, the Museum and the new Mint, the latter one of the finest buildings in Rio. The municipal taxes are few, and it is not easy to find a surplus to be employed in ornamental works. As regards the railways, I must reserve my notice of them till my return from the Plate, as at present my sojourn in the Empire is limited to a couple of days in the capital.

The terrible ravages of the cholera in the River Plate brought me back to Rio de Janeiro sooner than I had contemplated, as there was nothing whatever to be done down there under such circumstances. At one period both town and country places were threatened with absolute decimation, and the daily tales of horror exceeded almost anything on record. In many cases, when no one could be found to bury the dead inside ranchos, or cottages, they were set fire to as the only way of disposing of the bodies therein. In the Province of Buenos Ayres alone the loss of life is computed at 25,000, and other provinces suffered almost in an equal ratio, so that the actual loss of life and property in the

Argentine Republic must have been something enormous. In the Banda Oriental the losses were severe, and at one time the mortality at Monte Video itself was almost as great as at Buenos Ayres. Farms were in many cases abandoned, and sheep and cattle left to roam at large; crops rotted in the ground, growers of fruits and vegetables were ruined, the markets for these products being closed, and their entrance into the town prohibited. In fact it appeared as if the destroying angel was passing over the devoted land; nor do I believe, from all I could learn on the spot, that cholera was the only form of disease. It rather resembled the fearful destruction of the Israelites, when Moses and Aaron "stood between the living and the dead." How soon, however, such fearful visitations are forgotten. Except from the general appearance of mourning when I returned to the River Plate about three months later, and the crowded state of the cemeteries, no one could imagine that Buenos Ayres and Monte Video had gone through such a fearful ordeal. Everything went on as usual, and people looked after their farms and their merchandise as if nothing had happened, though doubtless many feared the return of the hot season, before which very little will have been done in the way of sanatary precaution. That the cholera will become a permanent visitor in the River Plate seems unlikely, if we are to judge from its erratic course in other parts of the world, but no one can say that the scourge will not prevail until the cities and towns are effectively sewered and drained. The climate itself is healthy enough, but then this is no safeguard against epidemics, which have their origin in impurities allowed to accumulate until cities become pest-houses.

On my return from the River Plate, in the beginning of

February, I availed myself of the opportunity to ramble about the city and suburbs, to visit old friends, and to go over the railways, an account of which will be found under its proper head. The weather was still very hot, with frequent heavy thunder storms, some terrifically grand—more so than I ever remember during a two years' residence here. From my room window, at the Hotel dos Estrangeiros, I could see the whole heavens lighted up with frequent flashes, and now and again portions of the bay and of the mountains stood out as if from a sea of fire. Then the awful crash of the thunder, followed by instant and utter darkness, and with reverberations shaking the house to its foundations, all combined to heighten the grandeur and sublimity of the scene. As for sleeping in the midst of such turmoil, it was simply impossible.

Both February and March were very wet, stormy months, and on one occasion some large trees were blown down about the city, and much damage done to the roofs of houses, many of which are not very well protected from such visitations. Similar weather followed me to San Paulo, but on my return to Rio, after again visiting the River Plate, the weather was delightfully cool, fine, and pleasant, equal to the most agreeable portion of our summer weather in Europe. There is no doubt the climate of Rio de Janeiro is a healthy one, and it is a striking fact that scarcely any cases of epidemic have occurred since the sewerage of the city was completed, nor any visitation of cholera, notwithstanding sick and wounded were constantly arriving from the seat of war, and that the quarantine was merely nominal. I am convinced the very thunder storms to which I have alluded tend to purify the atmosphere. The deluges of rain of course exercise a great cleansing power, and it has been noticed in years when thunder storms did not prevail that much sickness followed. One requires to go closely over the city before he finds out improvements which have been effected in Rio, which are nowhere so palpable as when passing through the great public thoroughfares. With such a number of narrow intersecting streets, no adequate idea of the size or extent of the city can be formed until some of the hills about it are ascended, such as that of Santa Theresa. It is, however, from the top of the Corcovado that its dimensions are most striking, from whence also the spectator can form a fair notion of the extent of the bay.

I have before remarked on the defective state of the landing-places, that most used, near the custom-house, being a very dirty, dilapidated wooden jetty, about which the rabble of the city seems to collect, and it is always a scene of much uproar and confusion. There is quite a Babel among the boatmen and their black hangers-on. There are some other landing-places, with stone steps, in front of the large square, whence the ferry-boats across the bay take their departure, but these are not very convenient, and the untidy state of the public market which stands here is a disgrace to the municipality. Indeed nothing can be more derogatory to a large city like Rio de Janeiro, possessing the finest harbour in the world, than such landing places, which create a most unfavourable impression on strangers. The Custom-house, with its wharves and warehouse, the Marine Arsenal and Building-yard, together with the private wharves, occupy a large portion of the water frontage, but there is still sufficient space left, if it were properly laid out, as I believe is intended before very long, for decent landing-places for the public. Speaking of the Custom-house, the source from whence a large portion of the revenue of the country is derived, it is an unsightly building, though immense sums of money have been spent, and are still being spent, in order to obtain adequate accommodation for the increasing trade of the port. Hydraulic lifts and machinery of every possible kind are in course of erection, and a few years will doubtless see the Rio Custom-house take its stand as the finest building of the sort in South America The old Praça do Commercio, or Exchange, with its dismal vaulted roof, remains unchanged since my last visit, but when the Custom-house is completed I believe it is intended to construct an exchange more worthy of the place, with suitable accommodation attached. This, as well as a foreigners' club, is much required at Rio, where the foreign population is numerous and influential, and ought to be represented in a manner consistent with its importance.

When I lived here in the years 1848 and 1849, there was much sociability,—amongst the English residents at all events—but this appears to have quite died out, and even ceremonial visits are now rarely exchanged. The only society worthy of the name existing in Rio is that associated with the diplomatic circle, which is of course more or less exclusive in its character. I must nevertheless notice one institution in which I found a great change for the better. I mean the English Church. A good deal of money has been spent in connection with this edifice, entirely raised by private subscriptions, and certainly it has been well spent. The recess built out for the communion table is very pretty, and the organ is well placed, in a line with the body of the church. There is a good choir, the whole arrangements being very complete, and the service efficiently performed. The Rev. Mr. Preston is chaplain

Whilst in Rio, I went to the Palace of Sao Christovao, and had the honour of being presented to the Emperor, whom I was glad to see looking well, but thinner than when I last saw him, fifteen years since. The Palace is well situated, on a rising ground, with a good prospect, and appears to be comfortable enough, but without any gorgeous display. The Court is very simple in its habits, and the democratic tendencies of the people render access to it comparatively easy.

With regard to politics, the Government has generally an opposition party to contend with, both in the Chamber and in the Senate, but without impeding the regular proceedings of these bodies, which, on the whole, are conducted with great decorum, and the speeches are very fully and fairly reported,* occupying whole pages of the daily papers. The *Jornal do Commercio* still stands pre-eminent in the Rio press—as the *Times*, in fact, of the Brazilian Empire.

The political discussions in the press, which are perfectly free, are often pursued with considerable acrimony. At the same time there is a degree of reticence observable which some of our newspaper writers would do well to imitate. Brazil does not lack parliamentary orators or able statesmen, but public business is trammelled with too much of red tapery as at home. The current of popular feeling does not run very deep from the fact that the bulk of the community are too much absorbed in their business occupations to leave them much time for political discussions, to which a large portion of Englishmen devote themselves because they have little else to do. It must not, however, be in-

---

* The difference between reporting proceedings of the Brazilian and English legislatures is that the latter appear daily, whilst it takes many days before speeches in the Brazilian Chambers are published, and frequently a large double sheet is issued to make up for arrears.

ferred from this remark that Brazilians are indifferent to what passes inside the walls of the Senate or of the Chamber. The support the Government has received in carrying on a long and costly war proves that the honour and well-being of the Empire is as dear to them as to the most patriotic people.

I am glad to have to record the abolition of passports in Brazil unless specially asked for. I had occasion to notice the inconvenience caused on a late trip to the River Plate, and it is gratifying to see that Brazilian statesmen appreciate the march of events in this respect, as I trust will also soon be the case in facilitating the despatch of passengers' luggage. As a rule, passengers do not carry with them articles subject to duty, though, of course, a surveillance in this matter is quite necessary. At Buenos Ayres there is a custom station on the mole or landing place where passengers can bring their luggage, which is at once examined and passed, thus saving much time and trouble. The Post-office is on the whole pretty well managed and letters are promptly delivered on arrival of the mails. The building is, however, quite unsuited to the requirements of so large a city as Rio de Janeiro, and I learn that it is intended to erect a fine new post-office in a square facing the Bay, which will be a great convenience to the public.

I found the population on the opposite side of the bay had not increased as much as I expected, although the facility of crossing by the large American ferry steamers is a great convenience. Nitherohy is a large straggling place, supposed to contain a population of about 20,000, but there are many houses uninhabited, nor do the Rio people show much partiality for a residence there even at a much less rent. Some handsome villas have been built there, and it is intended to light the place with gas, which would be a decided advantage to the residents. Some of the islands in the upper parts of the bay are now cultivated and inhabited, and numerous small craft ply between them and Rio de Janeiro, bringing down fruits and vegetables.

In the appendix to this volume will be found sundry official documents and statistical information in reference to the resources and commerce of Brazil. The institutions of the Empire are very favourable to mercantile development, and the great progress made within the past half century is indicative of a highly prosperous future.

THE WAR IN PARAGUAY.

LEAVING for the moment the narrative form, I devote a chapter to this lamentable struggle, which has entailed such serious consequences on Brazil, and which at the time I am writing is yet undetermined. Writers have differed much as to the origin of the war, but none have shown how it could have been avoided. I may observe *en passant* that so far from having entertained any prejudices against Paraguay, my sympathies have always been in favour of that country as evinced during my visit to the River Plate in 1853, at which period the elder Lopez was alive, and there appeared to be dawning in the future, not only an era of internal development for a very fine, fertile territory, but also a relaxation of the iron rule under which the people had so long groaned, by encouraging, to a limited extent it might be, commercial relations with other countries. Lopez had joined Brazil in putting down the tyranny of Rozas and in restoring a free government to the Argentine provinces; the rivers were to be opened by treaty to all nations, and an era of peace and prosperity appeared to be the natural result of these arrangements. The visit of the younger Lopez to Europe, it was thought, would have instilled into his mind the fact that all the wealth he saw there emanated from commerce, and that his first object would be to render Paraguay a commercial country. Unfortunately, however, he seems to have become more enamoured with the martial attitude of France than anything else, and determined on his return home to develop the military instead of the commercial resources of Paraguay. His ambition was centered in organizing a large army, fortifying the river approaches to Asuncion, and creating a small but efficient steam fleet. The experience of the past was thrown away, and on succeeding his father in the dictatorship, it became evident that his policy was to be one of aggrandisement, if it meant anything at all, and that, in other respects Paraguay was to continue isolated from her neighbours, and to stand aloof from participation in the business of the world. Paraguay had no enemies, nor was there any desire to trouble her; her territorial position secured her safety from attack, and it is impossible that all this military and naval preparation on the part of Lopez could have been merely intended for purposes of self-defence. The truth is, that Lopez had always coveted that portion of territory called the Missions, formerly a great stronghold of the Jesuits, but now part of the Argentine Confederation; and the possession of this would bring him close upon Uruguay, where the sea port of Monte Video afforded a tempting prize. At the same time, all this involved the prospect of a collision with other Powers, against which it was necessary to provide, and this I believe to be the true reason for the great military preparations of Lopez. I have already said that Paraguay joined with Brazil in putting an end to the tyranny of Rozas, and entered into a treaty by which the navigation of the upper rivers was to be free and the independence of Uruguay to be recognised. If ever Brazil had any sinister design on the latter State this was the time when she would have been most likely to assert it, but no such disposition was evinced. On the contrary, it was the wish as well as the interest of Brazil to keep Monte Video a free port, and the rivers open to the flags of all nations. Unfortunately for the peace of South America, Monte Video has never had a strong and independent Government, and during the presidency of Berro disorders broke out on the frontier. The persons and properties of Brazilian subjects were exposed to the inroads of lawless marauders from Uruguay, until at length the patience of the people of Rio Grande was exhausted, and they threatened to take up arms in their own defence, if the Imperial Government did not at once interfere for their protection. This statement has been personally confirmed to me by large landed proprietors who were themselves on the spot and suffered from the causes here referred to. Brazil was, therefore, compelled to send troops to the frontier and to follow the marauders into Uruguay, until such time as she could obtain fresh guarantees from a Government which had proved itself totally incompetent to deal with the matter. Then came the Colorado movement, headed by Flores, and further complications ensued, which might have been settled by the timely intervention of foreign Governments, but the men in power were quite deaf to all friendly remonstrances. The flag of Brazil was grossly insulted, trampled on in the streets of Monte Video, and the treaty with her publicly burnt. Recent melancholy occurrences in that city have shown what excesses can be committed from party spirit, and how difficult it was at the period I allude to, to avoid an armed intervention. How these acts affected the interests of Paraguay it is not easy to conceive.

Brazil agreed to recognise the independence of Uruguay, and she left it in that condition, stronger than it had been for some years previously. It is true that about this time Lopez had given notice to Brazil that any interference in the affairs of Uruguay, or the entry of Brazilian troops into Uruguayan territory, would be considered by him as a *casus belli*—a piece of impertinence that Brazil might well disregard, as the rights of nations allowed reprisals for injuries received, and this was all Brazil carried into effect. Up to the point mentioned Lopez had, therefore, no real or ostensible cause of war against Brazil, but she stood in the way of the consummation of his ambitious designs, and so he made what he termed an interference in Uruguay the pretext for setting his legions in motion. Without any declaration of war, he seized and took forcible possession of the steamer Marquis de Olinda whilst on a peaceable errand up the River, with Carneiro de Campos, the President of Matto Grosso on board, and has retained him prisoner ever since; he marched a division into Brazil, and occupied the frontier town of Uruguayana, simultaneously sending his fleet down, no doubt to co-operate with his troops, but this was prevented by the gallant action of the Riachuello, in which the Paraguayan navy was nearly destroyed by the Brazilians. The proceedings of Lopez towards Brazil were, therefore, offensive and insulting in the highest degree, and still more so towards the Argentine Republic, which had really given him no cause of offence beyond daring to remain neutral, and consequently refusing to allow the passage of troops through its territory. Upon the refusal of General Mitre to grant such permission, he crossed the Parana and invaded Corrientes, seizing two Argentine vessels as well as the persons and property of Argentine subjects, on whom he levied black mail. These extreme measures taken by Lopez towards both countries were in pigmy imitation of the first Napoleon, whose tactics Lopez affected to follow by seizing the persons, property, and territory of his neighbours before it was possible for them to offer any opposition. Such an offence against the laws of nations could lead only to an alliance against him as a common enemy, with the condition that the aggrieved nations would not lay down their arms until the offender was punished by expulsion from Paraguay. In Europe this course was adopted against Napoleon I. and in South America, under nearly identical circumstances, an equally strong measure was rendered necessary for the future peace and security of the allies. If a case in point was required on the spot, Paraguay itself had joined in the expulsion of Rozas, because no security existed for any one so long as that tyrant dominated at Buenos Ayres. That neither Brazil nor the Argentine Republic anticipated such conduct on the part of Lopez is evident from the unprepared state of both, the latter being at the time literally without army or navy; indeed, the first check given to the advance of Lopez was by the late General Flores, at the head of a gallant little band of Oriental troops in conjunction with those of Brazil. No impartial person can question, therefore, that Lopez has been the sole cause of this long and bloody war, and that he committed a glaring act of violence towards his neighbours, who were compelled in self-defence to enter into a league for the expulsion of so dangerous a character. To have made peace on any other terms would have been only playing with a firebrand.

It is not my purpose in this chapter to criticise

the manner in which the war has been conducted, or to point out mistakes which may have been made. Intelligent Brazilians believe that, instead of sending a large army by sea, it would have been better to have made a diversion by marching across the country to the interior of Paraguay, direct to Asuncion, leaving Humaita blockaded. Thus a large amount of money would have been expended in Brazilian territory. Whether this would have hastened the conclusion of the war it is difficult to say, but the direct advantages in other ways would no doubt have been considerable. However, Brazil is not the only country that has blundered in carrying on a distant war, as we know to our cost. That they did not anticipate so vigorous a resistance is certain, nor was it possible to suppose that any section of the Argentine people, whose nationality had been grossly insulted, would have been lukewarm, or have desired to make peace until the object of the struggle was accomplished.

THE PROVINCE OF SAN PAULO.

Availing of an opportunity to accompany a friend to this province, we left Rio on Tuesday, the 18th of February, on board the steamer Ptolemy, with a remarkably smooth sea, and a light, but cool breeze. We reached Santos early the following morning. The steamer was at once moored alongside an iron wharf, facing the Custom House, and Mr. Miller, one of the railway officials, came on board with the unpleasant information that the railway was stopped, owing to the heavy rains, which appeared to have prevailed here as at Rio. The town did not look very inviting under the influence of a hot sun, but Mr. Miller kindly offered us rooms at the station, where he himself lived, and made us very comfortable. There was every prospect of our being obliged to walk up to the top of the Serra, but fortunately, on the 20th, a telegram came to announce that the line would be opened to San Paulo the next morning, when we started with a small train, arrived at 2.33, and drove to the Hotel d'Italia, where rooms had been engaged for us.

The province of San Paulo has played a distinguished part in the history of Brazil, and has latterly attracted much notice from its production of cotton, in addition to the large quantity of coffee grown and shipped from the port of Santos, both of which articles are expected to be greatly increased by the railway facilities. There can be no doubt that the province offers splendid scope for emigration, if properly applied, and this important subject will be specially treated of after I have collected together the requisite materials. Certainly the size, extent, and evident prosperity of the city of San Paulo surprised me, no less than its superiority in most of the comforts and luxuries to places more favourably situated by their proximity to the sea; but the large number of old churches, convents, colleges, and public institutions date its origin from the time of the Jesuits, who must have been very industrious and wealthy to have found the means for building such huge places, with the object of perpetuating their order, and for the spread of the Roman Catholic religion. I much regretted that the stoppage of the railway, and very unfavourable weather—constant thunder storms, with deluges of rain—prevented me travelling some distance into the interior, where the coffee and cotton plantations lie, but the accounts received from others, who possess a thorough knowledge of the localities, enable me to speak most highly of its resources.

His Excellency, Saldanha Marinho, the President of San Paulo, and who by his affability and business habits has won the esteem and affection of the people, received me kindly during my stay here. He is a determined supporter of every practical measure having for its object the improvement of the city and of the province. Respecting the great work of the railway, on which so much of the future welfare of the province depends, I will endeavour to give a tolerably ample description; but to begin with, it may not be out of place to quote as follows from the work of Mr. Scully, entitled "Brazil and its Chief Provinces":—

"Passing over the Mugy river you arrive quickly at the foot of

THE PROVINCE OF SAN PAULO. 53

the gorge formed by the two out-jutting spurs of the buttress-like mountain, and the black defiant ravine is suggestive of anything but a railway course. Here the line climbs boldly up the side of the Mugy spur, at a usual ascent of one in ten, crossing mountain torrents, leaping gloomy chasms, cutting through solid rocks, holding hard on to every foot gained, until it attains a resting-place upon the table land, 2,600 feet high, after five miles of gigantic excavations, removing 1,100,000 cubic yards of granite rock and earth.

Here we must give a slight idea of how this daring plan is utilised, which was at one time laughed at as an engineering impossibility, and which even yet stands pre-eminent among similar works.

This entire and almost straight ascent of upwards of five miles is divided into four "lifts" of about a mile and a quarter each, having a level platform of some 400 feet in length between them. On these lifts, as in general on all the line, the track is single, except at the upper half, where it is doubled to admit of the ascending and descending trains passing each other. At the upper end of each platform is placed a powerful stationary engine of 200 horse-power, whose two cylinders are 26 inches diameter and 5 feet stroke, calculated to haul up 50 tons at the rate of ten miles an hour, which are supplied by five Cornish boilers, three of which suffice for the duty.

A steel wire rope, tested to a strength far exceeding the requirements which will ever be made upon it, passes over a friction-wheel on each side of the fly-wheel drum upon which it is wrapped round, and, one end being attached to an ascending and the other to a descending train, it is intended to make the "lift" partially self-acting, as it now wholly is at one of the inclines which is not supplied with its stationary engine, the weight of the descending train drawing up the ascending one. Powerful breaks that will stop a train instantly are supplied to guard against a breaking down of any part of the machinery, or a rupture of the rope. From this short description our readers can form an idea of the mechanical contrivances for effecting the ascent.

Throughout these wonderful inclines the most majestic and wild scenery is observed along the slightly winding way. On the third lift occurs a ravine still more gloomy than the rest, which is called the Boca do Inferno (Mouth of Hell); that, having a width of 900 feet, is crossed by an iron viaduct, which lies on rows of iron columns resting on stone piers 200 feet below in the centre of the line."

I have great pleasure in endorsing all Mr. Scully says as to the excellent qualities of the railway officials, and can also affirm that to Mr. Aubertin and Mr. Hutchings is due the extraordinary development that has been effected in the production of cotton.

THE SAN PAULO RAILWAY.

I WILL now proceed to describe the railway in my own terms, without reference to the statistics or the reports that have been published about it. My impression on leaving the station was that of setting off on an adventurous journey—not merely ensconcing oneself in the corner of a railway carriage and taking a comfortable nap. Curiosity was excited to the utmost, after the accounts I had heard, and the temporary stoppage of the line by recent heavy rains washing down some of the slopes of the cuttings rather added to the interest of a first visit. There was a tolerable amount of bustle at starting, but away we went about eleven o'clock, over low, swampy ground. For seven miles the rails run parallel with the old road to Santos, and the bridge at Cubitao (an arm of the sea) is passed, beyond which for a further distance of six and a half miles (making $13\frac{1}{2}$ miles to the foot of the Serra) it becomes a dense mass of forest and jungle, which it must be difficult to convert to any useful purpose; indeed, the curse of the country is this mass of useless forest, only fit for the haunts of wild animals and reptiles. How they have hitherto been able to carry on the traffic between Santos and San Paulo is a mystery when we look at the country and miles of wood passed through. However, we are now in sight of the first rise of the mountain, which looks grim enough, and the train comes to a stop at the station, after passing an open space of ground, on which stands a house, built and formerly inhabited by the contractors, with almost a little village about it, occupied by their staff, &c., where, I understand, cricket was often played to while away the leisure hours after the labours of the day. Now everything is going to wreck, and if the land is not kept clear it will soon be a jungle again : such is the quick growth of vegetation in this country and so rank does it become. The station at the foot of the Serra is a good substantial sort of house, the station master being a young German, with a wife and family, very comfortable adjuncts in so lonely a spot ; and the house was surrounded by fowls and other live stock needful to family wants. We stood contemplating the height we had to be dragged with a certain kind of awe, and presently we saw the train descending, which it did steadily enough, bringing Mr. Aubertin, the general manager, Captain Burton, her Majesty's consul, and some other notabilities of San Paulo. The former gentlemen returned with us, adding materially to the interest and pleasure of the trip by their intelligent knowledge of all we had to see and pass through.

Well, the signal is given, and we are off, mounting an incline of about 1 in 10 for a distance of some 800 yards, where there is a curve, and we are shut out from the lower level of the line, steadily ascending the mountain, until we reach the first lift, about 1¼ miles. After a short delay, we were hooked on the second lift, and as we mount the scenery becomes grander, the shadows of the mountains deeper, and the work becomes heavier. I was surprised to find so many curves, which are an additional strain on the wire rope, as well

Bridge Viaduct on the San Paulo Railway.

as an additional risk, requiring close attention to the break, where we rode in order to have a good view of everything. Mr. Fox, engineer-in-chief, and Mr. Welby, locomotive superintendent, were with us, and we got down to look over Fairburn's splendid stationary engines, which are of 200 horse-power, embedded in a granite foundation, about 40 feet deep, with five boilers to each, three being generally used. The curves continue on the third lift, close to which, entering the fourth lift, is the wonderful viaduct across a chasm in the mountain, which makes your head giddy to look down. The bridge is certainly a great engineering achievement, resting on iron pillars with a stone foundation, the centre being nearly 200 feet deep. We are accustomed to great altitude of railway bridges at home and elsewhere, but there is a peculiar aerial look about this one which makes one glad to be over it. At one point in this fourth section is a fine view of a deep valley behind us, the opposite mountain one dense mass of forest, and the scene is inexpressibly grand. To have made the lifts straight would have necessitated frequent tunnelling and added another half million to the cost of construction. On reaching the top of the Serra, a distance of about five miles from its base, the break is detached, a locomotive takes hold of the six carriages which have come up in two lifts, and away we whisk for some time through a thickly wooded country, for a distance of about 48 miles, stopping at several stations. Some miles before reaching San Paulo are the Campos, or level plains, covered with a short grass, and rather swampy, but no cattle are to be seen, owing, I believe, to the number of insects which fasten on them, causing sores, and being otherwise injurious. It is, however, a great relief to the eye, after the dense forests passed through, to come upon plains,

From San Paulo the line passes on to Jundiahy, a distance of 44 miles, or a total length from Santos of 88 miles, the chief interest of course being centred in the gigantic works of the Serra. The San Paulo Railway is undoubtedly one of the grandest works yet made with English capital in Brazil, and it is destined to play a very important part in the future development of this fine province. Engineering mistakes have, undoubtedly, been made, and the want of a personal superintendence of the engineer-in-chief, at all events during the construction of the important works of the Serra, is amongst the complaints made by the Brazilian Government, as also the manner in which the contract was executed It is also questionable whether another and less costly route could not have been selected to be worked by locomotives, instead of the old fashioned but dangerous lifts. However, for the present, this is mere matter of controversy or opinion. The railway is made, though far from being complete or perfect, and it is evident that a considerable expenditure has to be faced before sufficient traffic can be carried on to realise the expectations of directors and shareholders, few of whom know anything about the undertaking or are able to comprehend the difficulties it has still to pass through.

It is curious that the real traffic is only tapped at the extreme end of the line (Jundiahy), where only commences cotton growing, and the great coffee plantations are some 30 miles further on, to which district a private company is now trying to get the line extended. One advantage possessed by the existing company will be in having their mileage rate for the bulk of their traffic over the whole of the line, and of course it will be an additional advantage to present shareholders if the line should be continued to Campinas, which is, I believe, a large and thriving place, the abode of many wealthy proprietors. Passenger traffic can only be limited for some time to come, from the absence of a resident population along the line; at the same time it will naturally increase between Santos, San Paulo, and the upper part of the Province, particularly when the line is extended in that direction. The stoppage of the line is between San Paulo and Jundiahy, where the cuttings have given way to some extent, a contingency, I fear, they will always be exposed to, from the heavy rains which prevail, and I believe I am justified in adding, the imperfect manner in which some of them have been constructed. Whilst expressing my admiration at the courage and enterprise of the resident engineer and superintendent, who jointly succeeded in getting the line opened, I cannot conceal from myself the difficulties they have still to overcome in order to carry on an adequate traffic and get the line accepted by Government. One thing is very certain, that had a deputation of shareholders been sent out to look over the intended line before fairly concluding the contract for making it, they would have returned so scared and frightened as to have led to an immediate dissolution of the company, and San Paulo would hardly have had its railway in this generation, so far as English capital is concerned. I well remember the kind of awe with which I looked over the plans and sections of the line before it was commenced, nor has this effect been diminished by a personal inspection of the works up to this place. That the railway will be a grand thing for the province there can be no doubt, and this consideration ought to render the Government lenient towards a company which, apart from its other difficulties, has suffered so much by maladministration at home.

In describing the works of the Serra, I have omitted to allude to the double rails which are laid near approaches to the stationary engines, so that the trains can pass each other, which, of course, they are constantly doing, one up and the other down, on the several lifts. I was at a loss also to understand how they could work their goods traffic to a large extent with the amount of trains running. I now find the latter applies only to the passengers, and that produce is dealt with separately, collected at the top of the Serra, and sent down during the day, three waggon loads at a time, the waggons being collected together at the foot of the Serra, and taken on to the station at Santos as convenient. These arrangements necessitate a large amount of rolling stock and extra shed accommodation, which I believe is about to be supplied. Another feature in the works of the Serra is the loose kind of material they have had to go through instead of granite rock, which they expected, the former being apt to crumble away from the effects of rain, although latterly the road has stood very well in this respect. Some of the embankments crossing the gorges of the mountains are almost perpendicular, and involved a heavy amount of labour and expense. It is quite frightful to look down them. Of course the traffic of the Serra can only be worked from sunrise to sunset, but a large amount of produce can be brought down during that time.

I have now to record a trip over the remaining portion of the line to Jundiahy, the terminus. An announcement had been issued that traffic would be resumed over the whole line on the 2nd March, but a continuance of wet weather caused further and serious impediment, so I availed of the kindness of the officials, who were making a survey of the state of the works, to go to Jundiahy in the best manner circumstances would permit. We started about 8 a.m., on Tuesday, the 23rd March, in a carriage attached to the engine, having, amongst others, Mr. Aubertin, superintendent; Mr. Fox, engineer-in-chief; the fiscal, or Government engineer; the Postmaster-General, Captain Burton, and other persons, with some luggage belonging to them, and some small stores for the use of the line.

My impression was that I had seen the heaviest works on the line, but this was a great mistake, as I soon found out. The first few miles were not of much interest, but afterwards, as we approached the mountain scenery, the view became very fine,—the bold outline of the Jaraguay, a mountain where gold mines exist, but long since ceased working—deep gorges began to open out, and huge hanging forests towered above us, in their wildest and most primitive form. At the first station I got on the engine with Mr. Fox, and certainly it is difficult to imagine a country less adapted to a railway —making it against nature, as some one significantly observed. It is a succession of deep cuttings, high embankments, curves, and heavy gradients the whole distance, at times with an incline of 1 in 45, and only occasionally what may be termed a bit of straight road. It is really wonderful how people could be found to make such a railway in this country. Scarcely a human habitation to be seen along the whole distance, except the rough mud huts for persons connected with it; and about three stations between San Paulo and Jundiahy. The stations themselves are barely sufficient for the station master to live in, though probably adequate under present circumstances. At one of them (Belem) a small quantity of cotton was stored, having gone there direct, but no means of forwarding it on at present.

The ordinary mule road to Jundiahy crosses and runs parallel to the railway for some distance, and a wretched state it appeared to be in—deep mudholes and quagmires, through which the poor mules have to struggle.

I must now refer to some of our difficulties, resulting from the state in which we found the road. The first actual gap occurs some seventeen or eighteen miles from San Paulo, where the river current has carried away a large culvert, the rails and iron bowls (sleepers) attached to them hanging suspended for some twenty feet. They were at work rebuilding another culvert. We had to leave the carriage, cross the stream, and, walking some little distance, to get to another engine, which with a ballast truck was waiting there. On we went again, at times having to pull up or go slowly over slippery places, until we passed the tunnel, with water dripping from the roof. On the other side of the tunnel occurs the most serious stoppage, the whole side of a huge hill having apparently moved forward, the advanced portion of it blocking up the road. Some under current has raised the rails several feet in places, notwithstanding the immense piles of timber that have been driven in to prevent encroachment. The conclusion is that a mass of quicksands, swollen by the heavy rains, has forced its way under the hill side and under the bed of the railway. The labour here will be very great, by having to remove the falling mass, and the uncertainty is when the movement may subside. The "mountain in labour" has brought forth no "ridiculus mus" in this case. After walking past this obstruction, we again mounted on the ballast truck, and went along until we came to a place where the river had quite overflowed the rails, and the engine had to force its way through two or three feet of water, of course at a very slow and cautious pace; here they are raising the road so as to escape, if possible, future inundations. Once through this last impediment, we rattled along over a good hard bit of road at a good pace to Jundiahy, the end of our adventurous journey. The station is a little distance from the town, which stands on a hill, and after partaking of some solid refreshments, which we fortunately found ready at the Railway Hotel, in half an hour we were again on a ballast truck going through the same process of changing from one truck to another, walking over slippery ground, until we finally again joined the carriage on the opposite side of the broken culvert, before arriving at which a thunder storm came on, accompanied by torrents of rain, and most of us were thoroughly wet through. The storm continued nearly to San Paulo, but it is amongst the gorges of the mountains it comes down most furiously.

It is not my intention to comment further on the errors that have been made in the construction of this railway. No doubt obstacles had to be met at every step; nor can shareholders be supposed to know much about engineering details of this kind. They subscribe their money on the faith of a Government guarantee, believing in the estimates, and that of course the line will, under any circumstances, pay its working expenses. The late Mr. Brunel used to repudiate the existence of engineering difficulties. It was a mere question of money; but I think had he surveyed the intended line of the San Paulo Railway he would have said both these points were involved, the result being that the original estimates are greatly exceeded, and the works still require a considerable outlay before they can be permanently relied on. The thing certainly appears incredible, if it were not the fact, that to work a line consisting almost entirely of short curves and heavy gradients, the directors should have sent out rigid locomotives suited to a first-class English railway, without even bogie frames attached, causing great wear and tear to both engines and rails. I quite believe that with suitable locomotives the line may be safely and properly worked, and it seems exactly a case in point for such engines as Fairlie's. The question as to maintenance of way must always be a very important one; whether in such a mountainous country, subject at seasons to heavy rains and flooded rivers, and with a treacherous soil, the nature of the works is such as can be relied on, for unless this is the case, as the public journals of San Paulo justly observe, the real utility of the railway is destroyed. Coffee growers and cotton planters have been looking to it as a sure and certain means of getting their produce down to Santos, and unless this can be depended on they will have to resort to the old, cumbrous, and expensive mode of carrying it upwards of one hundred miles on the backs of mules as heretofore. It is a momentous question for this province whether or not they can depend on railway conveyance, which I think may fairly be looked for when the line becomes consolidated, but both shareholders and the Government must be prepared to make sacrifices of no common kind before this end is finally attained. That the officials and managers of the line in Brazil are doing all they can is very certain, and it is for the company or the shareholders to provide them with everything required to ensure the permanent success of the company. They entered into a solemn contract with the Brazilian Government and the Provincial Government here, which it is their duty to fulfil, no matter at what sacrifice, and the sooner the shareholders look their position in the face the better, instead of being guided entirely by directors, who could only appreciate their position if they came out in a body and personally inspected the line. One thing is very certain, that if it had not been for the great liberality of the Baron de Mauá in coming to the rescue of the concern, the works might never have been completed or the line opened.

THE CITY OF SAN PAULO.

If it appears a long time in reaching here after passing the wonders of the Serra, I was not disappointed either in the first peep at the city or by a more intimate acquaintance with it. One cannot help marvelling how the adventurous handful of men who originally penetrated the forests and founded these cities in South America had the courage and perseverance to do so; but I believe they availed, in many cases, of the Indian tracks, and doubtless of Indian assistance occasionally. The city has rather an imposing aspect as you wind round it to the station, being built on a ridge of high ground which overlooks the River Ticté—a stream rising in the neighbouring hills, and after traversing nearly the whole of the province, eventually finds its way to the Parana and the Paraguay. At the railway station sundry omnibuses and carriages were waiting to receive the passengers. We drove to the Hotel d'Italia, where a friend had taken rooms for us, and found ourselves tolerably comfortable in a large house rather the worse for wear, and, like most things in this country, allowed to get out of repair. During the construction of the railway it was the head-quarters of the engineering staff.

The first thing we did next morning was to pay our respects to the President of the Province, who received us very graciously. He is a man of a very expressive, benevolent countenance, and I believe he administers the affairs of the province in a most satisfactory manner —not the easiest of tasks in such troublous times as the present.

A ramble over the city impresses one favourably: good wide streets, paved with a material resembling macadam. It is obtained from one of the neighbouring hills, and forms a capital road. The sides are well made of large flags, much superior to those of Rio de Janeiro, although the pavement there is admirable. There are several fine churches, an extensive new public market, and, as a rule, the houses are well and substantially built. The shops are also numerous and well appointed with all the requisites for convenience and comfort suited to a city of 20,000 to 25,000 inhabitants. There are several national colleges here, with a number of young students, who help to enliven the place. The Province of San Paulo has always held a good position, from the enterprise and spirit of the people, the latter owing in some measure to the cool climate, which even now occasionally renders woollen clothing and blankets at night desirable, and a few months hence it will be positively cold, with ice in the morning. Previously to and since our arrival it has been raining so much that a vast tract of land bordering the Tieté is overflowed, and travelling must be very bad. We took a drive to the church of Nossa Senhora de Penha, a few miles distant, on elevated ground, from whence a good view of the city and surrounding country is obtained; but unfortunately rain came on, and we had only to make the best of our way home, the carriages nearly sticking fast in a quagmire. Otherwise the road is a pretty good one.

I may here allude to the kind hospitality of Captain and Mrs. Burton, which rendered our visit an exceedingly agreeable one. On the occasion of this visit to Nossa Senhora de Penha, a curious incident occurred. On our way out Mrs. Burton took a fancy to some geese which were quietly feeding by the road-side, and she determined to make a purchase of them on our way back, although it was raining heavily. After some bargaining the geese were bought, their legs were tied, and each of us took charge of one or more. They were quiet enough until we reached the city, where the people began to pelt us with wax water balls, as it was the Intrudo time, when such pastime is still carried on to a great extent in an old fashioned place like San Paulo. The geese became alarmed, struggled to release themselves, and after some difficulty and much amusement we got them safely disposed of in the yard attached to the Consulate. Geese are very plentiful in Brazil, but there is a prejudice against them amongst the natives as food, from an idea that they eat snakes and other vermin, but a few weeks good domestic feeding is calculated to do away with any objection of this sort, as we had occasion to find in the excellent quality of these very geese when we afterwards dined at the Consulate.

A ridge of mountains forms a background to the north-west of San Paulo, in some of which are gold mines that have been long abandoned, nor is the mineral wealth of the province at all developed. The railway may bring with it new enterprise of this kind, but it will be slow work.

I went over the San Bento Convent, where only one priest appears to reside in an enormous building, a portion of which has lately been fitted up with considerable taste The church is also kept in good order, but it seems absurd for only one man to occupy such a building. The wealth of religious orders in Brazil is by no means insignificant, and it would be to the advantage of the country and of the people if this was made available for national purposes. Religion would be better appreciated, and the State would be able to form colonies in some of the richest lands of the Empire, which naturally enough fell into the hands of religious bodies.

It is said that the Tropic of Capricorn passes close to the city of San Paulo, but of course the exact spot cannot be defined. There is plenty of fruit and vegetables to be had, grapes are abundant and very cheap, good milk and fresh butter are easily obtainable, the cow going round to the houses in the morning with a bell attached to her, and generally the calf following. Indeed, a great many of the comforts and conveniences of life are to be found here which do not exist in other Brazilian towns, whilst the climate is infinitely superior. For many months of the year the thermometer ranges about 60°, and at times goes down to 40°; on the other hand it is sometimes very hot, but of short duration. This morning I saw a black boy in the street engaged in the occupation of shoeblack, with his little box and brushes very much after the London style. In fact there is a more general inclination to work when it is not so intensely hot. There goes the railway whistle, the train starting for Santos, and it will return about 3 p.m., bringing the passengers by steamer from Rio, which left there yesterday. There are two fast steamers a week between Rio and Santos, so the communication is well kept up.

The number of old fashioned waggons or carts on two solid wooden wheels, drawn by teams of oxen according to the weight carried, and the constant passage of them, and of mules and horses, the former with tinkling bells, all laden with country produce, indicate the nature of the traffic which existed prior to the opening of the railway, rendering the streets of the city a busy scene. The railway being closed between this and Jundiahy no doubt increases this traffic for a time, but it must always exist to a greater or a less degree, as everything for the consumption of the city has to be brought into it by these means. The bulk of the through traffic of coffee and cotton must, however, inevitably find its way on to the rails and be taken down the Serra, as it is impossible mules can compete with a railway for so great a distance. The troops of mules, horses, and carts assemble at shops or warehouses in streets where their business is carried on, their produce discharged, and a certain portion of the animals loaded back to their respective destinations. Hence the perpetual tinkling of bells and creaking of wheels; at the same time a number of carriages and tilburys are constantly in motion, conveying passengers about the city or outskirts, causing a degree of activity one would otherwise hardly expect to find.

Yesterday, Sunday, being the first Sunday in Lent, there was a grand procession, consisting of a large number of figures of saints, carried on men's shoulders, after the old style of chairing an M.P. at home. Sundry children were dressed up as angels, and there were also a military band and some few soldiers; for, as the latter have been drained by the war, only a sufficient number remain to keep guard, &c. The figures are as large as life. They were collected together at the church of San Francisco, a large and rather showy building, and at five o'clock the procession started, amidst discharging of rockets, ringing of bells, and other demonstrations. It passed the street in front of the hotel, and, being a tolerably long one, it had rather an imposing appearance. After traversing the principal streets of the city, it came back by a side one, which also skirted the hotel. A thunder storm had been gathering, and broke over the city just as the procession was reaching the church from whence it started. An indescribable scene of confusion ensued. The pace was quickened, angels were lifted on the shoulders of blacks, the carriers of saints hurried along as fast as the weight permitted—in fact, it was a race with the saints —each trying to pass the other, to the imminent danger of an upset. The only part of the procession which retained a show of decorum was that in charge of the Host, where the high priest walked under a canopy with a number of other priests, accompanied by attendants, swinging censers; and as the Host passed, all the spectators knelt down. Fortunately the rain kept off until the greater part reached the square, and the saints escaped a terrible wetting, as it came down in torrents, with loud peals of thunder and lightning, such as I have rarely met with.

The storm continued in this way for several hours, and curiously enough in the midst of it came a telegram from the Government of Rio de Janeiro, announcing that the iron-clad fleet had succeeded in passing the fortress of Humaita, while a division of Brazilian troops had also taken a redoubt, &c., particulars of which will doubtless shortly reach England. Excitement was at its height, and spite of the thunder, lightning, and rain, houses began to light up, rockets were flying about, and later on, a band of music, with many followers, paraded the streets, playing and shouting vivas, with other joyous demonstrations quite edifying under such an accumulation of atmospheric difficulties. On Monday evening the city was entirely illuminated with candles, lamps, and Chinese lanterns, the latter very pretty, and the effect altogether striking. A full military band paraded the streets, followed by crowds of people; indeed, nearly the whole of the population, male and female, turned out and paraded the streets to a late hour, the wonder being where they all came from. The demonstration continued for three days, or rather nights, but not on so extensive a scale, nor was the firing of rockets so profuse. The news from the seat of war has, therefore, created quite a sensation, the Paulistos being somewhat a martial people, and proud of the exploits of their countrymen before Humaita, though further advices are needed before the war can be considered at an end. A drawback accompanied the war news, namely, the cruel assassination of General Flores at Monte Video, and the sanguinary proceedings that followed on the occasion.

I may mention having attended a sitting of the Provincial Assembly, in a very pokey, close room attached to the palace, with a miserably low gallery at each end for the public. The proceedings, however, were orderly and dignified, and good speeches were made, one by Senhor Leite Moraes, a tall, handsome man, who appears likely to distinguish himself as an orator. The subject under discussion was a complaint against the conduct of the Roman Catholic priests. There are thirty-six members of the Provincial Chambers, who annually attend for a period of two months, and some of them come from considerable distances at much personal inconvenience to themselves. I believe they are to have a larger and better place for conducting their business, which is certainly very desirable. I also visited, in company with Captain Burton, English Consul, one of the seminaries or schools, presided over by French monks, who received us with attention, showed us over the extensive building and well laid-out gardens, and entertained us afterwards with some good English beer. The college, to which a good sized garden is attached, contains accommodation for about one hundred youths, who come here for their education, and remain several months, being comfortably lodged, and, I believe, well cared for.

This is only one of the many similar establishments in San Paulo, which, in this respect, answers to our Cambridge or Oxford. The view from the college is very extensive and picturesque—the city on one side, the large plain in which the city stands, with mountains in the distance, and close to the railway station. We heard the locomotive whistle, and saw the steam a long way off, reaching the station in time to see the train come in with 115 passengers, quite a large number, it being about the period of the students returning. It also brought a company of performers from one of the Rio de Janeiro theatres, who are going to afford the inhabitants a month's display of their artistic skill, so that in all respects the city will be very lively during the season of Lent, one of the eccentricities connected with the Roman Catholic religion. I went to the public gardens, which are at only a little distance from the railway station, and cover a large space of ground. They are in tolerable order, with flower beds and a piece of water in the centre. A considerable sum of money must have been originally expended on them, but not keeping things up is one of the major defects of the system in this country.

K

I thought processions were over for the present, but last evening there was one of some magnitude, conveying a saint from one church to another, and spite of wet streets after the heavy rain, a large number of people turned out to witness and follow the participants in the ceremony. To-day, however, being Friday, the 6th of March, was set apart for a special occasion—a meeting, not a race of saints; and, for a wonder, the day and night have been remarkably fine, a beautiful bright moon now shining after the great bustle is over and the saints gone to rest, though the illuminated altars in various parts of the city are still glittering in all their tinsel, with numerous worshippers, after depositing in a plate their offerings in the shape of "dumps," a slang phrase for copper coins. Preparatory symptoms have been going on for some days at a sort of large closet, or "hole in the wall" of the house opposite, belonging to an old nobleman, whose wife departed this life to-day. The folding doors had been opened and a large blue cloth thrown over the sanctuary from a balcony above, but still it was easy to see that something unusual was in progress; and to-day, about the time of the procession, the doors opened, and the curtain was withdrawn, revealing a very pretty altar, with a cross and small figures of saints at the top, the back parts and sides being covered with gold and silver tinsel, and groups or garlands of artificial flowers tastefully arranged, the whole lighted up by an immense number of candles, many of them in silver candlesticks, provided or lent for the occasion by devotees. There were about a dozen or more of these old cupboard altars decked out, each apparently vying for supremacy in effect. But I am forgetting the procession itself, which began to form at five o'clock, accompanied by the usual paraphernalia—a number of young girls dressed up as angels, bands of music, soldiers with fixed bayonets, the President of the Province, and all the dignitaries, with the high priest under a canopy and his attendants as before, whilst in front and behind walked the multitude. The meeting of the saints took place close to the hotel, where a halt was made, and a stout ecclesiastic (the bishop's secretary, I believe), for whom a very large pulpit had been temporarily erected at the corner of four streets, addressed a very energetic discourse to the multitude, until his voice began to get rather squeaky, nor could very much be made of what he said beyond that his listeners were a very bad lot, and required all the intervention of the saints before them to save them from perdition. The sermon ended, some music and singing took place before the altar opposite to our hotel, after which the procession went on, passing all the street altars, and this part of the ceremony ended when the saints were fairly housed. For hours, however, before the bright gaudy altars, and the still brighter moon, the whole population of the place passed in review, making their reverence and depositing their "dumps" or offertories

Whether or not these ceremonies are conducive to the maintenance of the Roman Catholic Religion I cannot pretend to say, but certainly they are preserved here in all their original stage effect (for it can be called nothing else) just as I first recollect them in Brazil. I understand that in other parts of the Empire they have much fallen off. San Paulo has been more or less isolated, and it is only since the opening of the railway that the foreign element has been introduced. Formerly a voyage to Rio de Janeiro was quite an undertaking; now, by rail and steam, it is an affair of two days. One thing is very clear, that processions and religious observances of this kind are very popular here. It is quite astounding to see the number of people filling the streets, mostly dressed in their best garments, but to-day the ladies wore chiefly black. On the other hand, the black women—the "swells," as they are called—prefer bright colours, and generally in good taste—white and coloured muslin, with gay shawls thrown over their ample figures, many of them very tall, fine looking women. Considering the dull, monotonous life here, these religious festivals are unquestionably a great relief to the female portion of the population, with whatever motive they may attend them; nor can one help being struck with their apparent earnestness of worship to dumb idols, and the constant stream of "dumps" poured into the plates by high and low, rich and poor, the latter bestowing their mite freely. A parade over the city on such occasions in their best attire, and the opportunity for showing off, has no doubt some influence, but this may be combined with religious feeling, according to their interpretation of it. Amongst the numerous votaries present I may mention the hardy, bronzed, country race, men who travel over the country with mules, leading the life of gipsies, and not unlike them, wrapped in a kind of coloured "poncho," similar to that worn in the River Plate. They almost live in the saddle, and are a very fine class of men—true Paulistos. But I see they are putting out the lights at the altar opposite, so it is time to extinguish mine and go to bed, as the clock is just striking midnight. To-morrow the folding-doors will be closed, and appear as the ordinary appendages of the house, leaving "not a wreck behind," except a few leaves of dead flowers scattered about the streets.

After a night's rest, I find that things have assumed their usual quiet course, enlivened only by the continued favourable news from the seat of war, which keeps the church bells going, rockets firing, and bands of music parading the streets at night. These public demonstrations have been of the most lively kind, assisted by a bright moon, without a cloud in the sky; indeed you can see to read by its rays. Moonlight nights are agreeable in any country, but in these tropical countries they seem to have an influence both on body and mind, refreshing the physique and raising the spirits. The atmosphere at this elevated spot is so cool at night that, however hot the day, you sleep in comparative comfort, and awake to enjoy the cool breeze of the early morning.

I took a ride in company with Mrs. Burton in the direction of what is called the Luz, past the railway station, where are numerous country houses, and a handsome bridge over the Tieté, after which the road goes through low ground, now entirely flooded, forming a swamp of many miles in extent. A couple of miles further on brings you to a rather sharp hill, on which is a small, rough-looking chapel, never finished, where people come on a kind of pilgrimage, or to enjoy the beautiful view from it. Looking back, the city of San Paulo is seen to much advantage, and to the left, some thirty-five miles distant, appear the spurs of the mountains, past which the railway runs to Santos. In the opposite direction, and apparently much nearer than they are, you see the chain of hills through which the railway proceeds to Jundiahy, the celebrated Jaraguay (or gold mountain) to the left of them, standing out very boldly in the light of the setting sun. Altogether it is considered one of the prettiest short rides about the place, there being a great variety of them. The site of the chapel also enjoys the reputation of being in the exact line of the tropic of Capricorn, so that San Paulo is just outside it. We reined up a short time to enjoy the prospect and then cantered back for dinner.

A perusal of accounts from England by the last mail, and of those from the River Plate, form a very agreeable diversion to the otherwise monotonous life one has to lead here, although my visit has been an exception to the rule in this respect from the occurrences detailed in previous pages. It is impossible to read the official and private communications from the River without feeling deeply grieved at the tragic scenes that have lately been acted there. The correspondent of the *Jornal do Commercio* at Monte Video gives a very graphic account of the assassination of poor General Flores and the events arising out of it; and I incline to believe that, however deplorable, they nipped in the bud a very formidable conspiracy, which, had it been successful, would have deluged Uruguay with blood for a long time, and might otherwise have complicated the position of things, as there can be little doubt the first act of the Blanco party would have been to do away with the Triple Alliance, so far as Monte Video is concerned, and to institute a renewal of their insulting conduct towards Brazil. The changed aspect of the war, with a prospect of its speedy termination, will strengthen the hands of the Colorados, and, it is to be hoped, maintain peace and order in the little Republic. The writer already mentioned goes into very minute details of the passage of Humaita by the Brazilian ironclads; and there is quite a tinge of romance attached to their performances, which certainly reflect the highest credit on the gallantry of the commanders and crews; nor less so the victory obtained by the Marquis de Caxias, the combined effects of which must lead to the occupation of Asuncion and to the ultimate surrender or destruction of Lopez himself. That his resistance has been wonderfully stubborn no one can deny; still less the pertinacity which has distinguished the conduct of the allies under difficulties pronounced by some first-rate military authorities to be insurmountable.

I have not yet referred to the theatrical performances now going on here, with a company from one of the Rio theatres, which draws crowded houses in a building almost as large as Covent Garden. It is in a very improvised state, but sufficiently got up to answer the purpose; and in a climate like this external appearances are not much thought of provided there is enough ventilation, which is certainly the case in the San Paulo Theatre. A stranger cannot help feeling surprised on entering to see so large a place, having three tiers of boxes, filled chiefly by well-dressed ladies, and a gallery for what we term the "gods," the gentlemen being in the pit, which holds fully 500 people and was quite crowded. Each one has what we call a stall, but here cane seats, with backs, divided by arms, so that you are very comfortably seated. The large attendance is explained by the circumstance of the city being dependent on casual performances, and of course everybody is anxious to take advantage of the opportunity. There is no regular company attached to the theatre, but the attendance, appearance, and dress of the ladies of San Paulo on these occasions will compare favourably with what is presented in any city of South America. As to the performance, it is usually a compilation from some French rubbishy novel; but the acting is tolerably good, and the audience attentive, sitting patiently for

the five or six hours commonly occupied by the piece
—a very great objection.

To-day—March 16—is the first of term at the College, where a strong muster of students took place at an early hour of the morning, and I believe that some of the ceremonials that occur on such occasions at Oxford and Cambridge also prevail here. The presence of nearly a thousand students gives a tone of animation to the old city, and is a set-off to the constant creaking of waggon wheels and the tinkling of bells of mules, which indicate its commercial character. Brazil is chiefly indebted to this city for a swarm of lawyers, many of whom have been, and continue to be, distinguished men, but it would be far better for the country if many of them were brought up to agricultural or commercial pursuits.

In the seaport towns the Portuguese continue to act as the chief traders, but in the interior the latter are mostly Brazilians. There is now the army, the navy, and the engineering pursuits open to the youth of Brazil, and I have no doubt they will by degrees take up positions more beneficial to their country than that of mere disputants, or lawyers, which characters are sadly too numerous.

Took an early ride to the north of San Paulo on the 17th, from whence there was a fine view of an extensive valley, where the mist was rising and floating away to the distant hills on the other side. We met troops of mules coming in with their drivers in their picturesque coloured ponchos, and also a group of women approaching the city. Skirting a wood to the left, through some pretty looking scenery, we came upon the new Santos road, made a few years back at great expense; and a most admirable road it is, but, it appears, not much used since the railway was opened, passing through a most admirable road it is, but it appears, not much used since the railway was opened, passing through a poor, uncultivated country. If the large amount expended on this road had been laid out at the terminus of the line at Jundiahy, towards the coffee producing districts, it might have been of much greater importance to the Province. Odd enough, it was made in opposition to the railway, although it must have been evident that the latter would take a large portion of the traffic, and that that by mules from San Paulo to Santos would be greatly reduced. The projectors, who were chiefly large coffee growers of the Province, might have supposed a good road to Santos would keep a check on the railway as to charges of transit, and be used in case of any partial stoppage of the railway; but unfortunately the heavy rains which shut up the latter for a time also injured the common road, rendering it impassable in places.

Before leaving the City of San Paulo, where I have spent several pleasant weeks, I went over what is called the House of Correction, but is in fact a criminal reformatory for the Province and admirably managed. The building is in a fine open space near the railway station, enclosed on a large square plot of ground, surrounded by high walls, inside which are gardens beautifully laid out, and kept in order by the inmates. The main portion of the building converges into a central point by means of arched roofs, lighted from the top, the cells abutting on the corridors which lead thereto. Here there is also a circular raised stone altar, on which mass is performed, and heard in all the cells through an open iron grating with which each is provided. The workshops are apart, leading off the garden, and consist of various trades suited to the acquirements of the criminals; there being also a school, where they are taught to read and write. They come to these workshops from the main building in groups, each individual having a mark or number to distinguish him by, and they are accompanied by a guard. The workshops have doors with open gratings, but secured by a strong lock and key, a sentinel doing duty during the time the men are occupied at labour, with a time master seated in a kind of elevated pulpit to see that the work allotted to every individual be properly done. In approaching or leaving the workshops the men all walk with folded arms, and the whole being on the silent system of punishment, no one is allowed to speak, except, I conclude, when some question has to be asked through the warder or other officer of the establishment, the discipline of which is admirably maintained. The inmates are about 120 in number, most of them convicted of serious crimes; they have here a dejected look, but I believe, on the whole, the system is found to be a very efficacious one, and does really lead to reformation of character. No female criminals are admitted, but I understand a ward is to be built for them. We were conducted over the establishment by the Governor, a retired colonel in the army, accompanied by Senhor Leite Moraes, a distinguished member of the Provincial Assembly. Much attention was shown us, and some refreshment was provided for us in the Governor's room. Near to the reformatory, abutting on the railway station, are the public gardens of San Paulo, on which a good deal of money has been spent. They are well laid-out, but not kept in order, one of the chronic defects of these kind of places in South America generally.

SAN PAULO TO SANTOS AND RIO DE JANEIRO.

We finally left San Paulo after a very agreeable visit, on the 25th of March, by the 9.30 train for Santos, with a tolerable number of passengers, and some friends who kindly accompanied us on our journey. Between San Paulo and San Bernardo station, a distance of about ten miles, the road is tolerably level, and the country more or less open, though uncultivated save in small plots. At this station I got upon the engine with Mr. Fox, and came upon sharp curves and many cuttings until we reached Rio Grande Station, after which, for a distance of seven miles, the works are very heavy, some of the inclines being one in fifty and one in sixty. Nothing near but dense forests, without a human habitation to be seen. Approaching the top of the Serra, it appeared completely shut in by the range of mountains in front of us, the road winding and twisting till we suddenly reached the small platform, whence the descent of the mountain begins, and a glorious prospect opens out of the valley below, with the sea in the distance; yet not without a vague feeling of anxiety as to the novel position in which we find ourselves placed. I was allowed to ride on the break again, and it is certainly a wonderful sight, whilst being slowly let down the lifts which I have before described. The day was light and the atmosphere clear, the light and shade on the dense mass of foliage with which the mountains are clothed appearing to great advantage, like a huge carpet spread over the face of nature. It is decidedly worth a visit from Europe to go over the railway, and few can help wondering how it was ever made, under what must have appeared almost insurmountable difficulties in such a country and such a climate; the pioneers obliged to live in the forests and often short of the necessaries of life. Without traversing the line it is impossible to form any idea of the magnitude of the undertaking, or how the boilers and machinery for the stationary engines were dragged up the mountains, almost without a track, much less a road, for a total height of 2,600 feet above the level of the sea. The Paulistos ought to be proud of their railway, and Englishmen of the skill and endurance of their countrymen in making it; at the same time, it cannot be denied that many errors of construction have been committed, and even at the present moment the working power of the line is crippled for want of locomotives, besides which those on the metals are not adapted to it, as I have previously explained. Red-tapery and official conceit have produced the same result here as in other places, to give way eventually to a practical common sense view of things; not without entailing, however, losses upon the unfortunate shareholders. The line being again open throughout, a considerable arrear of traffic is waiting to come down from Jundiahy, which will severely tax the insufficient rolling stock and locomotive power at the disposal of the manager; but at all events it is satisfactory to know that the traffic is likely to be a steady one, with a considerable future prospect when once its requirements are fairly met by the company.

We reached the foot of the Serra before noon, and at one o'clock we were at Santos station, the whole distance from San Paulo to Santos being 48⅛ miles; rather a long time on the way, but the Serra itself takes an hour, and there are several stoppages at the stations. Some time is also occupied in waiting at the foot of the Serra for the second portion of the train (it is divided into three carriages each lift) to come down and join before proceeding forward. This process of course takes place both ways. Contrast this system, however, with that of pack mules, and what an immense stride does it represent in the means of transit and communication.

Santos was cooler than when we went there before, and the day was fine and bright. The steamer did not sail until four o'clock, so we strolled about and got some dinner. The departure was punctual, and sailing down the river to the bar the surrounding scenery, tinged by the glowing afternoon sun, gave everything a very cheerful, though grandly picturesque aspect. The friends who had kindly accompanied us from San Paulo here left us in a boat, to land at the bar, which is a favourite watering place, and where many nice cottages are built. We steamed on, passed the small fort, and were soon in the open Atlantic, the boat dancing about more than was agreeable to some of the passengers, who soon disappeared below. The Santa Maria is a powerful boat, steaming her twelve knots an hour, with very good accommodation; but the wind and sea being against us, we did not get into Rio harbour before noon the next day, taking 20 hours for a distance of about 180 miles.

TRIP TO JUIZ DE FORA.—THE DOM PEDRO SEGUNDO RAILWAY.

To estimate the resources of a country with such an enormous extent of territory as Brazil by the quantity of cotton, sugar, coffee, or other products she actually exports, or by the extent of the towns and cities on her seaboard, would be to form a very inadequate idea of what those resources are capable of becoming by means of imported labour, the extension of railways, and other transport facilities in the shape of good roads. Even with the present limited population, railways are calculated to swell enormously the amount of Brazilian productions, as they naturally lead to the opening out of other modes of intercommunication, and draw towards them subsidiary streams of traffic, which have hitherto been unable to find a vent. It is only when a railway penetrates the primeval forests, and goes into the heart of a country, that an adequate idea can be formed of what it is capable of being made, or that the state of existing cultivation can be seen under all the drawbacks arising from the want of labour, added to the difficult and expensive means of transport. This has been very clearly shown in the case of the San Paulo Railway, which, with the proposed extension to Campinas, will reach at once the great producing districts, and enable the cultivators of them to make their calculations to a nicety as to the cost of laying down their coffee or cotton at the port of Santos, and whether or not it can repay them to extend their production with the means at present under their command. The result will doubtless be a very large addition to the exports from Santos.

But to return to the Dom Pedro II. Railway. On the day previous to my leaving Rio, I had made the acquaintance, through the introduction of a friend at home, of Dr. Gunning, who, I found to my surprise, lived some fifty miles up the line, and he very kindly invited me to remain the night with them, instead of going on direct to Entre Rios. Accordingly at noon the next day, (the 4th April), we started by a train that only runs at that hour on Saturday, the ordinary ones being at 5 a.m., which involves getting up in the middle of the night to those who are any distance from the station. The train was a very full one, and I had to be content with a seat on my own portmanteau at the beginning of my journey, the carriage being open, and built in the American style, with sofas and chairs round the sides. The station is large and commodious, with plenty of sheds and warehouses for receiving produce. The pace was pretty good; the train passing the suburbs of the city, then the abatoirs, where cattle are slaughtered, with hundreds of the large black vultures hovering about; afterwards going through the Emperor's grounds and not far from his palace. Many fine country houses are near the line, which become fewer in number until we reach the first station called Sapepomba, at a short distance from which is a fine estate belonging to the Baron de Mauá, whose name is a household word in Brazil. This estate is worked by an American, who married an adopted daughter of the Baron, and has now a very large tract of sugar cane under cultivation. It presents in other respects all the evidence of good management. The public road runs close to the station. We proceed through lowlands, with cattle grazing on some of them, until we reached the station of Machabamba, in the neighbourhood of which the Baron de Bomfim has also a large sugar estate as well as ground for grazing cattle. At this station, as at most others, were so-called hotels, where eating and drinking is carried on much after the fashion in other countries, and a number of passengers got out apparently to spend the Sunday in the country.

After traversing some fine open country, bounded by mountains on all sides, we crossed what is called the dismal swamp, where so many people lost their lives during the construction of the line; this part of the line reminded one of the swamps about which so much has been written in connection with the Panama Railway. The next station we came to was that of Belem, an important place at the foot of the great mountain rise. I may perhaps observe that many plots of land, after we left the suburbs of Rio, were cultivated with mandioca, the great staple article of food in this country, and doubtless much of what is now a waste will soon be brought into requisition for the production of this commodity. At Belem there was a good display of refreshment, substantial and light creature comforts evidently being appreciated by the Brazilians; oranges, figs, and sweets of various kinds were brought also to the carriage doors. Here we exchanged the ordinary English locomotive for one of the powerful American description, calculated to mount the hills, which we began to ascend immediately after leaving Belem station, and here commences the really interesting feature of the works. The American "horse," as it is termed, began snorting, the whistle making a frightfully loud noise,—a sort of steam gong, which can be heard at a very great distance. The train now twists and turns round the sharp curves, the scenery becomes grand and imposing as we go up, and at one point, after proceeding eight or ten miles through a succession of tunnels and embankments, a stone could be thrown across the ridge to the place we left. The views of the valleys, with the spurs of the hills planted with coffee and Indian corn, are very pretty, and one is called Paraiso, or paradise, though I think that title might be much more appropriately applied to the valley opposite Dr. Gunning's house, which is called the Valley of Monkeys, I suppose because many exist in the woods there. The elevation attained on reaching Dr. Gunning's station was upwards of 1,300 feet, in about $2\frac{1}{2}$ hours from Rio, and here I was persuaded to rest over Sunday, resuming my journey by rail on Monday morning.

Dr. Gunning's little colony, for it quite amounts to that, took me quite by surprise, as I was utterly ignorant of its existence. As I said before, the valley which it overlooks might justly be termed that of Paraiso, instead of the other we passed in ascending the mountains. It takes a range of some 20 to 30 miles, with a series of hills or spurs rising from it, backed by the mountains which tower over Rio de Janeiro. The house is built on the foreground, with an extensive balcony in front, where you sit in a rocking chair in a state of quiet ecstacy and wonder how such an enchanting spot can be so little known in a great city comparatively so near to it. From the balcony you can see the trains moving upwards, popping now and again into the numerous tunnels, there being no less than thirteen between the house and the foot of the mountain and sixteen or seventeen over the whole line. The Doctor has constructed two or three neat cottages on his land, and there is also within hail a charming one erected by Mr. Gotto when he was out here as Engineer of the Rio Improvements Company. It is situate at a point which also commands a fine view of the noble valley, and is at present occupied by an American merchant. The Doctor is about to build other cottages on his land, and is laying out the site for a hotel, which ought to be very attractive to Rio residents in search of fresh air and renovated health. It is difficult to conceive a more lovely situation, or one surrounded by more attractive scenery. Before dinner we took a walk in the fine shady woods below the house, and at night enjoyed the effect of a splendid moon from a balcony where the scene in Romeo and Julliet might be admirably enacted, a place of all others adapted for the interchange of "lovers' vows." We were, however, a very sober-minded, but pleasant party, and enjoyed ourselves with "sweethearts and wives" over a glass of toddy. On Sunday morning I rose early to look at one of the greatest natural curiosities it is possible to conceive. A light vapoury mist, "white as the driven snow," covered the entire valley; with here and there the tops of hills appearing like islands in a sea; indeed, one could hardly believe that what one saw was simply mist, and not something more tangible and substantial. This gradually disappeared as the sun topped the heights, and then all became bright and verdant as on the previous day. Residents in the valley feel wrapt in a kind of shroud whilst the mist is over them, but no evil effects appear to result from it. An American missionary, Mr. Black-ford, who was for some time stationed at the city of San

Paulo, and was, with his wife, a guest of Dr. Gunning, read a portion of the Church Service in Portuguese and preached a sermon in the same language to the household and a number of people employed about the place, after which we wandered about, dined, and enjoyed another quiet moonlight evening looking over the happy valley. There is quite a little society of Americans residing about here, which renders it anything but a solitude.

I left this hospitable retreat on Monday, by the train which passes at 8 a.m., and continued to find a series of wonderful curves and tunnels until we reached the station of Barra, where a good comfortable breakfast was waiting for such passengers as chose to avail of it.

I was joined by the son of Mr. Ellison, head engineer of the line, who is making a branch near Disengano station, in the direction of San Paulo, with which it is eventually intended to connect this province. He made himself very agreeable, and gave me much valuable information.

I should not omit to allude to the really beautiful scenery passed through between Entre Rios and Barra, where the passengers breakfasted. I walked to look at a very handsome bridge erected over the River Parahyba, which becomes here a considerable stream, running the whole distance to Entre Rios, where it meets the Parahybuna, which comes down from Minas Geraes, the latter emptying itself into the sea at San Joao de Barra, after passing the important town of Campos.

The railway, which is here 122 miles in length from Rio de Janeiro, is to be extended to another point on the Parahyba called Porto da Cunha, making a total distance of about 160 miles, the latter portion tapping valuable sources of traffic, as the river is only navigable a short way from its mouth. Besides its 16 tunnels, small and great, the railway is crossed by several handsome bridges, first to one bank of the river and then the other, as the gradients were found favourable, and there is one very fine station, called Disengano, a portion of the cost of which was contributed by the Marqueza de Bependi, who has a magnificent fazenda near to it, and numerous large picturesque fazendas are seen at different bends of the river, which rolls along in its rocky bed, with a succession of small rapids, the hills above it being covered with coffee, Indian corn, and mandioca, all now ripe. Where this cultivation does not exist either virgin forests or cattle grazing form the variety, and the former still occupy a large portion of the country we passed through, particularly between Uba station and that of Parahyba do Sul. I am told that Vassoura, a city about seven miles from the station of that name, is prettily situated and interesting, but of course it is impossible to see everything in so extraordinary a range of country.

We reached Entre Rios station before noon, and found the stage coach waiting; also a tolerable dinner, which the flies tried to participate in, being only held in check by boys with large feather fans. The place, I believe, is infested by flies from the number of mules kept there; but the company is improving and extending the accommodation for passengers, the head station being 800 feet in length. The guard of the "Mazeppa" summons the passengers, and away we started with four good mules, amidst dust and bustle, by a regular stage coach of the old English type, the first stage being along the banks of the Rio Preto, coming down from the mines. The road was all that had been described to me and more; a perfectly good, smooth, macadamised one, fenced in with groups of bamboo on the river side and aloes on the other, along which we drove at the rate of nine to ten miles an hour. I was inside at starting, but some passengers left at the second station, Parahybuna, when I mounted on the front seat for the remainder of the journey, and enjoyed as fine a ride, for good travelling and good scenery, as it is possible to conceive.

The road belongs to a Brazilian company called the "Uniao e Industria," started some few years back, and now carrying on a large and profitable traffic, chiefly in merchandise; but the stage coaches are a very important feature as regards accommodation for the public. The stations where they change mules are large and commodious, with warehouses for receiving produce, and that of Parahybuna is in a most picturesque situation, a huge granite mountain on one side and in front of the river, which rushes down over rocks, forming cascades here and there, with a long bridge which we had to cross. A good many dwelling houses are built about these stations, belonging, I conclude, to people connected with the road. Our next station was Simon Pereira, about which there is a good deal of woodland scenery, reminding one of parts of Wales, with the road winding in and out round the hills; and on this stage is a very fine fazenda known by the name of Solidade, the property of the Baron Bertiago, comprising, I am told, an immense district. Here we again come upon the mountain stream, which runs through the valley, always forming a rapid current as we keep ascending.

The next stage was Barboza, where we came up with another diligence, also from Petropolis, with a party, having a band of music outside, and Portuguese and Brazilian flags flying. They kept ahead of us, but at the last stage, Ponto Americano, a most romantic spot, we started almost together, our companion still keeping the lead, at a strong gallop, which our coachman imitated, and it was anything but an agreeable race into Juiz de Fora, to say nothing of the dust we had to take up in the wake of the front diligence. Nothing could be more beautiful than the scenery for the last stages, coffee and Indian corn plantations succeeded each other, mingled with virgin forests, grazing ground, waterfalls in the distance, entire trees covered with purple and yellow flowers, a perfect galaxy of tropical vegetation in its most attractive forms. The evening was pleasantly cool,—so cool as to cause one to button up his coat, and there was a sensation of freshness in the air like that of an autumn evening at home.

As the two coaches approached Juiz de Fora a large number of its residents turned out to see the arrival, which I believe was that of some new settlers, who must have been gratified with their reception. We drove on to the coach station, where I found that the gentleman I was anxious to see had gone to his fazenda that morning, some leagues distant; so I determined to await his return and went to a small hotel close to, called the "Union," where I made myself as comfortable as the limited accommodation would permit.

Juiz de Fora is pleasantly situated on an elevated plateau, some 2,600 feet above the level of the sea, with a background of fine cultivated hills and a very picturesque waterfall. The originator and director of the flourishing company "Uniao e Industria" has built a magnificent house on an elevated spot which overlooks the whole valley, and his grounds are beautifully laid

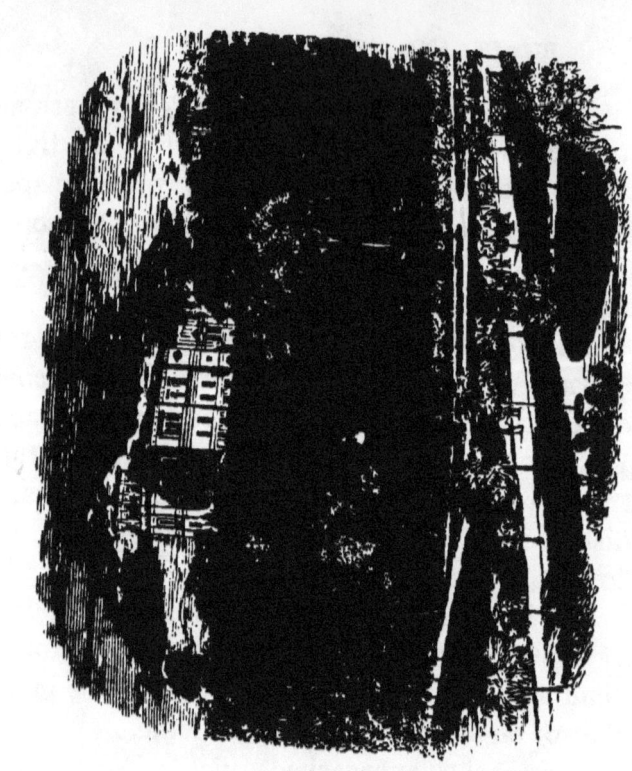

Residence of Senhor Lage.

out with every species of tree to be found in Brazil, as well as those brought from other countries. There are ornamental waters, with swans, rare specimens of water fowl, and numbers of valuable birds, fowls, monkeys,—in fact, a little Zoological Garden of itself. Everything in the establishment was in keeping, evincing the good taste of the owner and the liberal manner in which he expends his large fortune. I had also the opportunity of going over a new building called the School of Agriculture, where modern agricultural implements are to be collected, as well as samples of live stock to improve the breed of cattle. There is a capital English stallion, two years old, descended from the celebrated Stockwell, brought out from England at great expense; another one of Norman breed, besides brood mares, bulls, Alderney cows—in short, the nucleus of a respectable cattle show, which it is intended to become, and the Emperor has announced his intention to visit the place in June next, though it will take some time to make it complete and in a state of efficiency. An intelligent Swiss gentleman presides over the School of Agriculture, and an English groom is very proud, as he may well be, of the silky coat and the healthy appearance of the descendant of Stockwell.

There is a nice little German colony at Juiz de Fora, mostly artisans in the company's employ, who live in very snug cottages, with little gardens attached to them, the women keeping cows, selling milk, &c. A death had occurred the day I was there, and the funeral was attended by all the elders of the colony, men and women, dressed in their best clothes, forming a very interesting group. The company employ some 3,000 mules in the traffic of their line, the breakers of them, as well as the coach drivers, being Germans. Mr. Treloar, jun., arrived from Rio with his wife and family during my stay here, leaving the next day with a large troop of mules, on a seven days' journey up to the mines.

Having seen all of interest in Juiz de Fora, I started on Thursday, the 9th of April, to return to Entre Rios, and thence on by the same "Uniao e Industria" road to Petropolis, a total distance of about 107 miles. I found the second half of the road as interesting as the first half I had gone over—all in the same perfect state, some parts between Entre Rios and Petropolis passing through splendid mountain scenery. Near Entre Rios the river is crossed by a very fine iron bridge. We reached Petropolis at dusk, amidst a shower of rain, the first I had met with on the whole journey, during which the weather was remarkably fine and cool in the higher ranges of the road, though hot and dusty on the level parts. For nearly the whole fifty miles the road winds by the bed of a rapid mountain stream, descending from the mountainous district about Petropolis, going to swell the river of which it is the source, forming a succession of cascades, the noise of whose waters makes "music to the ear," enhancing the grandeur of the scenery through which it passes as well as cooling the atmosphere.

I should not neglect to mention the extensive cart traffic over the road, which constitutes the real income of the company, and has enabled it to pay the large dividend of 10 to 14 per cent. These carts are all of one pattern, with names and numbers on them, drawn generally by five mules, with a spare one attached. We were constantly meeting them going up and down, and whether they have got more into the way of it, or the mules are now better trained, we met with no such in- conveniences as Mr. Hinchcliffe describes in his book, though the windings and turnings of the road are often of such a nature as to require a "bright look out," and the use of a shrill whistle—the horn being only sounded on approaching the end of the journey. By means of the rail and coach, Rio morning papers are delivered at Juiz de Fora, a distance of 170 miles by rail and road, the same evening. Formerly it required a week to communicate between the two places. A large quantity of stone is collected along the road to keep it in order, and at certain distances are men breaking them in the most old fashioned manner possible. They are chiefly Portuguese immigrants.

I had not been at Petropolis for twenty years, during which time there has been a large increase of building and population, but I was sorry to learn that this prosperity is likely to be evanescent, in consequence of the soil suitable for cultivation by the German colonists being worn out, and still more by the Dom Pedro II. Railway turning the stream of traffic, which previously to its opening to Entre Rios had continued to flow from the mines through Petropolis and down the splendid mountain road, conveying goods and passengers to the Mauá Railway, and thence by steamer to Rio. Of course, the railway from Entre Rios to Rio de Janeiro, though longer as regards mileage, is quicker and more direct, with a saving in expense to travellers, even if produce and merchandise were conveyed at equal rates by the two roads, but it must be the interest of the country to keep both the roads open, as, in the case of accidental stoppage, the Petropolis one is always available. It is not unlikely that terms will be come to by the two companies so as to prevent injurious competition, as the country has had to pay large sums of money for the installation and maintenance of both roads.

I remained over Sunday at Petropolis, but it turned out a very wet day, and I was not able to go about much, or to take advantage of the splendid view there is from the top of the mountain down to the Bay of Rio de Janeiro. We started at 6.30 on Monday morning in a carriage with four mules, and descended amidst heavy rain and a dense mist, so that none of the beauties of the locality were visible. At the foot of the Serra, the railway train was waiting, and we soon reached the place of embarkation by steamer, arriving at Rio about 10.30, after a week's absence, during which I have acquired a better knowledge of the progress and resources of this part of the country than any other means of information could have supplied. As regards the great internal road on which I have dwelt so much, it is decidedly one of the marvels of Brazil.

RIO DE JANEIRO TO THE RIVER PLATE.

SECOND TRIP.

On my return to Rio on Saturday, the 11th of April I found the City of Brussels had arrived after a very quick passage from Falmouth of twenty days, and she was leaving next morning (Sunday) for the River ; so I resolved to go by her and complete my visit, which had been so recently unfortunately interrupted. A difficulty occurred, owing to the police requiring me to give three days' notice in the public papers of my intention to leave, and they refused to *visa* the passport I brought with me, though it had already served on other similar occasions. The only way to get over the obstacle was to take a surety to the police office, who would be responsible for any debts I might have contracted, and after driving backwards and forwards for some hours, at considerable trouble and expense, this requirement was satisfied. This absurd and vexatious system of passports is one of the old relics of barbarism which Brazil ought to do away with, and the sooner the better ; nor is it any protection against roguery, as every one knows how easily such regulations are evaded in the latter case. Countries like Brazil ought to be as free as the air, and all possible facility given to travellers who only come for information or amusement, and have no business relations. Passports do not exist in the Great Republic of the North, and France has abolished them, so let us hope Brazil will follow in the wake, and evince equal liberality in dealing with passengers' luggage.

We were to leave at 8 a.m. on Sunday, but were detained for dispatches until ten, and finally passed the fort at 11 a.m., with a light wind but much swell, indicating a southerly wind, of which we got the benefit the next day. I may mention that the City of Brussels is a splendid new steamer of Tait's line, and made the first departure under their contract with the Belgian Government. At Antwerp a grand entertainment had been given to the authorities on the day of her departure, and on Saturday a party was entertained on board at Rio.

After encountering rather a strong southerly gale, we made the River on Thursday night, and came to an anchor off Monte Video early on Friday, the passage having been run in five days. It blew so hard, with so much swell on, that it was some time before we got on shore, on reaching which I went to my old quarters at the Gran Hotel Americano, meeting several old friends there. The aspect of Monte Video was greatly changed for the better since my last visit, when the cholera was making such fearful ravages and an air of activity pervaded the place, notwithstanding the sad tragedy which had occurred in the assassination of General Flores. Rumours of political troubles still prevailed, but there was nothing on the surface to indicate them, and the nightly gathering on the Plaza to hear the band had been resumed, although for some time after the murder of the President the Plaza was held by troops and guns planted at the corner of it.

A visit to Buchentall's quinta occupied the greater

part of one day, and a delightful place it is, enclosed in spacious grounds, provided with choice trees, beautiful exotics, a large conservatory, and other glass houses; in fact, with everything which a cultivated taste can devise. There is a large kitchen garden attached, and quite a plantation of pear trees, loaded with splendid pears, for which Monte Video is famous. The stables and farm buildings are extensive, and, like the house, they are in the Swiss cottage style; they are tenanted by fine horses, valuable cows, and other descriptions of cattle. Everything is in perfect order. The view from the upper ground, at the back of the house, is very fine —the city, the harbour filled with shipping, and the mounts at its entrance, the waters of the La Plata glistening beyond in the sunlight. It is a bright, beautiful day, and certainly at this season the climate is very agreeable, so different from the intense heat experienced in the month of January. After leaving the quinta, we extended our drive, passing by many pretty country houses, some of peculiar but tasteful architecture, and stopped at a house on the road side, kept by a Frenchman, where we got an excellent cold luncheon and drove back to the city.

Expecting the steamer to sail the same night, we embarked before dark, but were disappointed, the cargo not being all discharged. We did not get away until next evening. Had we known this we might have seen the races, which took place the following morning, to see which I believe more than half the population turned out, the Custom House and public buildings being closed. South Americans are fond of excitement, though horse-racing is comparatively a new amusement for them, being chiefly got up by foreigners. Whilst at dinner on Monday afternoon, the wind, which had been blowing moderately from the north, suddenly veered round to the south, and soon after we left the harbour increased to a pampero, causing a nasty cross sea and a very disagreeable motion in the ship, which sent most of the passengers to bed early. It is not a very pleasant navigation in such weather, with banks lying in the way, and shallow water in many places, and we were glad when daylight came to find ourselves near the outer roads of Buenos Ayres. This exposed roadstead, having to lie so far from the shore, is a great drawback, rendering the expense of discharging and loading very heavy, but there is no help for it, nor any prospect of improvement in this respect. They have very fine boats and lighters, with first-rate boatmen, and, as a rule, accidents are rare, unless when the fierce pamperos drive everything before them.

This is my second visit to Buenos Ayres, after a lapse of 15 years, and, although from the sea no remarkable change appears to the eye, yet, after landing, the enormous increase of the city soon becomes apparent, about which I shall say more presently. The Mole and Custom House were new to me, as also the landing pier for boats—a very great convenience and improvement on the old carts, into which you had to get from the boat. The weather, which had been cool at Monte Video, became positively cold here, cloaks and great coats being the order of the day. It is now approaching the coldest season of the year, with some sharp frost at night, which has blackened the potatoes and other vegetables outside the city; and the sunny side of the street is decidedly preferable to the shady one, a very different state of things to that which existed when I was at Monte Video, in January, with the heat frequently above 90 degrees.

CITY OF BUENOS AYRES.

It is not an easy task to describe the great changes that have taken place in this city since my visit fourteen years ago. At the same time they are so remarkable as to require a special notice.

My views at that time were sanguine as to the progress of these River Plate countries, but they have been more than realised, notwithstanding political and other drawbacks. Suffice it to say that Buenos Ayres has nearly doubled in size since I was last here, and, although no public census that I am aware of has ever been taken, the population of the city and environs must almost have augmented in the same ratio. The difficulties of the roadstead remain, but a forest of masts, extending for many miles in the outer and inner roads, together with a considerable number of steamers (the latter particularly in the inner roads) meets the eye, and two piers, or moles, have been erected, one exclusively used for Custom House purposes, the other for boats and passengers, but a large portion of the traffic is still carried on by the carts which go alongside the boats with cargo or to take it away. Landing at the mole, a busy scene presents itself in the conveyance of passengers' luggage, which is taken charge of by the peons or porters, and carried for examination to the little depot at the entrance to the mole. Afterwards it is allowed to proceed in carts or carriages to its destination.

Being built in squares, the increase of the city is not very apparent until you get fairly into it; but the numerous two or three-storied houses, the large new hotels, the fine shops and warehouses, and the great movement in the street, all indicate a thriving place of business, which Buenos Ayres unquestionably is. Most of the streets running direct from the river are now three miles in length, and they cover an equal breadth, so it is easy to judge the extent of the ground covered; besides which, very many handsome quintas, or country houses, are to be seen in every direction outside the city. The streets generally are badly paved, and make very rough work for carts and carriages passing over them, but these manage to get along with considerable wear and tear of wheels and springs, as well as horses' feet, which, however, appear to be quite a secondary consideration. After the well-paved streets of Rio de Janeiro, both Monte Video and Buenos Ayres cut a very poor figure; but the worst feature is the absence of sewerage, and the refuse of the town is at times very offensive to the olfactory nerves, and destroys the appellative "good airs," which is otherwise a characteristic of the place under ordinary circumstances, or as nature intended it to be. The inhabitants seem to have had a wretched municipal system; but for this there is no reason why the city should not be well drained, well paved, as well as properly lighted with gas, which latter is now the case.

Strangers have a choice of really very large and commodious hotels, and there are boarding and lodging houses of various kinds, but at seasons accommodation in them is very difficult to obtain, such is the constant increase of demand by visitors as well as by permanent residents; in fact, the requirements of the population are constantly overtaking the facilities of the city, and there appears to be no reasonable limit to its extension north, south, and west, the river facing eastward. The chief increase, however, has been westward, or in a straight line from the river frontage into the country. Owing to the necessities of an augmenting population, the price of building land in or near the city has been driven up to a very high figure, and rents, as a matter of course, are excessive. Increased population has been followed by enhanced luxury, which manifests itself in the style of architecture, in the splendid shops, in the number of private carriages as well as those for hire, but naturally this has been attended by an inflated expenditure. Living in Buenos Ayres is now quite as expensive as in London or Paris; perhaps more so as regards luxuries, the import duties on which are very heavy. Generally, Buenos Ayres is a dear place to live in. Amongst other new buildings is the large theatre called Colon, and a Music-hall, the latter erected by private subscription. It is lofty and light, tastefully decorated, and I believe very well filled when concerts are held there, being also occasionally used for dinners.

The busiest part of the city, commercially speaking, is down by the Custom House and on to the Boca, the latter the rendezvous of lighters conveying produce to the ships in the outer roads, as well as of small steamers bound up river, and I understand that 300 lighters are now engaged in this work, many of them of good size and decked over. It is in contemplation to deepen and enlarge the Riachuelo, as the stream alluded to is called, and a most useful work it will be, as it is almost the mainstay of the port. At the other extremity of the city, which borders on the Northern Railway, washing of clothes is carried on among the willow trees which border the river; it is quite a sight on a fine sunny day. On the high ground about and beyond the Retiro, numerous handsome villas have been erected and the Retiro itself has been planted with trees, forming a pleasant promenade. In addition to other improvements and conveniences, omnibuses now ply from the city in various directions, so that locomotion is greatly facilitated, and people can live out of the city without the trouble of keeping conveyances, if they object to this, or have not the means to maintain them. Commerce is extending rapidly, and the Custom House revenue has doubled itself within a very few years.

BUENOS AYRES TO COLONIA.—
ESTANZUELA.

The invitation of Mr. William White to spend a few days at his estancia took me over to Colonia, from which it is distant about 15 miles, amidst the beautiful undulating country of the Banda Oriental. Three to four hours is the time usually occupied in crossing the river, almost in a direct line from Buenos Ayres, and the steamer in which I embarked had very comfortable accommodation but few passengers on board. There was a small boat in opposition to the one I was in, and we arrived very close together.

Colonia is one of the oldest settlements in the River, being built upon a peninsula jutting out into the stream, with a snug little harbour, which is in course of improvement. The town presents a dilapidated and neglected appearance, which is accounted for by its having, until recently, been fortified, and made the head-quarters of different factions during the long civil wars. There is a large church, with three high towers, visible at a considerable distance, and a lighthouse for the protection of vessels passing, as several low islands are situated close to the harbour. Some good looking houses have lately been erected, and the site of a new town laid, but it will be many years before it is likely to assume any importance. I noticed an old gateway, with an inscription dated 1724 over it.

I found Mr. White's carriage waiting for me at Colonia. It was drawn by four horses, the road being heavy for a few miles, but after that we got into a good one,—a kind of beaten track over what is called the campo, and for the first time I realised the pleasurable feeling of travelling over a sea of land, if it can be so named, where, excepting an occasional *puesto*, or shepherd's hut, not a human habitation is to be seen. The undulations of the land are here very like the long roll of the ocean, by which it is supposed to have been formed, and you are at once in the midst of cattle, horses, and sheep, with grass and thistles growing everywhere, the thistles in many cases being masters of the situation.

It was getting foggy before we reached Mr. White's estancia, but the light of the moon assisted our course across an apparently trackless country. I found Mr. White's quinta a very pretty and comfortable residence, surrounded by trees and evergreens, all of which have been planted by the present owner. The whole place is in fact the creation of some ten years, showing what can be done in this country by a judicious application of capital and labour. The house and estate cover a space of some nine square miles, the former being built on an elevated spot, called "Monte" (or the "Mount,") and occupying with grounds about 50 acres of good rich soil, overlooking an amphitheatre of hill and dale, which stretches as far as the eye can reach, with "puestos" or shepherds' cottages at regular distances, where the cattle and sheep are collected together at dusk and let out again at daylight. This is a most interesting process, which I have seen described, but it

Mr. White's House at Estanzuella.

can only be realised personally. It is something like marshalling a scattered army and bringing them into a given square. The shepherds or peons go galloping about until the cattle and sheep are gathered together, when they all, as by a kind of instinct, find their way to the corral or fold. At dawn the following morning they are let out again and roam for miles over the estate. The arrangements at a good estancia like that of Mr. White's are very complete, and every one understands his work, but of course the eye of a master is required to see that the work is properly done. The stock on this estancia consists of about 30,000 sheep, upwards of 1,000 head of cattle, and some 100 horses.

My first day was employed in visiting several of the stations, and very agreeable it was cantering over the springy turf, clothed with grass and thistles, where the sheep and cattle were quietly feeding. Buttercups glittered in the sunshine, but we missed the modest daisies so familiar at home. We were on horseback five hours, and I returned to dinner highly delighted with all I had seen. The second day we took the carriage and a gun, as partridges are plentiful and innumerable flocks of doves. Paid a visit to the estancia of Mr. Giffard, about six miles distant in a direct line, but further by the course we had to take, partly over the open campo. Returning we came close upon some half-dozen ostriches and Mr. White shot at and wounded a very fine male; but it was a painful sight to see the struggles of the poor bird, and we were obliged to get one of the men from a neighbouring station to dispatch it with his knife. Many of these noble birds are still to be met with in the campo, where they are pursued by the natives for the value of the feathers. I was presented with a portion of the feathers of the ostrich killed as described. The third day we were again on horseback for several hours, with a boy carrying a gun and some refreshment. We rode along one of the running streams with which the campo is favoured, to look for some ducks, but the streams were very low, and we only succeeded in bagging one. These streams are invaluable for cattle, and the Banda Oriental in this respect is more fortunate than Buenos Ayres, and in consequence suffers less from drought. Finding game so scarce, the boy was sent home, and we cantered on to visit some of the other stations I had not yet seen, the weather throughout being beautifully fine, clear sunshine, with a bracing and most exhilirating breeze.

There are some curious collections of rocks mostly on the margins of the streams. Huge boulders, thrown up it would seem by some convulsion of nature, and between which trees and enormous cactuses have forced their way, in cases even splitting the stone, especially present a most singular appearance. About Mr. Giffard's quinta there is quite a large formation of this kind, and a collection of very fine ombu trees, several with immense trunks and evidently of great age.

To-day, the last of my visit, has been spent in riding about the quinta, watching the operation of lassoing and bringing into the corral a refractory bull and cow that had left their companions and roamed miles away. The dexterity of the peons, and the way they manage their horses on these occasions, is something wonderful, and fairly exhausts the strength of the animals.

This is the finest season of the year in these countries, and it is impossible to imagine anything more pleasing or more cheerful than the present aspect of the campo. The next two or three months constitute the winter season, which is rainy and cold. September and

October (their spring) are generally fine. The heat of summer is, of course, considerable, but it is not so much felt in the open country, where a fresh breeze, as a rule, prevails; it is the towns that are most disagreeable at that period.

To-morrow, I return to Colonia, highly gratified with all I have observed, and with the kind hospitality I have experienced. As I have said, partridges are abundant, but they commonly go singly, and without a pointer they are difficult to follow. Mr. White, however, shot two brace close to his house, when we were walking out before breakfast, and several single ones on other occasions. They are prettily marked birds and delicate eating. He did not happen to have a suitable dog by him at the time. The shepherds all keep fine dogs, mostly of the retriever breed, to assist them in managing their flocks, and there were a good many attached to the house and out-buildings; one of the former, a Scotch terrier, and myself becoming very great friends.

TRIP ON THE CENTRAL ARGENTINE RAILWAY.

I AM writing this on board the "Lujan" steamer, built in Buenos Ayres, with engines by a Glasgow house. She is a comfortable boat, with good accommodation for passengers, and the "vivers" excellent, including even champagne at dinner, which in this country is rather an expensive luxury. After a lapse of fifteen years I find myself once more ascending the noble Parana river, which at that time was almost unknown in Buenos Ayres, the little "Argentine" being the first commercial steamer that ever navigated its waters. I predicted the results a few years would bring about, and my expectations have been more than realised, the river being now as freely navigated by steamers as some of those in the United States, with the difference of course that there is not the same amount of population on its banks —population being still the great want of this boundless region.

The station for passengers for the up-river boats is now the terminus of the Northern Railway, at a small stream called Tigre, which is reached in something over an hour's time. We left the station at 10 a.m., and arrived at the wharf alongside which the steamer lay at 11.30. All the passengers, with their luggage, were soon on board, and we started, wending our way through the small branches of the Parana, in many places not wider than a canal, the steamer brushing against the overhanging trees. A couple of hours brought us at last into the wide embouchure of the river at a point named Palmas.

The advantage of the Tigre as a starting point for steamers is that it avoids the disagreeable boating in the roads of Buenos Ayres and crossing the bay for Martin Garcia; in every way it is a desirable arrangement, alike beneficial to the steamers and to the railway. Upwards of a dozen steamers were laying outside the Tigre, in a stream called Lujan (after which this boat is named), two of them large double-decked Yankee river boats and nearly all of them without occupation—a terrible sacrifice of valuable property. Having discussed a solid *dejeuner à la fourchette*, I came on deck to enjoy the scenery. It was blowing a fresh breeze, dead against us, with a strong current and very cold, cloaks and great coats being a necessity although the day was bright and sunny. For several hours we steamed along, passing only jungle and dense masses of trees, with numerous sailing craft at anchor, laden with cargo, many bound upwards, no doubt with stores for the army in Paraguay.

Just before sunset we passed a very fine quinta, belonging to the Minister of Education, Senor Costa, built on a beautiful barranca, or elevated ground, a short way from the river, the horsemen on the heights presenting a very picturesque appearance.

Dinner was announced, which occupied fully an hour, and afterwards I went on deck and enjoyed a night on the noble Parana. The wind had gone down, and the stars shed their light over the still water, on which the shadow of the trees was reflected, our course being occasionally close to them, though at times we had to take the mid stream. Now and again the sky was lighted up with fires, caused, I believe, by the burning of wood for charcoal, a process which might go on for centuries without exhausting the illimitable extent of wood. A large traffic is carried on in this material by river craft to Buenos Ayres and Monte Video. We stopped to land passengers at a station called Hermanos, and soon after passed two or three steamers at anchor, with some sailing vessels near them, no doubt connected with the war services. Our passengers are a motley group, speaking all languages, and amusing themselves by playing cards, chess, and dominoes, the while talking and chattering away at the top of their voices; some ladies amongst them as merry as the rest. Many Italians, French, and Germans are met on board these steamers, but comparatively few English, who remain more in the cities and towns, or at their estancias when resident in the country. After a fine, clear, starlight night, the latter part aided by a bright moon, the day broke grandly, and we soon came to anchor at the little port of San Nicolas, where we landed and took in some passengers. Then came a good, substantial breakfast, and at about eleven o'clock the large saladeros near Rosario were in sight. We brought up alongside a coal hulk, where the steamer had to take in fuel before returning to Buenos Ayres the same afternoon.

A number of sailing vessels and steamers were laying at anchor at Rosario, making quite a busy scene. I landed in a small punt to find my way to the house of a friend. The aspect of Rosario was not much changed, looking at it from the river, with the towers of the church in the background, the town itself being more or less concealed by the high barranca. On entering it, however, I was quite lost. Streets have been extended in every direction for more than a mile, and I should say it has doubled or trebled in size and population since I was here. Whatever prejudicial effects the Paraguayan war may have produced in other respects, there can be no question that Rosario has largely benefitted, the place being one of call for steamers and sailing vessels up and down; and it also supplies a considerable quantity of stores for the army. The value of land and property has gone up to a high figure, and the poorer portion of the population are obliged to squat wherever they can find room to build a rancho, or kind of mud hut. Gauchos galloping about in their picturesque costume showed that we were in a new province, and although civilisation has extended itself here somewhat after the fashion of Buenos Ayres, there are evident signs that it is intermingled with much of the wild habits of a life in the Pampas.

The great object of my visit here was of course to see the Central Argentine Railway, and certainly those accustomed to the imposing appearance of railway stations at home will hardly be impressed with the rough and ready wildness of the scene which presents itself here. A few disjointed wooden sheds in an open plain, one side bordering on the river, some carriages and covered waggons on the rails, at this time constitutes the terminus of a line already carried 158 miles into the interior; but all this is merely temporary and will give place to the permanent station now in process of formation, and upon which hundreds of labourers are at present constantly at work. The material is all there in readiness, and the station would have been much further advanced had it not been for the cholera, which caused such terrible devastations here a few months ago. Internal commotions have also tended to retard progress. Happily these scourges are for the time at least passed away, and it is to be hoped nothing will again interfere to prevent the completion of a line of such vital interest in connection with the material development of the country between Rosario and Cordova.

I was curious to see the first arrival and starting of the trains, which did not indicate much traffic; but this can hardly be looked for until the metals are carried through and the railway possesses all the needful appliances, not to speak of the prejudices of a people who have been accustomed to gallop over the wide plains like the Arabs of old, and use those antique structures drawn by bullocks, which are yet destined to be abandoned to rot in their final resting place, or be removed further west to bring traffic to the Cordova station. Engineeringly speaking, it is the easiest possible task to make a railway through such a country as this, but other drawbacks and difficulties exist in the absence of population and of conveniences to which we are accustomed in England. It is a refreshing sight in Rosario to see so large a mixture of the foreign element. New banks and large establishments are in operation and Estanceiros constantly coming into town to transact their business. Among the visitors at Rosario are many Englishmen from the districts round about, who have not been murdered by the Indians, notwithstanding the stories prevalent to that effect, and I hear of numerous thriving colonies in the neighbourhood, which I regret time will not permit my visiting, as the extent of my ramble must now be confined to going over the railway. I repeat that my impression as to the future of Rosario, after all it has lately gone through, is favourable, and I am perfectly satisfied of the go-a-head nature of every thing in this prosperous province.

The train for Rosario starts at 8 a.m., and is due at Villa Nueva, a distance of 158 miles, at 6 p.m., travelling at an average speed of nearly sixteen miles an hour, including eight stoppages—quite sufficient for present purposes, with a train composed of waggons and two American passenger cars, one for first and the other for second class. We got off a little after eight o'clock with a good long train and the cars were pretty well filled. For the first two or three stations the ground is slightly undulating, covered with good pasture, on which numerous herds of cattle, flocks of sheep, and horses were feeding; afterwards, or about half-way between Rosario and Villa Nueva, there are few cattle seen, though the food for them is there in any quantity. At Roldan, the first station from Rosario, some tents were erected, and horses collected, in course of training for the races to be held on Monday next, the 25th of May, at which there is generally a large gathering of sporting characters from that and other districts, as also of spectators from Rosario. It is an English club, with the usual array of stewards, umpires, &c. The meeting is expected to be a very good one. The next station is Carcaranal, near which the river is crossed by a handsome iron bridge, the river itself flowing for a very long distance through the province of Cordova and Santa Fe, ultimately merging its waters with those of the Parana. These first two stations are mere mud huts, being only temporary, but Carcaranal has the additional disadvantage of being placed in the midst of a black, dismal, dry lagoon, where a butcher's establishment is kept for supplying a portion of the company's workmen on the line with meat. The rancho, or station for the passengers, might as well be removed, however, a few hundred yards further back, the engine going on to get its supply of water at one of the tanks placed here, instead of the olfactory nerves of the passengers being exposed to an ordeal of no agreeable character. I believe the nuisance is much complained of and will soon be removed.

The next station, Canada de Gomez, is a very respectable brick-built one, well kept, where we found some excellent partridges just cooked, which soon disappeared amongst hungry passengers, who had not time to breakfast before leaving, and there were also other refreshments. About this and Tortugas station is some very good land, and numerous English estancias in the neighbourhood, which I am assured are in a thriving condition, the aspect of the country being also more cheerful. We saw the plough at work, and I believe a large quantity of corn will soon be grown in this district. Further on, about Leones station, the country becomes more monotonous, one dead sea of brown-looking grass, without cattle or any appearance of cultivation, and not a shrub or tree to be seen. We passed a long train of carts from Rosario, filled with merchandise for distant places; also troops of laden mules going in the same direction, as the facilities offered by the railway are not yet sufficient to do away with this cumbrous and expensive mode of transit. This, however, is only a question of time. As we approached Frayle Muerto station, trees began to appear, and we passed through quite a forest, which was very pleasant after the long stretch of land bare of shrub or tree. The station at Frayle Muerto is a substantial brick building, and will be very commodious when completed. We had plenty of time to get some dinner here, and being rather behind, it was dark when we reached the present terminus at Villa Nueva, where I was kindly received by the manager, Mr. Lloyd, who gave me a shake down for the night at his comfortable little cottage close to the station. There I found a nephew of Mr. Wheelright and Senor Don Gonzalez, late Minister of Finance, with his family, waiting to proceed to Cordova next morning. I was fortunate, too, in having for fellow-travellers on the line Senor Moneta, the Government engineer, and Senor Crisofuli, both proceeding to Cordova on business connected with the railway, so the journey passed very agreeably and was anything but fatiguing for the distance. There is ample room in the carriages, which also have the advantage of enabling the passengers to go from one portion to the other and conversing with acquaintances who may happen to be there. This is much better than being stuck in a close carriage without any chance of relief. Indeed, I think for all South American railways the American saloon carriages are the most suitable as well as the most economical.

I was up early next morning to see the train start at seven for Rosario, and diligences for Cordova, Rio Cuarto, and other places. The last was a most comical sight. The mode of conveyance has been frequently described by travellers, so I will not enlarge on the subject. The diligences remind me of the old French *malle poste*, only the gearing is all hide instead of rope, and they are drawn by six horses, all mounted by peons, with very long traces, each horse seemingly independent of the others. The poor brutes, mostly with sore backs, are first driven into a corral close to the diligence station, where they are lassoed one by one, a halter thrown over their necks, and then taken to be saddled.

The diligence station is a very busy place at this time, several starting at the same time for Cordova and other distant places; there are also private carriages, and all goes to show how extensive the passenger traffic will be when the line is open to Cordova. The time occupied in this latter part of the route is so long that a large supply of vehicles is required, as well as horses, but the latter may be had almost for the catching; at all events their cost is very trifling. After seeing the start, I went over the railway station works, and found evident signs of considerable traffic, even with an unfinished line. A large space of ground adjoining the station was filled with bullock waggons, some discharging cargo into railway waggons, while carts conveyed merchandise brought up by train from Rosario to other bullock waggons at a short distance, as there was no space for them about the station, where a large commodious brick warehouse has been built and works on a large scale are in course of erection, which will greatly facilitate the traffic now carried on. In fact, all was bustle and traffic under difficulties. Amongst the produce brought down was wool in bales, dry hides, wheat, large bars of copper, fruit, and other articles, not even omitting fowls in large coops, which had been brought all the way from Cordova.

The day was very fine and sunny, and after breakfast I accompanied Mr. Lloyd on horseback to visit a large forest and lake two or three leagues distant from the station. Here the wood used for locomotives is cut. It is found to answer better than coal, and is of course much cheaper. We passed over the newly laid rails and earthworks intended for a continuation of the line, along which piles of cut wood, extending at least a quarter of a mile, were laid, as well as a large quantity of wooden sleepers of excellent quality, to be used, I believe, between this and Cordova. We then struck across the campo to the forest, soon after entering which we came upon one of the most picturesque lakes I remember to have seen. We rode along the margin, which is chiefly sand, seeing numbers of wild fowl and black-necked swans. The water was beautifully clear. There are numbers of otters here, and at the upper end are immense rushes, which are gathered for roofing the ranchos built for the company's peons. We then struck into the forest again, and with some difficulty worked our way through it, the lining of my coat being torn off, as I was hardly got up for such an expedition. The forest is partly the property of the railway and of one of the religious establishments at Cordova, and it is capable of supplying sleepers to make the line to that city, as well as to supply fuel for the locomotives for years to come. The railway has quite a little colony here cutting wood, which is conveyed to a small steam saw mill on the line, and dealt with most expeditiously there.

On our way home we visited the company's farm, where the plough was at work, turning up a rich loamy soil, and next year it is expected a good crop of wheat will be taken, besides potatoes, Indian corn, grass for the horses, &c. In short, it will soon become a very productive farm, being also completely fenced in so as to keep out cattle. The plough was being driven by a young Somersetshire man, who evidently understood his work.

At length we finished our tour of inspection of about twenty miles very much pleased and gratified with what I had seen, and much impressed with the important future that awaits the landed property of the company, in addition to the line becoming a great main trunk one across this part of South America. Seeing is believing, and if shareholders who are sceptical as to the future could take a trip out here to satisfy themselves, they would be quite re-assured on this point. Many doubts have been thrown upon the enterprise, which I have never entertained, from my previous knowledge of the country, and my confidence is much increased by a personal inspection of the line itself and the traffic which evidently exists ready to come on the metals when proper provision is made for it. The company are about laying down the telegraph wires, which will be a great advantage and prevent accidents, besides establishing a valuable means of communication and saving much time. Indeed, no line can be efficient without it. I return to Rosario to-morrow, having only a few days to spare before embarking for England; otherwise I should have gone on to Cordova and spent some time in this interesting region, whose only want is population to render it one of the most productive of the globe.

When I made a hasty visit to Rosario in 1853 I formed a very strong opinion of its future importance from the position it occupied in connection with the river navigation and the traffic of the Western provinces; but the establishment of the Central Argentine Railway has immensely added to the other advantages of Rosario, and accounts for the great increase that has recently taken place in building and population. Thus far, however, the benefit is in a great measure prospective, the railway being still incomplete. Nevertheless, there can be little doubt that the sanguine views of speculators on the future will be realised so soon as the line is finished.

It is only in traversing the streets that one becomes aware of the great extent of the town, which is built in squares after the usual manner in this country. Several commercial establishments, some banks, and many really good shops now exist, and there is difficulty, I am informed, in finding house room for the numerous settlers in the town. I was surprised to find so large a number of cafés crowded at night by all classes, and there is also a little theatre, where, in the absence of regular performances, masked balls are frequently held. These are not of the most edifying description, but the people will amuse themselves in some way, and better this than political conspiracies, of which Rosario has often been the scene.

As I have before said the port presents quite a busy appearance; but there are no facilities in the way of wharves and landing places, which would be a vast convenience to traffic, as everything has now to be done by boats. Some gas works are in course of erection, on the river side, but owing to bad foundations or want of care the chimney fell down and only the skeleton walls appear. It will be a great blessing to the town and suburbs when they are lighted with gas, as on dark nights perambulation is difficult even with the aid of the miserable oil lamps at present in use. There is an American Missionary Chapel near the railway station, and recently the nucleus of an English Protestant Congregation has been formed under the auspices of the Rev. Mr. Combe, appointed by the South American Missionary Society. Service is just now performed in a room, but efforts are being made to build a chapel, as the number of English residents continues to increase. Mr. Combe also holds service at Frayle Muerto, where some sixty Englishmen reside on farms within a few leagues of each other.

I had occasion to visit the Protestant burial ground at Rosario to attend the funeral of a young Englishman who died under melancholy circumstances, and was sorry to notice that it presented a very forlorn aspect and was situate in a very inconvenient locality. Many interments took place here during the cholera, which was very fatal to foreigners as well as to the natives, who were decimated, and the works of the railway were also retarded by this terrible scourge.

Before closing my notice of the railway, I may add that I had an opportunity, through the kindness of Mr. Woods, the company's engineer, of inspecting the plans of the new railway station, and of going over the ground, which will be enclosed to the extent of 3,200 feet in length, with a fine river frontage on the Parana, where there is a depth of 18 to 20 feet of water close alongside. This will be a great facility in dealing with the river traffic. As regards the materials for the use of the line, they have all been landed on their own wharf and drawn up an incline, as the bank on which the station stands is at a considerable elevation above the river. Eventually, I believe, it is the intention of the company to facilitate both their passenger and goods traffic by means of landing wharves, which would be a great saving of expense and time. One thing is very certain, that the Rosario station will be the finest and most complete in South America.

THE WESTERN RAILWAY OF BUENOS AYRES.

I HAD a very pleasant excursion over the Western Railway as far as Mercedes, in company with some friends. Mr. Emilio Castro, Government Superintendent of the railways in the province of Buenos Ayres, to the Government of which this line belongs, accompanied us, and he kindly provided a very luxurious saloon carriage for the occasion. We left the Parque station at 8 a.m., going over some curves of a formidable nature, and along streets until we came to the company's goods station and workshops. The latter are on a very extensive scale. After this we got fairly on the main line, which is single, except at certain stations where the trains cross each other. How any engineer could have been bold enough to construct such curves, or the Government could allow locomotives to run through the streets, it is difficult to conceive, as there must always be much risk both to the train and to passengers. There are also some heavy gradients before the goods station is reached, which increases the danger, but people seem to have become familiarised with it.

For the first twelve miles to Flores station the country presents a succession of quintas, or country houses, many large and picturesque, and Flores itself is quite a large and extensive town, though merely a suburb of Buenos Ayres. The town is called San Jose de Flores, and near it is a large Anglo-Argentine school, where the train stops. Flores station is a very good one, capable of being doubled, with a peculiar pattern of light ornamental roofing inside. In the summer season the traffic to and from Flores is very considerable, and there is also a large resident population. After leaving Flores, we got more into the open campo, with plenty of cattle, sheep, and horses about, and numerous farm buildings, until we reached Floreste station, close to which is a large fanciful looking building, originally intended, I believe, for a hotel, but it does not appear to have been successful as a speculation. San Martin is an important station, diligences and carriages being in attendance to convey people to the neighbouring villages of San Custo, Santa Lucia, and San Martin, one of which was called Rozas' Saladero, from the number of victims he is said to have sacrificed there at a prison established for his political enemies. Near this station are some fine, handsome quintas, belonging to the Madero family, the country being well wooded, with many farms, and the same features are observable as far as the Moron station, near which the battle of Caceres was fought, which decided the fate of Rozas. There is a theatre close to this station, and Moron is quite a large town, having grown up under the influence of the railway. A public road runs in proximity to the line for a distance of some fifteen miles, which is very objectionable, and the rails might just as well have been laid a few squares apart from it. After passing Moron we got more into the open campo, with large flocks of sheep, droves of cattle, and horses feeding all around, until we reached the ancient Spanish town of Merlo, which has a church, with a little steeple very like that of a village church at home. There is a nice looking two-storied house there, built by Mr. Boyd, planted with trees, showing they will grow well enough if people will take the trouble to plant them, and I understand Mr. Boyd was the first to introduce the gum tree, which now flourishes in many gardens in the neighbourhood. A branch line is shortly to be constructed from this place to Lobos, some forty miles south-west, through, I am told, a very rich part of the province, and from which district a large traffic is expected. A river, called Las Conchas, runs near Merlo, crossed by an iron bridge, the first I have seen on the line, there being only open culverts where the line crosses streams or watercourses. The next station we came to was Moreno, a new town built since the opening of the line. Midway between Moreno and Lujan is a small station called General Rodriguez. Lujan is one of the oldest towns in the province, a river of that name running past it to the Parana, joining the little stream of Tigre, the terminus of the Northern Railway, whence passenger steamers go up to Rosario. There is a large station and warehouse at Lujan, where a quantity of wheat was being loaded into carts, to be ground in a mill called the "Mill of the Virgins," a name which I conclude arises from an anecdote recorded as to the formation of the town. A travelling expedition, it would seem, while conveying an image of the Virgin, came to a standstill here, nor could the animals be made to proceed until the image was left on the spot. So it remained, and to this day it is a place of great religious festivities; and express trains are run from Buenos Ayres on these occasions. Whatever may be the real facts of the case, the Lujan Mills grind good flour. The wheat is grown in Chivilcoy, the present terminus of the Western line. It is small but hard. It was to

Lujan that General Beresford sent a detachment in 1807, when the first attack was made on Buenos Ayres, arising out of the war with Spain, and which was subsequently renewed under such disastrous circumstances by General Whitelock. I merely make this allusion to show that at that time it was a town of some importance. The little station of Oliveres comes next, but is yet only in course of erection, in the midst of an immense open campo, with large flocks of sheep and plenty of cattle to be seen in all directions. A fine stream of water crosses this part of the campo. The thistles, about which we hear so much, abound in most parts of the campo, but the dry season has kept them down, and they do not rise much above the surface, nor do they appear to prevent the growth of grass suitable for sheep and cattle. No donkeys are seen in this country to luxuriate on the abundance of thistles, and very few mules, horses being generally used and very badly treated. Their dead carcasses are frequently encountered, as, when "used-up," they are turned adrift to die in the campo. A few miles further brought us to Mercedes, a town of some 12,000 inhabitants, the terminus of the railway before it was lately opened to Chivilcoy, an extension of forty miles, making a total distance of 100 miles now open, and the number of stations denotes the amount of traffic carried on by this railway, for which it has a stock of 420 wagons and 20 locomotives, besides passenger cars, chiefly the large American description.

The Western Railway was originally a small passenger line to San Jose de Flores, but was afterwards continued and opened by sections, the point for goods traffic only commencing at the great open square called the 11th of September, where the goods traffic in bullock carts has always been carried on. A large number of bullock carts still find their way to that market.

We remained at Mercedes to enjoy an excellent lunch provided for us by the station master, who resides there with his family, as going on to Chivilcoy would have entailed the loss of another day, and having to sleep there with probably limited accommodation. The station at Mercedes is a very fine one, with iron pillars and a corrugated roof, brought from England; also a large roadside shed for the locomotives, workshops, &c. The large area of ground occupied by the station must be with a view to future requirements. Omnibuses and a diligence were waiting to convey passengers to the town, which is near the station, and to distant places. We did not go into the town, as it looked rather dusty and our time was limited, having to return by a special train at 1.30.

We rode some distance back on the engine, making twenty-one miles in thirty-five minutes over part of the campo, and reached the Parque station at Buenos Ayres about five o'clock, or three and half hours for a distance of about sixty miles; but we had to wait at two stations for the up train to cross, besides calling at most of the other stations, all of which involved a good deal of delay. The engines have to water frequently, and there was a scarcity of coal, so they were obliged to burn slack, mixed with cinders, causing some difficulty in keeping up steam. It must be admitted that the Government have shown real energy and determination in prosecuting this railway, which is of great benefit to the Province, and I believe well managed, yielding a good return for the capital invested. The rails used on this line are the Barlow, and they are in very excellent condition after being down several years. The line from Mercedes to Chivilcoy is laid with Griffin's rails, which I understand are not so rigid as the Barlow. There is no wood suitable for sleepers in this part of the country.

It is intended to carry on the line to the north end of Buenos Ayres, and to build a wharf out to the river, thus enabling the company to land and ship goods without passing through the city, which will be a great convenience and save expense, besides the advantage of opening up communications with the other railways by such a branch line. Eventually there is to be a Central Station on the beach for all the railways, so that goods and passengers can be conveyed from one to the other. As already observed, a branch is to be made from the Merlo station to the town of Lobos, and no doubt it will be carried further in that direction, so as to develop the resources of the country. All this will require time, and a large outlay of money, for which the Government is not prepared now, but it is sure to be accomplished later on, with many more urgent improvements required in this large and growing city.

We had a very fine day for our excursion, and enjoyed it much, thanks to the kindness of Mr. Emilio Castro, who made ample provision for creature comforts, and was exceedingly attentive. Mr. Allen, the engineer for the line, was also of the party, and gave us much valuable information. He has been many years out here, and with his brother, has worked his way to an important and responsible position.

In the Appendix will be found a very interesting description of the workshops of the Western Railway, which we extract from the columns of the Buenos Ayres *Standard*, an influential paper extensively circulated in the River Plate.

BUENOS AYRES.—SECOND NOTICE.

The more I look over this great city the more I am struck with its increase, as well as the luxury by which it has been attended, evinced in the style of building and in the large private establishments, some of which are really on a princely scale.

Speaking of public buildings, I do not much admire the opera house, called the Colon—it is badly formed and the decorations are too heavy. The gas-lights are ugly, being plain jets instead of small gas chandeliers. They give a very common-place look to the whole. The tiers of boxes look too much like *boxes*, and ought to be light and open, suited to the country. The entrances and corridors are also very rough and nearly as bad as the unfinished theatre at San Paulo, though the design of the latter is infinitely superior. On the other hand, the secondary theatres are cheerful little places, and the new Music Hall, built by private subscription, is a model for lightness and elegance. I attended an amateur concert there, and was much pleased; some fifty ladies and gentlemen forming the vocal strength, aided by a large instrumental orchestra. It was a sight not often seen at home, where *la mauvaise honte* would prevent so agreeable a gathering. The large hall was quite filled and the programme gone through most systematically. In alluding to this building, I may remark that it is precisely of the same dimensions as the new River Plate Bank, being by the same architect. This Bank occupies a large corner area of one of the most central streets in the city, and can vie in architectural effect with many of the new buildings in Lombard-street, with the advantage of being much better seen.

The churches have often been described, and the cathedral is now a finished, handsome building, very well kept up both externally and internally, and religious observances and masses are very frequent. The Clubs of Buenos Ayres hold a conspicuous place in connection with politics, and they occasionally afford opportunities for beauty and fashion to meet at the balls held in them. The Progreso occupies the first rank, the La Plata the second, and latterly a Club called El Temple has been established. I was up the country when the Progreso ball was held, and missed the invitation, as well as that for the Temple, but attended the ball of the La Plata, where 500 or 600 ladies and gentlemen were collected; a very gay and cheerful meeting, where all appeared to feel at home and enjoy themselves. South American society has the charm of being free from the stiffness and formality which exists in aristocratic society at home. The ladies, however, add great elegance of dress to their personal graces, which are very considerable, and they dance with great ease. With reference to the female population of Buenos Ayres, the *fêtes* held on the anniversary of Independence (25th of May) present an excellent opportunity for seeing them to advantage out of doors. The weather was fine, and the Plaza Victoria, as well as the leading streets, was filled with well dressed ladies, particularly at night to see the fireworks. The ladies go about very freely, those who keep carriages, or can afford to hire them, generally driving a short way out of town when they are not visiting their friends. Society in Buenos Ayres is decidedly of the free and easy, friendly style, and characterised by much hospitality. The democratic element in the constitution naturally stirs up a good deal of political feeling, but I do not find this to affect the private relations of life so much as might be expected. Party spirit runs high, and the "young Republicans" especially are very bitter towards those who differ from them; but of late years political animosity has not been stained in the Argentine Confederation with crimes such as those which have prevailed at Monte Video. The continuance of the Paraguayan war and the Alliance with Brazil have lately been the great bone of contention, and shows itself on the eve of the election of a new president, on the result of which the future peace of the country may more or less depend.

I looked over the Museum, where many fine antediluvian specimens found in this country are preserved, together with a variety of curiosities in natural history, animals, birds, &c., the whole being under the superintendence of Dr. Burmeister, who is a very superior man, and I believe remains there more from his love of natural history than for the remuneration attached to the office. He has travelled much over the South American Continent.

Numerous fine hospitals exist in Buenos Ayres, both native and foreign, and the English one, which I visited in company with Mr. Boyd, chairman of the committee, and the Rev. Mr. Ford, is a very good establishment, well deserving of support by the British community and by our own Government. The hospital was formerly an old quinta, and is beautifully situated at the east end of the city, overlooking the river, the Boca, Barracas, and the country round as far as the eye can reach. It has been greatly enlarged, forming three sides of a square, the fourth comprising a neat fever ward, run up last year for cholera patients, and it proved of very great utility. The wards, on both the ground floor and upper story, are kept very clean, and Dr. Reid, the medical attendant, resides on the premises, having occupied his position for six years. The building and ground are the property of the hospital and have much increased in value, but the difficulty is in meeting the annual expenses, which can only be done by voluntary subscriptions. What is required to keep up the establishment properly is a small tonnage rate on British ships, and inasmuch as sailors derive the chief benefit from the hospital, I cannot see why this should not be done. The expenses attendant on such an institution in a foreign country are considerable, if it is to be kept in a state of efficiency. Formerly there was a tonnage rate of this kind levied on British shipping, which may have led to some abuse, and been done away with from some "ignorant impatience of taxation," but there is no valid reason why shipping should not contribute to the support of hospitals, from which, as I have already observed, it derives the greatest amount of benefit, and without which sailors would be exposed to great hardships.

One of the disadvantages of the Spanish system of building their towns and cities in square blocks is that it creates a sameness in the streets, and narrows the approaches to them, leaving no scope for great leading thoroughfares, so that there is a constant turning of corners, and but for the names being pretty generally posted up it would be difficult for strangers to find their way. In reply to inquiries as to any particular house or locality, you are generally told that it is so many squares off, so that taking the right bearing or departure you can easily find out what you want. Then the houses are legibly numbered, which, combined with their plan of municipal taxation, ought to render a correct census easy, but there seems to be some strong objection to "numbering the people," which I cannot account for, and to this day no one is able to tell you the population of Buenos Ayres with any certainty; some calculations only giving 100,000, others 150,000, and even as high as 200,000. I believe the last to be a great exaggeration; probably the mean of 150,000 is nearest the mark. Again, the extension of the city by squares leads to the closing up of places for which a greater space should be left. As an instance, the English burial ground was quite in the country when first made, but the city is fast encroaching upon it, and notice has lately been given to have it removed, against which a strong feeling exists, as the ground was purchased, and is the property of foreigners; so the only plan to be adopted, if any alteration is made at all, will be to close the ground to future interments, the municipality giving a piece of land a mile or two further out. This, again, has its inconveniences, as the streets leading to the present burial ground are almost unapproachable in bad weather, and beyond their limits it would be still more so. I visited the English burial ground, which is pretty well kept up, but the huge square family vaults are very unsightly, and will be rendered useless in case the burial ground is removed to another quarter.

The great native burial place called Recoleta, adjoining a church of that name, is full of monuments of all kinds, some on a most elaborate and costly scale,—little temples, in fact, where the dead are laid on shelves, visible through glass doors. The cholera visitation compelled further addition to be made to the ground, which is in a very rough, disordered state, where medical students would have full scope if they were at a loss for subjects.

Altogether the municipal regulations of the city are very defective. An effort is now being made to obtain an adequate supply of water, and some works are in course of erection on the shore in the front of the Recoleta, on the plan of Mr. Coghlan, an engineer, who has been long resident at Buenos Ayres. The works will supply a number of fountains in the city, but no project is yet on foot to carry the water into private houses, which are supplied from their own patios, where there is generally a well or large tank underground which collects the rain water. A number of plans are before the Government for draining the city, one of the most urgent and imperative of wants, and without which it is impossible to maintain the public health. It is no wonder the cholera has made such ravages, and every one dreads a revival of it, or the appearance of some other scourge during the next hot season. These mysterious visitations are warnings to large populations that they cannot violate sanitary laws with impunity, and force lethargic municipal bodies into action. No city could be more easily drained and sewered than Buenos Ayres, but it requires a large outlay of money, which the Government can ill afford at present; and I believe the municipal and provincial taxes are already at their maximum.

House rent is very high, and with the exception of meat, all the necessaries are dear. Luxuries are especially high priced. One is forcibly reminded of our old watchmen by the prevailing practice in South

America of having what they call serenos, who go round calling the hour, some of them with most sepulchral voices, and they are about as useful as our "Charlies" were, only they are armed with a sword, and apt, I believe, at times to resort to it very improperly. In other respects the system of police appears to be pretty good, and considering the mixed and heterogenous population, with many bad characters about, there are less disturbances in Buenos Ayres than I expected, though, as a matter of course, many complaints are made as to the deficiency of police regulations. I was about the streets and suburbs of the city at various hours of the night and never met with the least molestation.

The city is well lighted with gas, only it is stated that the present works are inadequate to the supply, and another company is about to be formed. The charge for gas is extravagant; I am told about 24s. per thousand feet, and as a matter of course the shares are at a very high premium.

One of the most thriving occupations in the city appears to be the hire of carriages and horses. There are numerous large establishments of this kind as well as for the building of carriages; the latter as a rule are handsome and commodious. There are regular stands in the open squares, and cars are in attendance at the railway stations. For some time I could not make out what a great clatter of horses coming through the city about daylight meant; it sounded like a troop of cavalry, but I afterwards found it was the hired horses going to water at the river; indeed, horses are almost amphibious here in consequence of doing so much work in the river carts, and one day I saw an omnibus brougt down on the shore to be washed and cleaned, rather a novel performance.

River storms are not of common occurrence, but they occasionally take place with great violence. It had been hot and oppressive before, but it came on to blow heavily on Sunday night, and next morning the river had risen some 12 feet, the waves dashing on the beach in a most alarming manner, and the whole of the low ground between the city and the Boca was under water, with part of the Boca Railway washed away, as well as a portion of the Northern line, interrupting, of course, the traffic on both. It was a curious sight to see the waves dashing through the willow trees which are planted along the shore, and for a time suspending washing operations. Many houses on the low ground were invaded, and the wooden ones built along the Boca, on piles, looked like great bathing machines. The iron seats placed on the shore beneath the willows were knocked over and covered with seaweed. The storm lasted two or three days, during which no communication could be had with vessels either in the inner or outer roads, and steamers were compelled to run for the Tigre to land their passengers; also lighters with cargo—the whole forming a scene of much excitement and putting an entire stop to business. It delayed the departure of our steamer several days. After the gale subsided we had some fine sunny days, and the river fell as rapidly as it had risen. This gale was not what is termed a pampero, being from the south-east, beating on the shore. A pampero frequently follows after it from the south-west, or off the shore, causing the river to fall again.

The changes of climate here are sudden and said to be unhealthy. During the two months I was in the river until the occurrence of the gale nothing could be more delicious than the weather—cool, with bright sunshine and any amount of exercise agreeable. The nights were occasionally frosty, with ice in the mornings in some places. Dust storms are terrible things during the summer, but happily are rare, and generally the forerunners of a pampero, accompanied by heavy rain, which refreshes the thirsty soil. Droughts are serious afflictions to the sheep and cattle, which often perish from their effects. Water is the great desideratum for the campo, and without it the prospects of the estanciero are blighted. As I have said before, the Banda Oriental is less subject to drought, being more undulated and better watered, but the pampas, or plains of Buenos Ayres, grow a more nutritive grass and rear finer sheep and cattle.

During my stay at Buenos Ayres the Provincial Chambers met, as well as the National Chambers, and I attended a sitting of the latter, where an unusual excitement prevailed owing to a motion put on the books as to the retirement of President Mitre from office, and whether or not this would put an end to the alliance entered into for carrying on the war with Paraguay. The building is small, exactly like a theatre minus the stage, and was crowded to excess by strangers, the pit, or lower part only, being used for the business of the Senate. There was so much demonstration from the galleries as to promise a stormy meeting, but when the speeches began the speakers were patiently listened to, with occasional cheers by their respective supporters, at which the President rang his bell. Dr. Quintana and others maintained that their views were correct, and that the retirement of President Mitre would put an end to the alliance. The Government, represented by Senor Elizalde, Minister for Foreign Affairs, maintained the contrary, and defended his colleagues with considerable acumen and ability, the result being that nothing was got by the motion and things remained in *statu quo*. The custom is for members to speak sitting upon their benches, which greatly detracts from their oratory, and must be very inconvenient, as you can only hear a voice, and are puzzled sometimes to know where it comes from. On another occasion, when the Senate was in committee with explanations going on, half-a-dozen members would be addressing or interrogating the Minister at the same time, which appeared very absurd, as well as unfair, it being impossible to reply to more than one at a time, or at all events to collect the observations of half-a-dozen members speaking in the same breath. Senor Elizalde, however, defended his position with much coolness and ability, and was assisted by his colleague, Dr. Costa, Minister for Education, &c. The audience became so troublesome on another occasion that the Senators decided to meet with closed doors, having only reporters present, rather a trial to democratic forbearance, but it did not seem to produce any sensation out of doors. As in our own Parliament, a great loss of time is caused by the professional speech makers, and the business of legislation retarded accordingly, as they only sit in the day in these countries. Whether or not such an arrangement would suit in St. Stephen's is another matter. Outside, and apart from public sittings, no doubt a deal of intrigue and jobbery takes place in South American assemblies, as in other countries, but I think on the whole their legislation is fair and conducted with moderation. There is not the same value in "loaves and fishes" to operate with, nor the same amount of honour and reward to look forward to as in England; besides, the members of Government out here are very poorly paid, so they are obliged to look to their professions, mostly as lawyers, unless they happen to possess private fortunes. Republicanism is not endowed with more gratitude than Royalty, and deserving men who have faithfully and zealously served their country are too often left in the "cold shade," and forgotten in both cases. The Provincial Assembly meet in another part of the city, where all the provincial business is carried on. It was formerly the town residence and head-quarters of Rozas, from which many a bloody mandate has been issued. The municipality occupy large premises in the Plaza, attached to the old Spanish cabildo, or prison, on which the date of 1722 is still to be seen.

PROGRESS OF STEAM NAVIGATION ON LA PLATA.

If there is one subject more than another on which I am entitled to express an opinion it is that of steam navigation on the great South American rivers, and especially as regards the fluvial waters of the La Plata. In my book, published in 1854, pages 314 to 316, occur the following remarks :—

These are sentiments, however, which the reader may naturally think are not very pertinent to a purpose like the present, and not exactly in keeping with an occasion expressly connected with the commercial opening-up of those streams by the instrumentality of English enterprise, in a form so indicative of progress as steam. So, too, thought the writer after a moment's rumination of the " cud of sweet and bitter fancy;" for he reflected that these magnificent regions, first discovered by Cabot—English, born and bred, though of Venetian parentage—had stagnated, not under the rule of that " good olde and famuse man," but under the rule of those in whose service he had found out a river which might, indeed, have proved worthy of the name the avaricious Spaniards had bestowed upon it— La Plata, the River of Silver—had they been imbued with a particle of the spirit which has converted " icy Labrador," the first territory discovered by the same glorious adventurer, into a comparatively industrial paradise. I augured, I hope with no unjustifiable audacity, that now the descendants of Cabot and of his companions had been brought into direct relationship with the people of the Parana, something would be done to render that " Mississippi of the South " not altogether unworthy of some slight social and political comparison with the Northern "Father of Waters" before many generations should roll by; and I deemed it a not altogether impossible contingency that the younger members of our crew might live to cast anchor in certain riverine ports hereabouts, amid a forest of masts and funnels belonging to all the maritime states in the world, not one of which countries but may find produce of some kind or other profitably suitable to its markets on these fertile shores.

I will leave it to my readers, acquainted with what is going on at the present time, to say whether my views were too sanguine. It may be said that the war in Paraguay has hastened the development of steam navigation up the rivers, which is true enough, but at the same time I am satisfied that without this war there would have been steady progress, particularly had the policy of the despotic ruler of Paraguay been in a pacific direction, encouraging, instead of throwing every difficulty in the way of free transit to the country lying beyond Paraguay, and into the interior of Matto Grosso. The exigences of a war of the nature carried on for the last three years, where the troops, amumnition, and supplies of all kinds had to be sent forward by steam, would naturally create active employment for steamers, and it has tended to familiarise navigators with every nook and corner, sand bank, or other impediment that may have existed unknown to any of them. The war at an end, steamers will be organised to run to the different towns and stations, in response to the requirements of traffic, as well as to facilitate postal communications, so much needed in those countries; and Rosario, being the terminus of the great Central Railway, must of necessity become the rendezvous of all river steamers ascending the Parana, the Uruguay having already a pretty good organisation in this respect. In a country so widespread, and so dependent on internal communication by rivers, steam is now a primary necessity, and therefore it may fairly be assumed that this will be one of the first objects of the Government, as well as of the Central Argentine Railway Company; the latter to facilitate traffic to and from their line, and to regulate the departure of their trains, a matter of much moment to travellers. It may in truth be said that steam navigation on the waters of La Plata and its affluents is only in its infancy, dating from the commencement of the Paraguayan war. One of the great requirements of civilised life is rapid intercourse, not only for persons, but for correspondence, and the task of arranging the latter is one that must be strongly pressed on the Government by commercial bodies, who are so much interested in the question. Brazil sets an example in this respect that other Governments ought to follow. In process of time telegraphic wires will doubtless be added to steam facilities, and probably be carried across the Andes to join the West Coast line to Panama, in connection with the great Atlantic cable to England.

When I remember the sensation created by the little "Argentina," and her trip to Rosario in 1853, I must say the progress of events has indeed been rapid. To this day the "Argentina" is remembered at Buenos Ayres and Monte Video, and her subsequent loss was regarded as a serious calamity.

I subjoin in the Appendix some particulars showing the increase of steam tonnage in these waters, which will be interesting to those who contemplate visiting the regions of the La Plata.

In connection with the up-river steam traffic, the Northern Railway to the Tigre is a great facility, as passengers can walk on board the steamers without encountering the often disagreeable boating at Buenos

Ayres, and the passage through what is called the Capitan is very pleasant, but if the railway was extended a few hundred yards further, to the bank of the River Lujan, it would be far more convenient, as large sized steamers would then resort there, as also vessels with cargo for Buenos Ayres to be sent on by rail. The Tigre is so small and so shallow that a few steamers block it up, but the Lujan is wide and deep, and it might be made a valuable adjunct to the port of Buenos Ayres, at present suffering so much for want of accommodation. In my general report on the railways this subject will be again alluded to.

RAILWAYS IN THE RIVER PLATE.

There are two classes of railways in the Argentine Confederation, inaugurated by Provincial and the National Governments respectively. I will begin with the Province of Buenos Ayres, as the railroad system has there acquired the greatest development. The first line established was the Western, which has now reached the town of Chivilcoy, a distance of 100 miles from the city, and it is proposed to effect a further extension to the frontier fort of Melincue. I need not repeat here the details already given in reference to this enterprise.

Next in importance comes the Great Southern Railway, seventy-one miles in length, which was made by an English Company, under a Government guarantee of 7 per cent. on £700,000, but the capital actually raised was £750,000, the contractors taking £50,000 in unguaranteed stock on certain conditions as to their participation in dividend. The expenditure has been further increased to nearly £800,000, owing to additional disbursements for goods stations and for increased rolling stock. The line was opened throughout in Dec. 1865, and the traffic has gone on steadily augmenting, with improved receipts, the result of the first year showing a net profit of nearly three per cent.; the second year a fraction over five per cent.; and the present year promises fair to reach the seven per cent. guaranteed by the Government, when it will be self-sustaining and free of all the drawbacks necessarily incidental to a condition of dependence on State aid. This enterprise has a prosperous future before it. The great question which remains to be decided has relation to an extension of the line further south, or in a south-westerly direction, so as to intercept the large amount of traffic which still comes forward by the ordinary bullock carts. One disadvantage of the Southern Railway consists in its chief station at the Plaza Constitucion being so far from the central points of the city, which are only partially reached by a tramway, but this ought to be extended, and even then it will be difficult to meet the requirements of passenger traffic. The following particulars are taken from a private letter sent home after a very pleasant trip over the line, accompanied by the Local Committee and Manager:—

My first stop after arrival here was to visit all the Railway Stations, as they are generally a pretty good index of what is behind them, and I found the Great Southern far in advance of all the others as regards provision for the traffic it has to carry on. The money which has been spent in shed accommodation was only an absolute necessity, and is of that practical character which quite meets the case. The single-roofed shed into which the wool is discharged from the railway trucks on one side, and taken out from the other, is most convenient, and to look at the sheds, which are divided into compartments, and all numbered, you might fancy yourself at one of the warehouses of the London Docks, with which you are familiar. The booking offices, refreshment rooms, &c., occupy the centre of the station, with the platform in front for passengers; the warehouses occupying the two wings. There is also a goods receiving shed, with stabling for horses used on the tramway. The only thing I see in the distance is that more station room will be required. Leaving the station by a double line of rails, you soon cross the handsome bridge over the Riachuelo and arrive at Barracas station, situated near the centre of a large population, and connected with the Boca, where a large portion of the business of the port of Buenos Ayres is carried on, the place being studded with saladeros and large warehouses, where the produce of the country is deposited, a great drawback being the abominable stench arising from dead carcasses and offal strewed about, and nests of piggeries which are allowed to locate spite of all municipal regulations to the contrary. After leaving Barracas the line strikes at once into the campo, or open country, the first ten or fifteen miles being studded with quintas or farms, and establishments of one kind or other, when you reach the great plains covered with sheep, cattle, and horses, and at this time the pastures look green and healthy, though at the same time they could do with rain. The line is nearly a dead level with few curves, the stations well built and commodious, and of a very durable nature, easily added to if required; in fact, I do not see how a railway in this country could be better adapted for its work; the rails, permanent way, as well as the rolling stock, all appear to be in good order. Although the line may be said to traverse a sea of land, and does not pass close to any town of importance until it reaches Chascomus, there were many more estancias (farms) in the distance than I expected to find. We saw Mr. Glew and Mr. Donsellear (after whom two stations are called) in *propria persona*. The Somborambon bridge, crossing a river of that name, is a fine work, and at the Chascomus station are evident signs of considerable traffic, with machinery for hoisting the bullock carts on to the railway trucks after their wheels are taken off, and the cart with its contents (wheels included,) brought into Buenos Ayres. Chascomus itself is a large straggling town, situated close to a picturesque lake, on the banks of which Mr. Crawford (agent for Messrs. Peto and Betts during the construction of the line) built himself a large comfortable house, now converted into an hotel, at which we enjoyed a very good dinner. During the career of Rozas Chascomus was a military station, and many people from the neighbouring districts came to spend some months of the year at the town, but its glory in this way has departed, and it does not look like a very go-a-head place at present. On the whole I returned much impressed with the soundness of the undertaking and the favourable prospect before it.

The Northern Railway, originally called the San Fernando, has been very unfortunate from its birth, arising in a great measure from its being made on a strip of land adjoining the river, where it was subject to inundations in consequence of sea storms. Had it been carried over the bank, within a few hundred yards to the left, it would have been entirely out of the reach of such casualties, an instance of which occurred a few days before I left Buenos Ayres, when a portion of the earthworks was again washed away. Soon after my arrival out I made a trip over the line, accompanied by Mr. Crabtree, the new manager, Mr. Ford, locomotive superintendent and engineer, Mr. Santa Maria, consulting local director, and Mr. Horrocks, the traffic manager. The station at the Retiro is a plain, modest building, which answers the purpose well enough, though rather open and exposed. The locomotives and carriages are in limited number, but sufficient apparently for existing wants, as the large American carriages hold many passengers. A tramway from the most central point in the city, passing along the beach, carries the passengers to and from the station in a much more convenient manner than to any of the other railways, and there can be little doubt that if the line could be rendered safe from the encroachments of the river on the occasion of great storms, fortunately "few and far between," it would be a very prosperous enterprise, as it affords accommodation for the most populous suburb of the city. It also touches a branch of the river where a large portion of the steam traffic is likely to be concentrated. I found the rails in tolerable order, and altogether more life in the concern than I had expected, considering the drawbacks, financial and otherwise, with which it has had to contend. The first station is Palermo, the old paradise of Rozas, but which is now allowed to go to ruin and decay, the beach from the Retiro to Palermo being almost entirely monopolised by what has been termed "an army of washerwomen." The next station is

Belgrano, where Mr. Matti, the great steamboat agent, has a most fantastic quinta, glittering in green and yellow colours, but of what style of architecture it would be difficult to determine; nevertheless it is a pretty place, and evidently no expense is spared to keep it in order. It is, however, too close to the railway. Directly opposite is the hotel of Mr. Watson, where I can testify to a first rate dinner being provided for those who want a little relief from the closeness and monotony of the city. After Belgrano comes San Isidro, near which are also many handsome quintas. There are two or three other stations before arriving at San Fernando, about which there is a large, scattered population. Here a new branch is being made to the Parana, by a small company of which Mr. Hopkins is the head; the intention being to build a new wharf and some warehouses there; but I question whether the enterprise will ever arrive at maturity, as the most natural point for the construction of such works is undoubtedly the mouth of the Rio Tigre, on the Lujan River, as I have previously observed. At the latter place we found some dozen steamers, chiefly of large size, lying moored alongside the banks where there is deep water. At the Tigre station is a good restaurant, kept by a Frenchman, who provided us with a comfortable breakfast, and after two or three hours spent in a boat looking about the river, and rambling over the neighbourhood, we returned to Buenos Ayres much pleased with our trip.

The Boca Railway is a small line, made to connect the city with the important districts of the Boca and Barracas. It was laid on the beach, and is not unfrequently partially washed away by the river storms. The Boca is quite a little port on the banks of the Riachuelo, where lighters discharge and load, and where small craft are also built. Amongst other establishments there is that of the Messrs. Casares, the largest lightermen in the place, which is at all times very busy and generally crowded. A branch of the railway goes on towards Barracas, where an old wooden bridge crosses the stream, rendered exceedingly filthy by the refuse of the saladeros finding its way into the water. The effluvia arising from this cause are of a very offensive nature. Attempts, however, are being made to cleanse and deepen this valuable river, but the slow pace at which improvements are carried on here will probably postpone the event to a future generation. Most of the houses about the Boca are of wood, and are built on piles to avoid danger from floods, but there are also many large stone edifices in which produce is stored. A few days before I left a river storm laid nearly the whole locality under water, destroying a portion of the railway, and of course stopping the traffic. The replacing of the rails is not, I understand, a very formidable undertaking. The whole line, which is only three or four miles in length, including the branch to Barracas, ought to have been built on piles or led through an iron viaduct, so as to be out of the reach of the floods; and under existing circumstances, not to speak of the cost of repairing the permanent way, the traffic is interrupted at the very time it would be of the greatest utility. The original plan, and that for which the concession was obtained, was to connect the Boca and Barracas with the city, running a branch to Ensenada, where it was proposed to form a new port; but this part of the scheme is still in embryo. Where the line is really of utility and would carry a large traffic is from the Custom-house to the Boca, and across the bridge higher up to Barracas, where the Government are making a large swing iron bridge to replace the old dilapidated wooden one now in use. An iron viaduct is about being laid to connect the Boca Railway with the Custom-house. If properly constructed the Boca Railway would command the whole traffic of this district, and direct communication might be established with the Northern and Southern Railways; but a large additional capital is required before this scheme can be realised. The bulk of the Boca traffic is carried on by carts, under great disadvantages and at a heavy expense; and it is a painful sight to see the poor horses struggling through the mud, or toiling under the lash up the steep, miserably paved streets which connect the beach with the warehouses and depôts at the southern end of the city. In fact everything in the way of locomotion is carried on under great difficulties, and the detention of shipping in the outer roads is a serious matter. When the river is low, the beach is covered with carts galloping backwards and forwards, bringing cargo from the lighters or taking produce to them—the horses up to their girths in water and sometimes swimming. Many of the carts have a hollow bottom made water tight to prevent damage to the goods; and at times, when there is not water for boats to the mole, passengers have still to embark or disembark in carts, as was the case when I last visited Buenos Ayres. Both this mole and that to the Custom-house, for which the latter is exclusively used, have been built since that time; but to show the great want of accommodation which still exists to carry on the trade of the port, there are upwards of 300 custom-house depôts in different parts of the city besides the Custom-house itself, and at the north end a large market is being converted into a depôt; in fact the trade of the port has entirely outgrown the facilities for its reception, the whole, as at Monte Video, being in a great state of confusion.

On the subject of railways generally in the Argentine Confederation there cannot be a second opinion that it is through their instrumentality the future development of the country must be looked for; and it is to the credit of General Mitre that so much has been done during his presidency, especially the great work of the Central Argentine Railway, which more than any other measure must tend to link together the provinces of the Confederation and strengthen their union. So soon as the line is open to Cordova the communication with the western provinces will be speedy, and produce will find its way to that city as a central point, thence to be brought down to Rosario, Buenos Ayres, or Monte Video, comparatively at great saving of time and expense. At present the cost of transit absorbs a large part of the total value, the effect of which has been to discourage any notable increase of production beyond the necessities of local consumption. The railway will in addition afford a more easy mode of locomotion, and will greatly promote intercourse, while emigrants can be at once conveyed to distant places where their services are required. On every ground, therefore, the promotion and extension of railways is the first duty of President Mitre's successor, and it is to be hoped Senor Sarmiento will not be remiss in this respect. At all events, the way has been paved and a good example set. The only other railway to notice, and which I had not an opportunity of seeing, is a small one from Puerto Raiz, on the Parana, to Galaguay, a distance of about six miles, which was constructed by Mr. Coghlan for a sum of £20,000, or about £3,380 per mile. I believe it is very useful and returns a fair percentage on the outlay.

EMIGRATION TO BRAZIL.

BOTH the Government and the people of Brazil feel the necessity and the value of promoting immigration to the fullest extent. Experiments have been tried, and small colonies of Europeans founded in some of the southern provinces, all of which have been more or less successful.

In my account of the Province of San Paulo I have alluded to the settlement of Germans on the coffee plantations of Senhor Vergueiro, and to the desire of other large owners of property to follow his example. I also instanced the case of a little colony of Germans at Juiz de Fora, in the Province of Rio de Janeiro, which I had an opportunity of seeing, and there are besides in the same province other colonies on a larger scale. Various efforts have been made by individuals in other parts of the Empire to introduce foreign labour.

Slave labour is of course an impediment to the more general influx of Europeans, but where lands are set apart and arrangements made for the location of colonists there is no reason why the latter should not succeed, and form the nucleus of a large future population. The assistance and pecuniary co-operation of Government is of course required to effect any decided progress in this direction; and considering that every labourer brought into the country contributes to the national revenue, as well as to national production, the primary expense of passage money is soon repaid.

Many of the high table-lands of Brazil are admirably adapted to agricultural purposes, the climate, owing to elevation, being also favourable to European settlement. Enormous tracts of such land are at the disposal of the Executive, but it needs some outlay in order to prepare the way for emigrants, as they cannot be expected to pioneer as in the case of the United States, on account of their ignorance of the language and the difficulty of access from the port of debarcation.

The time is fast approaching when slavery must cease to exist in Brazil; and it behoves the Government to anticipate this event by the introduction of free labour. It is morally certain that the negroes, even if they settle down under their new condition, will not labour so constantly as when in a state of servitude. The Government ought, therefore, I repeat, to adapt itself to the exigences of its position, and encourage by every means the accession of European agricultural labourers of a suitable class. Large landowners, whose estates are now only partially worked, might devote a portion of them for new comers, and, in connection with the Central and Provincial Governments, attain the desired end. Financial difficulties, caused by the long war with Paraguay, may be pleaded as an excuse for neglecting this great question, but the very drain that has thus taken place of men and money only renders the case more pressing. I believe the Emperor entertains the most enlightened and practical views, both as regards doing away with slave labour and replacing it by the introduction of emigrants; but the trammels of a war expenditure, and the degree of attention the struggle demands on the part of the Ministers, prevent their inauguration of measures which all must see are inevitable, if the Empire is to prosper as heretofore.

In our own colonies the Colonial Governments have naturally been the chief promoters of emigration, from exercising, as they do, full control over their own revenues and over public lands; but in Brazil the impetus must first come from the action of the Central Government, which receives and distributes the provincial revenues after payment of provincial expenditure.

In the southern provinces of Brazil the cultivation of coffee and cotton offers the greatest scope for European labour, and the Province of San Paulo alone is capable of wonderful development as respects the growth of these two important articles if only proper means are adopted to provide augmented manual power.

The northern provinces present greater difficulties, from the nature of the climate, which is more adapted to a people like the Chinese than to Europeans. There is, however, an objection to this industrious race in consequence of their desire to return home when they have accumulated a little money. A further introduction of the African race as free labourers would be very advantageous. Though this might be a great gain to the negroes themselves, whose lives in their own country are at the mercy of such wretches as the sable King of Dahomy, philanthropists object to the removal of Africans from their native soil on any grounds, entirely ignoring the miserable existence they lead there and the barbarities to which they are subjected. But let slavery be once abolished in Brazil, and there could be no objection that I can see to their settlement in those provinces where their labour would be most useful, say from the River Amazon down to the Province of Bahia. This, however, is only a casual remark, and does not come within the scope of my present inquiry, namely, as to the best mode of introducing European labour into Brazil. As I have already pointed out to the Government, the passage money of emigrants must be paid, or advanced, the selection of them must be carefully attended to, and on reaching Brazil they should be sent on immediately to their ultimate destination, where suitable accommodation should also be provided against their arrival. Every necessary arrangement can easily be made if the Government and landed proprietors would take some trouble and show their practical earnestness in the matter.

There is an Emigrants' Home, or temporary abode in Rio de Janeiro, where proper attention is paid to them, and an officer (Dr. Galvao) is especially appointed by Government to look after this department. I quite intended to have visited this establishment, but was unable to do so. I had, however, a conversation with Dr. Galvao on the subject of emigration generally.

EMIGRATION TO THE RIVER PLATE.

No country in South America is more favourably placed, or presents a greater field for European labour than the River Plate, notwithstanding the drawbacks which have to some extent retarded its progress and injured its character. It has an advantage over Brazil in the absence of slavery, and is of a milder climate, though it is very hot during the summer months, as I experienced when at Monte Video, in January last, at which time the cholera was at its height.

A friend, who has resided in Buenos Ayres for two or three years, chiefly out in the campo, has thus recorded his experience of the average temperature:—

20 Days	very cold	45 to 55 deg. Fah.
182 „	moderate	55 to 75 „
60 „	warm	75 to 88 „
45 „	hot	80 to 85 „
58 „	intensely hot	85 to 105 „
365 Days.		

The thermometer, in exposed places, reaches 110 Fah. in the shade, but such cases are very exceptional.

He also adds as follows some very useful remarks as to clothing:

> Flannel shirts are best; woollen drawers should also be used

> For working, clothes of such colour as will not show the dust are best.
>
> The thickness of the clothes for summer wearing may be very much the same as would suit in England during hot summer weather; they should be waterproofed before being made up.
>
> Indiarubber coats, although very useful in winter, are ruined in hot weather, and stick together and tear, so as to be useless.
>
> Good English boots are not to be had, and are therefore very useful.

As to food he says:—

> Be careful about eating and drinking, especially when newly landed, and avoid as much as possible unnecessary exposure to the sun.
>
> Fruit should not be taken in quantites at first. Peaches are said to be the best and most wholesome.

I may add from my own experience that where it is intended to frequent the campo a pair of good riding boots are very necessary, and a rough pea jacket would be a very good companion in winter. In town cloth cloaks are much worn, and in the campo chiefly *ponchos*.

The boundless tracts of open country are in a great measure occupied by sheep and cattle, and do not require much of the labour of man; but sheep farming having been carried to a large extent, the price of wool has much depreciated, and sheep can be bought very cheap. In consequence, agriculture is now much more attended to and will require labour. Good wheat can be grown in most of the Argentine Provinces, and now forms a staple commodity, which may be increased to almost any extent where railways afford the means of easy transport, and so soon as there are sufficient labourers to cultivate the soil. Indeed, there is no reason why wheat, as well as Indian corn, should not be largely exported, and I believe this will be the case in a very few years. Wheat crops are liable to injury from drought, but the price obtained for the product is a very remunerative one, and it is not subject to losses by depreciation as frequently occurs with sheep and cattle.

Foreign settlers in distant provinces have of late been much damaged by Indian raids, to prevent which the Government has done very little, owing to the drain of soldiers for the war and to internal discord, but this plague is merely a temporary one, and nothing would tend more to remove the evil than a large increase of population, of which the country stands greatly in need.

Emigration, at present, goes on to a limited extent, but chiefly of the class suitable for cities and towns, and not for an agricultural or country life. Several colonies, founded under arrangements with the Provincial Governments of Santa Fé and Entre Rios, are prospering, and those in the fine Province of Cordova will also do well when the National Government is able to repel Indian inroads and protect the settlers. Many young Englishmen have settled in Cordova during the last four years, with more or less capital, and have bought land, particularly near the line of the Central Argentine Railway, naturally looking to Government for protection, which unhappily has not been effectively extended. In many cases their stock has been carried off by the savages, and their prospects seriously injured. They are now turning their attention to agriculture, and I have every reason to think they will be successful.

Numbers of young men have come out to the Plate

with little or no resources, expecting to find employment on sheep farms, and failing this, have fallen into bad habits, often wandering about the country and undergoing great hardships and misery. To do any good in such a country steadiness of character is the most essential quality, nor is it at all safe to trust to the chapter of accidents. It is only by well organised arrangements, and great perseverance, that new comers can expect to overcome the difficulties attending their settlement in a new country, the very extent of which is a disadvantage until such time as the influx of population and the formation of communities do away with these inconveniences.

The Chilian Government have lately made a contract with a Hamburg house for sending to the port of Lota Swiss, Tyrolese, and German emigrants, on a principle that may be adopted with benefit in relation to the River Plate. The emigrants must be provided with good characters, viséd by the Chilian Consul at Hamburg, and on their arrival at Lota they are to be sent on to Arauco by the Government, and placed in possession of their land, according to the terms of the Chilian law lately published. The colonists are to be furnished with between-deck passages, and they will be allowed one ton of measurement for every adult, and half a ton for each person under 12 years, and they are to be treated on board in conformity with the Hanover Passenger Act. The Government also agree to pay 40 dollars (£8) for the passage of each adult, and 20 dollars for each child under 12 years of age. The contract is to last for four years, and if the scheme should meet with favour in Germany, the Government agree to contract for 100 families for the first year, 150 for the second, 200 for the third, and 300 for the fourth year, with liberty to the contractors to exceed these numbers to the extent of 25 per cent. It appears to me questionable whether the contractors can afford to take emigrants that distance for £8 passage money, but probably the nature of the land concession is an inducement to families possessing some means to augment this sum, in which case it becomes a scheme of assisted passages on terms arranged between the emigrants and contractors. It is, however, a step in the right direction, which other Governments will do well to follow.

At Monte Video there is an Emigrant Office under the management of a respectable committee, where every information is afforded as to employment, but there is no Home or Asylum. At Buenos Ayres there is a miserable building on the ground floor, called an Asylum, where emigrants are allowed to remain four days. It seems to have been formerly a large stable, and is indeed more fit for horses than human beings. It wants both ventilation and cleanliness, the latter at all events easy to provide, but, considering the vast importance of emigration to the country, a more appropriate place might be maintained at very moderate cost. It is not necessary, nor desirable, that emigrants should on landing find themselves so comfortable as to care little about removing, but there is a medium between this and the dirty place open to them at present. Of course the sooner the emigrants are sent off to the locality where their labour is required the better.

If ever there was a time when sheep farming ought to offer advantages to new comers it is the present, when the value of sheep has fallen so low that land may be stocked for a very small sum as contrasted with former years, and land itself can be bought or rented at considerably less than formerly. This has inflicted great loss upon the older residents; indeed the result has been sometimes so disastrous that sheep farmers here and there are giving it up altogether, and others putting as much of their land as possible under tillage. Everything is therefore in favor of new settlers who may choose to try their fortunes in this particular line, only they must make up their minds to rough it for a few years, and be content with a life in the campo.

The consumption of an article like wool can never be subject to any lengthened depression, and with railway facilities there will be increased means for utilising the carcasses of sheep, by boiling down, or otherwise disposing of them. On the other hand, in the ordinary course of things, more land will be put under cultivation, and agriculture as well as sheep farming is destined to play an important part in the commercial history of the River Plate.

As I have already remarked, the want of population is the great drawback under which this country now suffers, and is an impediment to progress in every way. This can only be remedied by emigration receiving the direct aid as well as the encouragement of Government. It is not sufficient that a few stray people find their way up the country, but centres of population and labour should be formed in the most productive parts of every province, which would lead to agricultural progress, and eventually to the formation of new towns and cities. The mere extension of existing cities will never bring solid wealth to the Argentine Confederation, nor develop political stability.

RAILWAYS IN BRAZIL.

UNFORTUNATELY the promoters of railway enterprises in Brazil, entered into with British capital, have looked more to the guaranteed interest offered by the Government upon the money to be expended than to legitimate sources of traffic, out of which a dividend might be earned. All the Brazilian Railways, with the exception of the little Mauá, at Rio de Janeiro, and to which reference is made in my former book, have been created since 1853, the first in order and time being the Recife, or Pernambuco, about which there has been so much controversy between the Company and the Government. Before submitting any comments of my own, I will quote the following from the report lately issued by the Minister of Public Works, Senhor Dantas, upon this and the other lines. The document is official, and therefore worthy of reliance :—

The annexed gives the length, receipts, and expenses of the railways in 1867. The receipts and expenses of the S. Paulo Railway include only nine and a half months :—

Name.	Kilos.	Receipts.	Expenses.
D. Pedro II	197.4	2,523:796$781	1,117:034$992
S. Paulo	139.0	1,236:423 702	305:140 286
Pernambuco	124.9	599:331 445	414:772 537
Bahia	123.5	263:323 292	517:870 760
Cantagallo	49.1	709:222 555	365:830 300
Mauá	17.5	297:595 347	172:297 628
Total	651.6	5,599:693 122	2,892:955 503

These figures leave a balance of 2,706:737$610 over the cost of working.

D. PEDRO II. RAILWAY.

With the Macacos branch the length of this railway is 203 kilometres, 56.6 kilometres having been added during last year in its prolongations towards the station of Entre Rios. Failing to come to an agreement with the Companhia Mineira for the extension to Porto Novo da Cunha, an offer was made by the Companhia Uniao e Industria to construct a cart road to that point, the final offer of this Company being to make it gratuitously if certain favours were conceded to it. However, its offers were declined, as a cart road was judged incompatible with the requirements of the railway. Under these circumstances, as the state of the finances did not permit the contracting for the extension, orders were issued to give it a commencement by administration; and at the present time the works of the first miles are tolerably advanced.

A proposition to construct and work the fourth section has been received from capitalists and planters of the district it would serve, and it is now awaiting solution.

The competition between the railway and the Uniao e Industria road being prejudicial to both, the directory of this road has proposed bases for a compromise as under:—The Uniao e Industria road company to give up all its traffic between its station of Posse and Rio, receiving as compensation certain advantages, the principal one being the duration of its contract for twelve years, and the receipt of 120 rs. on every arroba transported on the railway between Entre Rios and Rio, which, it is estimated, would give the company 324:000$ annually, and transfer traffic of 2,700,000 arrobas, or 1,000:000$ annually, to the railway. In order to facilitate this transaction the company proposes to lease the railway for twelve years and pay a dividend of four per cent. to the Government. It also proposes to make any extension determined on, that to Porto Novo to be finished in five years, the Government to furnish the money, and the company to receive no compensation for its trouble except what would arise from the 120 reis the arroba upon the traffic over the line from Entre Rios and Rio. On the completion of the Porto Novo branch, the company would receive 2,000:000$ out of the profits over the four per cent. dividend as indemnity for any loss, rights or advantages secured to it by the contract of October 29, 1864, and it would then commence the construction of the railway through the valley of the Parahybano towards the Serra of Mantiqueira, using for this purpose four-fifths of the net revenue received from the railway, one-fifth remaining for the company, this continuing until the end of the twelve years, and the company binding itself to make, at its own cost, the branch from Juiz de Fora to the railway station of Uba. If, however, the Government judge it better to construct a system of macadamised cart roads, centering at Entre Rios, the company will then pay six per cent. on the railway, and will construct within four years, twenty leagues of road to Porto Novo da Cunha, and on to Barra do Pomba, and will, within six years, macadamise the Serraria road as far as Mar de Hespanha, the road from the Parahybuna station to Flores, and that from the Uba station to Juiz de Fora; making also, during the last six years of the contract, the road to Barbacena, following as much as possible the trace drawn for a railway, and prolonging it to S. Joao de El Rei. Besides, the company will settle 2,000 families of colonists along the road from Uba to Juiz de Fora, and on that between Juiz de Fora, Barbacena, and S. Joao de El Rei. The company also binds itself to keep in order all the cart roads in construction, transporting freight and passengers on them at the rates provided for the Uniao e Industria road; and, in addition, to deliver up to the Government, at the end of the twelve years, the railway and roads in good condition.

Three proposals have been made for the prolonging of the railway to the waterside; that of the engineers, Senhors Bulhoes and Passos, proposes to bring the line to the Praia da Gambôa, and there construct large warehouses and furnish all facilities for shipping and landing goods; that of Senhor F. B. Jansen Lima and others proposes to pass by a tunnel through the Livramento Hill to the Praia da Saude; that of Senhor Feliciano José Henrique proposes to connect the Santa Anna station with the principal parts of the city wherein goods are now stored.

The capital employed in the railway having been 27,525:957$816 upon the 31st of December last, its net income of 1,422:434$402 during the last year represents a dividend of 5.16 per cent. upon its cost, which percentage should, when the Entre Rios traffic assumes a normal condition, rise to six per cent. in view of the greater number of stations now open, and if the Uniao e Industria freights pass over the line there can be no doubt that the percentage will exceed seven per cent. per annum.

The following table shows the progress of the railway since its commencement. The Macacos branch is excluded, it not existing in the first years:—

Year.	Revenue.	Working.	Per Cent.
1859	606:870$492	720:900$443	84.18
1860	611:402 672	920:765 784	66.40
1861	688:506 150	1,073:731 050	64.12
1862	800:934 211	964:996 982	82.99
1863	849:421 671	969:621 542	87.60
1864	964:199 300	1,211:615 205	79.57
1865	1,088:133 594	1,756:148 520	61.96
1866	834:057 521	1,848:783 351	45.11
1867	1,082:283 327	2,506:836 961	43.17

Net revenue of 1867... ... ...1,422:434$402

The stations opened during 1867 were:—Ubá on May 5, Parahyba do Sul on August 11, Entre Rios on October 13.

BAHIA RAILWAY.

The shareholders of this railway continue to suffer the consequences produced by the excess of expenses over receipts. Last year's balance showed an increase of 12:867$764 in receipts, and of 24:383$445 in expenses, giving a deficit of 218:630$092, more by 11:515$681 than the preceding year's.

This result is no doubt disheartening, but meantime I await the report of the commission I authorised the President of the province to appoint, whose investigations must have revealed the latent causes of this state of things, in order to take such measures as may be recommended for the purpose of placing the enterprise on the footing reclaimed by its and the public treasury's interests.

The construction of the feeding roads judged necessary for the improvement of the traffic could not be carried on rapidly owing to the financial condition of the province.

The register of cattle established at Alagoinhas is estimated to give the railway a further traffic of 24,000 bullocks and to augment the receipts by 40:000$.

In my opinion, however, the only measure which can save the capital employed in the railway is its prolongation, but unfortunately those causes subsist which counselled me to postpone surveys for the prolonging of this and the other railways, with the exception of the Dom Pedro II. line, whose existing conditions are different.

The debt of the Province of Bahia to the National Treasury for advances on account of the Two per Cent Guarantee was estimated at 1,516:862$220 up to the first half of last year, and at present must be more than 2,000:000$.

PERNAMBUCO RAILWAY.

Notwithstanding the elements of prosperity which the company already counts on, and those which the future reserves for it, its financial position is not at present satisfactory, nor have its shares been able to obtain in London quotations worthy of the destinies awaiting it. To such result that false position has contributed, besides other things, in which the company has been placed by the various operations through which the company sought to obtain its capital. As you know, part of this capital enjoys the guarantee of interest, another part was obtained by a loan effected by the Imperial Government, and finally, a third fraction, furnished by the shareholders, runs the risk of not realising the least return for a long time. The question of the increase of guaranteed capital, in discussion between the Imperial Government and the company, must indubitably have aided in augmenting the embarassments in which the company flounders. It would be very proper to put an end as soon as possible to every question delaying the prosperity of an enterprise whose capital has contributed largely to the development and riches of the Province of Pernambuco. It is needful to give a definite settlement to that question of the increase of the guaranteed capital of this railway which has been submitted to your deliberation. The directory in London is constantly reiterating its reclamations for a final decision. As we do not possess the needful means for undertakings of this kind, it is of much importance to us that foreign capital, which comes to try and to explore, may obtain advantages that may encourage other enterprises.

On the other hand, it is of very great interest to the State that companies which enjoy a guarantee of interest may prosper in such a mode as to dispense with the guarantee. The company having to meet the next payment of debenture bonds, whose time was ending, and neither having funds in hands for it nor the power of raising them in London, it recurred to the Imperial Government, asking for a loan of £40,000, but this the Government could not grant, as it was not duly authorised.

The question of the prolongation to the city of Recife has occupied my attention, especially since the engineer of the company presented the plans and estimates for the realisation of the project. According to them the direction of the line should run parallel to the streets of Santa Rita, Nova, and Praia, and the cost is estimated at £5,000.

Although the company comprehends the advantage it should obtain by this prolongation it is not disposed to undertake the works without a guarantee on the capital expended, or without some other pecuniary assistance. The advantages which this work will produce for the agriculture and commerce of the province, and the small sacrifice which its execution asks from the public coffers dispose me favourably towards it, and if, as I hope, the examinations I ordered into those plans and estimates do not change my opinion, I will at a proper time authorise a contract for this improvement.

In accordance with the dispositions of the law I authorised the Imperial Legation in London to lend the sum of £150,000 to the company, to be employed in increasing the rolling stock. The company proposing, however, to accept the loan without interest, and to amortise the principal with the excess of revenue over seven per cent., I declared the proposal inacceptable.

The revenue diminished by 47:917$011 from that of the preceding year, it coming to 599:331$445. The expenses on the contrary rose from 364:134$259 in 1866 to 414:772$537, an increase of 50:638$270 occurring therefore in 1867. This double result is partly explained by the diminution of the traffic in consequence of bad harvest in the localities profiting by the road, and partly by the need to promptly carry out the repairs of the road. Although it is desirable that this result had not occurred, it should not suscitate serious apprehensions for the future of the railway.

SANTOS AND JUNDIAHY RAILWAY.

This line was inaugurated on the 15th, and opened on the 16th of February, 1866: this road at once commenced to show an extensive traffic, which, augmenting day by day as the planters became convinced of its superiority over ordinary methods, prognosticates most brilliant destinies to it. However, notwithstanding its evident inferiority, the common road still maintains a serious competition with the railway and takes from it a part of the products which are sent to Santos from the interior, inasmuch as, out of 1,004,779 arrobas, at which amount the total traffic is estimated, 611,818 go by the railroad, and 392,961 by the highway. Despite this competition, and the difficulties with which every enterprise struggles at first, however well organised, the gross receipts of the Santos and Jundiahy railway, since its opening, up to the end of 1867, rose to 1,236:423$702, thus giving more than $4\frac{3}{4}$ per cent. upon the capital employed. It may be presumed that, when the short life competition referred to is overcome, and when the line is extended to Campinas, taking into account the natural increase of production in a province so favourably placed, the revenue would soon double, thus freeing the treasury from the onus of the guarantee of interest. The Santos and Jundiahy Railway is, therefore, one of those amongst us which promise best; and perhaps it may be considered the first industrial undertaking of the kind, if the serra service, by means of inclines, does not exact a constant outlay which will diminish the revenue.

During the past year the trains of the road transported 176,081 passengers, namely:

1st Class	19,078½
2nd „	26,033½
3rd „	130,952
Season tickets	17
Total	176,081

The plan of Engineer P. Fox for the extension of the line to Campinas having received the preference over the other traces presented to the ministry in my charge, the President of the province undertook to promote a company of planters and capitalists to carry this important benefit into effect. The company having the right of preference to the extension of the railway, I instructed our Minister in London to obtain an explicit declaration from the directory renunciatory of its right, in order that there might be no future doubts or reclamations. The directors replied that the company expressly desisted from the right, and, therefore, the association could proceed with its measures for the realisation of its object. In the opinion of Engineer E. Viriato de Medeiros the amount of capital expended up to the 30th of July, 1866, amounted to £2,548,434, but for payment of interest due it was estimated hypothetically at £2,650,000.

The provincial assembly not having empowered the President to pay the interest of two per cent. upon the guaranteed capital, to which the province had bound itself, it was necessary for the national treasury to take upon itself the satisfaction of the provincial promise. It is therefore requisite that the provincial assembly provide in the estimate of this year for relieving the public treasury from the charge upon its already too burdened coffers.

It will be seen from these reports that all the guaranteed railways are exposed to difficulties arising out of the special character of the relations existing between the various companies and the Government, and that Senhor Sobragy, the talented manager of the Dom Pedro Segundo Railway, has been sent to England to try to come to terms with the companies. In my opinion, however, nothing short of the Government taking over the railways, giving in exchange a guaranteed stock, can ever meet the requirements of the case, or bring these concerns out of their present unfavourable position. It would be useless to recapitulate here the causes of their failure. Certainly no fault can be laid to the charge of the Government, which has acted in perfect good faith towards them, and done probably more than any other Government ever did or would do to assist undertakings of this or any other kind. Rashness, ignorance, and bad advisers have led to most of their difficulties, and with such proofs of the mismanagement of railway directors on our home lines no one will be surprised at the unsuccessful result of their management of lines abroad.

As an evidence that railways can be made and properly managed by Brazilians I need only refer to the Dom Pedro Segundo, a line quite as important as any in the country. In separate chapters I have referred to this railway, and also to that in the province of San Paulo.

I believe it would be greatly to the advantage of the rising generation in Brazil if the young men were trained to become engineers, rather than lawyers or doctors, with which the towns and cities swarm. Brazilians are neither deficient in talent nor energy, if properly brought out, and the employés of the Dom Pedro Segundo are chiefly natives. The splendid road to Juiz de Fora furnishes an example of this, and I regret time did not permit me to make another visit there, which Senhor Mariano very kindly urged on me. Had it not been for the heavy expenditure of the Paraguayan war, the railway system of Brazil would doubtless have been much more extensively developed, and the provincial lines now in existence carried further into the interior, as it is impossible the latter can ever be productive of much revenue, or of much national benefit until they are prolonged to the chief centres of cultivation, which, as a general rule, lie upwards of one hundred miles from the coast. The provinces of Pernambuco and Bahia both attach great importance to railway extension to the river San Francisco, but it does not appear from the report of Captain Burton, who lately explored that river, that it is likely to yield so much traffic as is supposed. The want of population is the great drawback to railways, and until this want can be met by emigration of some kind, a large amount of internal wealth must lie waste.

My long detention in the southern part of Brazil and the River Plate prevented me visiting Bahia and Pernambuco, and judging from personal observation as to the state and condition of the railways there, or reporting on the new tramway from Caxioera to the interior, which promises to be of great utility to the country traversed by it, as well as remunerative to the shareholders interested in its future.

COMMERCE OF BRAZIL AND THE RIVER PLATE.

During the unfruitful dominion of Spain and Portugal, commerce with South America was limited to the exchange of commodities between the mother countries and the populations planted in the New World revealed to Europe by the daring genius of the great Genoese navigator and those bold spirits who after him traversed and explored strange oceans and seas unknown. The Courts of Madrid and Lisbon adopted the most stringent measures for the preservation of their monopoly and to prevent commercial intercourse with their colonies by the subjects of foreign States. So successful were the means taken to this end that very little was known with certainty in England concerning those immense regions until after the War of Independence freed them from the yoke under which they had so long groaned. I need not in this place indicate all the causes that led to this great revolution, but there can be no doubt the example of our own American colonists and the principles disseminated by the French Revolution exercised a potential influence in stirring the South American communities to liberate themselves from the oppressive restrictions with which they were fettered.

The marauding exploits of Admiral Drake, and the

rich prizes captured on the Spanish main, had given our countrymen some notion of the incalculable wealth of Chili and Peru, the Brazils, and the Rio de la Plata; and their erection into separate and Sovereign States was hailed as the advent of a new and prosperous era for the commerce of both hemispheres. With a liberality and promptitude which will always be remembered by the various South American nations, the capitalists of Britain responded to their demands for pecuniary aid, and loans were freely subscribed to enable the enfranchised peoples to establish popular self-government upon solid bases. It may be said that this still remains to be accomplished, and the frequently recurrent revolutions in Bolivia and Peru, and in some others of the nascent Republics, are certainly no manifestation of executive stability; but it must not be forgotten that their antecedents, under the Spanish and Portuguese control, were not of a nature to fit them for a wise and temperate exercise of political privileges. Year by year, however, with the growth of intelligence and the spread of education, the respective States are becoming less subject to internal and civil convulsions; and in this respect the rapid development of industrial and productive activity gives promise of a still more satisfactory condition of things in the proximate future.

Since the abrogation of the monopolies of Spain and Portugal and the inauguration of free intercourse with South America the commercial movements between that part of the globe and the maritime nations of Europe have assumed imposing proportions, and are every year increasing in value and importance. As elsewhere, England holds a high place both in the Pacific and Atlantic markets, as an importer of products and an exporter of manufactured goods. Our Board of Trade

Returns show the magnitude of British interests in those countries, and the necessity that exists for promoting the most cordial relations with the different Governments. But at present I must confine my observations to Brazil and the River Plate, and from a reference to the returns in question it will be seen that the former is our largest South American customer, taking commodities to the annual value of £5,822,918, while we in return receive Brazilian produce of the annual value of £5,902,011. The River Plate comes next in order, taking English goods of the annual value of £4,405,548, while it sends to us produce worth £2,146,079. It will appear, therefore, that the total movements between this country and Brazil and the River Plate are respectively of the yearly value of £11,724,929 and £6,545,627. And here I may state, without going into particulars, that the entire commercial movement between England and the whole of South America reaches the no inconsiderable sum of £34,566,405. The above returns are for the year 1867.*

The Board of Trade Returns, though they exhibit, in figures surpassing eloquence in their convincing power, the extensive character of our own trading relations

---

* It may be interesting to show the progressive nature of them by taking the Board of Trade figures in connection with those countries for the previous four years as follows :—

Brazil—	Imports.	Exports.	Total.
1863	£4,491,000	4,082,641	8,573,641
1864	7,021,121	6,369,359	13,400,480
1865	6,797,241	5,771,024	12,468,265
1866	7,237,793	7,358,141	14,595,934
River Plate—			
1863	£2,460,280	1,897,164	3,357,444
1864	2,285,486	2,788,653	5,074,139
1865	2,263,540	2,824,823	5,088,363
1866	2,613,263	4,250,470	6,863,733

with Brazil and the River Plate, of course convey only a partial idea of the commercial activity of the countries named.

Brazil and the Argentine Republic both carry on a large business with other European nations. With regard to the first it will be seen from the statistics we quote below that the Empire has large transactions with France and the Continent, as well as with the United States, to which the bulk of her coffee crop is shipped.

In the Budget of last year, submitted to the National Assembly by the then Finance Minister, Senhor Zacharias, I find the following:—

COMMERCE OF IMPORTATION, EXPORTATION, AND NAVIGATION.

The value of the import trade in 1866-67, according to the official data in the treasury, was 143,483:745$; 22,503:313$, or 18.6 per cent. more than the average of the five years 1861-2 to 1865-6, and 5,716:903$, or 4.1 per cent. more than 1865-6.

This importation took place in the various provinces in the following proportion, which is compared with that of 1865-6:—

	1865-66.	1866-67.	Over in '65-6.
Rio de Janeiro	80,709:067$	80,458:064$	
Bahia	17,598:941	17,878:203	279:262$
Pernambuco	21,083:655	22,211:290	1,127:645
Maranhao	2,946:760	4,028:383	1,081:623
Para	4,613:218	5,396:706	783:488
S. Pedro	6,514:928	7,746:076	1,231:144
S. Paulo	1,295:948	1,546:755	250:807
Parana	154:083	237:278	83:195
Parahyba	26:067	99:446	73:379
Ceara	1,924:546	2,586:973	662:689
Santa Catharina	449:246	630:912	181:666
Alagoas	62:250	219:537	157:287
Sergipe	63:177	17:390	
Espirito Santo	1:209	2:116	907
Rio Grande do Norte	30:853	171:654	140:801
Piauhy	293:157	252:957	
	136,766:842	143,483:745	6,053:893

Diminutions occurred in Rio de Janeiro 251:003$, Sergipe 45:787$, and Piauhy 40:209$; total, 336:990$.

The countries whence the importation came in 1866-67 were the following:—

Great Britain and possessions	58,276:905$783
United States	4,300:628 878
France and possessions	22,023:196 953
La Plata	12,325:712 734
Portugal and possessions	5,580:451 780
Hanseatic Cities	4,340:509 479
Spain and possessions	805:919 990
Sweden	222:194 583
Denmark	34:134 495
Russia	12:277 800
Coast of Africa	151:773 425
Italy	468:789 695
Chili	537:023 100
Belgium	1,333:855 778
Austria	910:268 440
Holland	3:017 850
China	23:400 000
Peru	680 000
Ports of the Mediterranean	29:744 000
Ports of the Empire	1,354:734 000
Fisheries	1:381 200
Ports not mentioned	30,747:145 332
Total	143,483:745 290

The value of the exports of native production and manufacture to foreign countries was in 1866-67 156,020:906$, 21,516:502$, or 15.9 per cent. more than the average of the five years 1861-2 to 1865-6, and less by 1,066:652$ or 0.67 per cent than in 1865-6.

The countries whither the exports of 1866-7 went were the following:—

Russia	460:660$717
Sweden	773:111 068
Holland	80:356 944
Hanseatic Cities	4,816:242 458
Great Britain and possessions	37,283:974 040
France and possessions	18,582:278 631
Spain and possessions	165:387 149
Portugal and possessions	4,847:275 259

Belgium	328:048$841
Austria	61:381 600
Italy	734:400 624
Chili	414:903 411
United States	31,188:066 047
La Plata	7,014:207 881
Turkey	149:347 716
Denmark	913:630 980
Coast of Africa	448:869 272
Channel	16,511:891 087
Ports of the Baltic and Mediterranean	1,363:562 864
Ports not known	30,335:659 000
Consumption	42:642 178
Total	156,020:906 766

The total of the direct importation and the national exportation abroad was in :—

1866-67	299,504:651$
Compared with 1865-66, namely	294,854:400
There was an augment of	4,650:251
Or 1.5 per cent., and, if compared with the average of 1861-2 to 1865-6, namely	255,483:836

There was an increase of 44,020:815, or 17.2 per cent.

The value of the importation with certificate (carta de guia) was in 1865-67 24,902:670$, 823:969$, or 3.4 per cent. more than in 1865-6, 2,448:821$, or 12.6 per cent. more than the average of the five years 1861-2 to 1865-6.

The re-exportation in 1866-7 rose to 1,786:052$, 447:993$, or 33.4 per cent. more than in 1865-6, and 377:686$, or 26.8, than the average of 1861-2 to 1865-6.

The number of national and foreign vessels cleared in the foreign trade of 1866-7 was :

Entered	3,439 vessels	1,245,214 tons		51,450	men.
Sailed	2,439 „	1,496,274 (*) „		49,655	„
Including nationals :—					
Entered	255 vessels	43,579 tons		1,953	men.
Sailed	209 „	47,703 (*) „		2,174	„

The products of Brazil are very varied, but the

* The "sailed" are toneladas of 1,728 lbs.

principal articles, and the relative positions they occupy in the commerce of the country, will be seen by the estimated quantity and value of the exports from Rio de Janeiro for 1867, as stated in the Official Report to our Foreign Office by Mr. Pakenham :—

		Quantity.	Value.
Coffee	lbs.	424,532,680	£8,776,590
Sugar	,,	8,980,960	106,752
Cotton	,,	9,240,000	350,000
Rum	pipes	3,865	40,000
Salted hides	,,	4,200,000	57,540
Dry hides	,,	250,000	8,250
Tapioca	barrels	11,294	25,066
Horns	,,	116,860	1,519
Tobacco	bales	51,615	154,845
Diamonds	oitavas	5,704	37,000
Total			£9,558,287

The exports from Pernambuco, Para, Bahia, Santos, and Rio Grande do Sul during the same period amount to about £7,000,000.

Mr. Pakenham, in the same report, also remarks :— "The Brazilian imports and exports for the last year for which there are Customs statistics amounted to £14,348,374 for imports, and to £15,607,090 for exports, and the total commercial movement with foreign countries had then increased 17 per cent. on the average of the preceding five years."

The trade statistics of the Argentine Republic are quite as encouraging as those of its Imperial ally. I have before me a valuable communication of Mr. Daniel Maxwell, of Buenos Ayres, addressed to the Sociedade Rural Argentina, in which he makes the following comparative statements as to the exports of produce during the periods mentioned :—

	From 1858 to 1862.	From 1862 to 1867.
Dry Ox and Cow Hides	5,554,417	6,798,152
Salted Ditto	1,972,755	2,325,084

	From 1858 to 1862.	From 1862 to 1867.
Dry Horse Hides	305,057	197,264
Salted Ditto	780,190	617,945
Bales of Wool	251,191	608,706
Bolsas Ditto	7,456	9,517

With the exception of horse hides these figures manifest a very material and striking augmentation in the productive energy of the Republic. The proportionate distribution is shown in the annexed tables :—

DRY OX, COW, AND HORSE HIDES.

	From 1858 to 1862.	From 1862 to 1867.
Great Britain	.233	2.816
France	11.936	8.054
Belgium, Holland, and Germany	25.847	11.585
United States	29.029	48.904
Italy	12.844	10.562
Spain	18.011	17.985
Sweden and Norway	......	.094
	100.000	100.000

SALTED OX, COW, AND HORSE HIDES.

	From 1858 to 1862.	From 1862 to 1867.
Great Britain	63.123	45.484
France	12.592	14.533
Belgium, Holland, and Germany	17.873	31.807
United States	2.626	1.889
Italy	3.482	4.893
Spain	6.304	.408
Sweden and Norway	......	.914
	100.000	100.000

WOOLS.

	From 1858 to 1862.	From 1862 to 1867.
Great Britain	10.273	7.235
France	27.508	25.109
Belgium, Holland, and Germany	39.784	45.433
United States	21.083	20.340
Italy	1.303	1.766

	From 1858 to 1862.	From 1862 to 1867.
Spain	.039	.030
Sweden and Norway		.087
	100.000	100.000

The number of sheep skins exported from 1858 to 1862 was 8,705,883 against 20,776,898 from 1862 to 1867; and with respect to the wool exported it may be desirable to explain that a bale of wool usually contains 34 arrobas, and that four *bolsas* or *chiguas* are equivalent to a bale. According to this calculation, the export of wool from 1858 to 1862 reached 8,705,883 arrobas against 20,776,898 arrobas from 1862 to 1867.

The war with Paraguay, though it has undoubtedly pressed upon the financial resources of the Republic, has in no manner arrested its commercial, industrial, and fiscal progress. This is very clearly apparent from statistics furnished by his Excellency Don Norberto de la Riestra in connection with the issue of the recent Argentine loan contracted in this country to cover the balance of the extraordinary expenditure caused by the protracted struggle with Lopez. I quote as follows from the document referred to, the value of which will be obvious:—

The official value of the foreign trade of the Republic through the port of Buenos Ayres alone in 1865 was as follows:—

Imports	£5,420,603
Exports	4,399,355
Total	£9,819,958

In 1866 it was:—

Imports	£6,453,817
Exports	4,605,942
Total	£11,059,759

The real value of the aggregate trade for 1866, including the other ports of the Republic, cannot be estimated at less than £16,000,000, and has continued since to augment.

The declared value of produce and manufactures exported from he United Kingdom to the Republic in 1867 has amounted to £2,838,037, taking in this respect the lead of all the other South American States, Brazil only excepted.

The export of wool, which is the staple article, from the port of Buenos Ayres alone was as follows :—

Season 1863-64	77,343,200 lbs.
,, 1864-65	104,688,000 lbs.
,, 1865-66	120,362,400 lbs.

and the same progressive increase is observable in the other productions of the country.

Referring to Brazil, every Parisian luxury is found in the cities, Rio de Janeiro being full of French shops, and the Rua d'Ouvidor, one of its principal streets, is almost exclusively French. Of course many important trades and industrial occupations are carried on, and in particular the manufacture of carriages, which equal in elegance and solidity those of any country in Europe. Iron foundries, iron ship-building, and other useful establishments also exist; but there are few cotton, woollen, or silk manufactories. Therefore the commerce of Brazil is almost entirely one of exchange.

As regards the River Plate, a large trade is maintained with France, Belgium, and other parts of Europe, where River Plate produce is extensively consumed. It is only necessary to look at the manner in which the ladies of Monte Video and Buenos Ayres dress to form an idea of the extent of French imports to those places. There are no manufactories in the River Plate beyond such as have been specified in regard to Brazil, carriage making being equally conspicuous.

It is a feature in the Board of Trade Returns that Paraguay, which has of late years caused such a noise in the world, makes no figure whatever. Now of course it is under blockade, but previous to that event the figures were almost *nil*. Had the ruler of that country used his energies to produce and export 5,000 bales of cotton annually, for which article the land and climate are admirably adapted, what would have been the state and condition of Paraguay at the present moment? It is not requisite to enlarge on such a topic.

Whilst adverting to the commerce of these countries, and to their internal wealth, their mineral products must not be left out of sight, and in this respect Brazil possesses a great superiority from the steady working of her gold and diamond mines, which have always been a source of considerable revenue, even though they are probably not yet very perfectly explored. To do this it requires a large outlay of money and the enterprise of private individuals or public companies. Formerly the mines were worked exclusively for the Crown.

The Argentine Republic has not yet given much signs of mineral activity, but there can be no doubt gold exists, as well as silver, in the Andine Provinces, and when the railway is carried on to Cordova we may hear a good deal more of the San Juan silver mines, to the development of which Major Rickards has devoted himself for so many years.

In the Banda Oriental gold has long been known to exist in the mountains of Canapiru, and the indefatigable Mr. Bankhart has succeeded in forming a company of Monte Videan shareholders to operate there. He is now in England obtaining the needful machinery and securing workmen for the mines. If successful it will be a great boon to the country, and may assist in providing a future metallic currency, from lack of which things now appear to be at a deadlock.

It will be seen from this short summary how closely our commercial interests are identified with those of the countries referred to, and how desirable it is, as at present, that the most friendly relations should be maintained with them. Nor are these likely to be again disturbed. In every port and city in South America are to be found British merchants and representatives of the country, the latter placed there, not, as previously, with a view to cavil, find fault, and threaten, but to see fair play and justice impartially administered to British subjects. The doctrine of non-interference in the political squabbles of other countries is now generally adopted, diplomatic meddlers are discouraged, and the post of foreign minister in South America is much more agreeable than formerly.

THE RIVER AMAZON.

As it has not been my good fortune to visit this mighty stream, I cannot, of course, speak of it from personal experience, but the Amazon is exciting so much attention in various parts of the world in consequence of the late voyage of Professor Agassiz that a brief notice may not be out of place here.

Most persons have read Mr. Bates' very interesting work, "The Naturalist on the Amazon," in which he has described in so graphic a manner the wonders of that country in the shape of animal and vegetable life. Since it was written a great change has taken place in the future prospects of the Amazon by the politic step of the Brazilian Government in throwing open its waters to the flags of all nations, from which will result much valuable information, if it is not immediately followed by commercial progress to the extent that some sanguine writers have foretold. This act has called forth in Europe and America the most gratifying tributes in commendation of the unselfish attitude thus assumed by Brazil towards the commerce of the world. The American journals are especially unstinted in their praise. With regard to the probable consequences of this measure one writer, the Rev. J. C. Fletcher, states as follows:—

The opening of the Amazon, which occurred on the 7th of September, 1867, and by which the great river is free to the flags of all nations from the Atlantic to Peru, and the abrogation of the monopoly of the coast trade from the Amazon to the Rio Grande do Sul, whereby 4,000 miles of Brazilian sea coast are open to the vessels of every country, cannot fail not only to develop the resources of Brazil, but will prove of great benefit to the bordering Hispano-American Republics and to the maritime nations of the earth. The opening of the Amazon is the most significant indication that the leven of the narrow monopolistic Portuguese conservatism has at last worked out. Portugal would not allow Humboldt to enter the Amazon valley in Brazil. The result of the new policy is beyond the most sanguine expectation. The exports and imports for Para for October and November, 1867, were double those of 1866. This is but the beginning. Soon it will be found that it is cheaper for Bolivia, Peru, Equador, and New Granada east of the Andes to receive their goods from and to export their indiarubber, chincona, &c., to the United States and Europe *via* the great water highway which discharges into the Atlantic than by the long, circuitous route of Cape Horn, or the Trans-Isthmian route of Panama. The Purus and the Madeira are hereafter to be navigated by steamers. The valley of the Amazon in Brazil is as large as the area of the United States east of Colorado, while the valley of the Amazon in and out of Brazil is equal to all the United States east of California, Oregon, and Washington territory, and yet the population is not equal to the single city of Rio de Janeiro or the combined inhabitants of Boston and Chicago. It is estimated that a larger population can be sustained in the valley of the Amazon than elsewhere on the globe.

Explorations have already been commenced by enterprising men from the Southern States of America, who have no doubt of the adaptability of the soil and of the climate on the banks of this noble stream for all the productions of the torrid zone. One of these pioneers, Mr. John W. Dowsing, has lately presented a most interesting report, with respect to the resources of Para, to his Excellency the President of that important province:—

May it please your Excellency, I herewith have the honour to submit a succinct Report of a recent exploration of a portion of the valley of the Amazon, and some of the tributaries of the Amazon river, by me, accompanied by Captain John B. Jones, George M. Sandidge, Charles H. Mallory, and Charles M. Broom, and all under the patronage of the Imperial Government of Brazil.

In accordance with instructions from the Minister of Agriculture to your Excellency, I was furnished with transportation, and one conto of reis to defray incidental expenses, and letters to various officials within the Province of Para to facilitate my explorations and secure as far as practicable every information I might desire in regard to the country, in order that I might more fully report to those of my countrymen in the United States who are now deeply interested in emigration.

Myself and party, consisting of the four above-named gentlemen, left Belem on the 9th of November, 1867, on board the steamer Soure for Cameta on the Rio Tocantins. After several days' preparation we ascended that river nearly to the falls; returning we ascended the Amazon and Tapajoz rivers to the town of Santarem and surrounding country, thence to the contiguous islands and up the Tapajoz, thence up the Amazon river to its junction with the Rio Negro to the city of Manaos.

From Manaos we made several excursions into the country. It was my purpose to go to Rio Branco, but utterly failing to obtain transportation, after remaining twenty-two days, I changed my course to Rio Matary and the lakes into which it leads.

The information I obtained at the various places visited would doubtless be of great utility to the commercial world. It would open up a new market for the various productions, and new fields for the employment of industry.

The trade up the valley of the Amazon, upon the great river and its numerous tributaries, is very considerable. Its full extent and value does not appear in the published statistics of your commerce.

The trade up this magnificent valley is susceptible of almost unlimited expansion. It stands alone in the inconceivable grandeur of its capabilities and the wonderful sublimity of its future destinies.

This magnificent valley, with its wonderful and inexhaustible resources, will form a great avenue of commercial communication between the Atlantic and the Pacific Oceans. It is an immense prolific theatre for the formation of colonies. There is no doubt but that the best route for many manufactures from Europe and North America to Peru is through the valley of the Amazon. The productions of this wonderful valley are necessarily very diversified. They include all the tropical vegetables and fruits, many kinds of furniture and dyewoods, many medicinal drugs, and in the elevated lands it is peculiarly rich in minerals. The great staples exported in which the commercial world is interested are indiarubber, cacao, sarsaparilla, tobacco, hides salted and green, various vegetable oils, cotton, deer skins, isinglass, urucu, rice, &c., &c.

The general surface of a great portion of the Province of Para is even and undulating while it is diversified with many rich campos and numerous beautiful lakes and streams, filled with every variety of fish and turtle. Elevated lands, rising here and there, impart variety, grandeur, and picturesque beauty to its scenery.

To expatiate upon the beauty, capabilities, and resources of the numerous streams tributary to the great basin of the Amazon, the country margining these streams, the general characteristics of the inhabitants, &c., would invite and justify a voluminous report. I will content myself, however, with a few reflections upon the brilliant future that awaits this favoured country.

My investigations disclose that the valley of the Amazon is one immense forest of valuable timber, woods of the finest grain, and susceptible of the highest polish: adapted to cabinet purposes. For building vessels there is no woods on the earth equal to those grown in the valley of the Amazon.

This is the country for indiarubber, sarsaparilla, balsam, copaiba, gum copal, animal and vegetable wax, cocoa, castanha nuts, sapucia nuts, tonka beans, ginger, black pepper, arrowroot, annetto, indigo, dyes of the gayest colours, and drugs of rarest medicinal virtues.

These immense forests are filled with game, and all the rivers and lakes are filled with fish and turtle.

The climate of this country is salubrious and the temperature most agreeable. The direct rays of the sun are tempered by a constant east wind, laden with moisture from the ocean, so that one never suffers from either heat or cold. I found the nights invariably cool enough to use blankets. With the succulent tropical fruits, the great variety of game, and the salubrious climate, this country is a paradise for the indolent man; for here he can maintain life almost without an effort.

The geographical position of Belem gives it many advantages.

It is in the direct route of vessels to or from European and North American ports and the Pacific and Indian oceans. Therefore this city could be made a half way station for vessels thus bound to receive orders.

With an interior river navigation of many thousands of miles, with a soil of great fertility, and a climate which allows tropical vegetation to develop itself in all its luxuriance, with varied and inexhaustible mineral wealth, the Provinces of Para and Amazonas are specially marked out by nature to become the most wealthy country on the globe.

Belem possesses the requisites for carrying on commerce on an extensive scale. The right steps have been adopted in inaugurating and securing a general commercial system for Belem by the establishment of the Amazon Steamship Company.

In order to build up this city and country, and make it what the future determines it to be, the mineral and agricultural resources must be developed.

The slave population is being rapidly diminished by the war with Paraguay and self-emancipation. How is this labour to be re-supplied? It can only be done by the immigration of the hard working, industrious yeomanry of the United States and Europe. The surplus population of Europe and the disaffected citizens in the Southern portion of the United States will find their way to this immediate section of the country.

The great exodus will as naturally flow into the vast arable area of the valley of the Amazon as did the tribes of Asia flow into Europe through the passes of the Caucausus.

Every advancing wave of population will lift higher and higher the gathering flood of human life, which the moment it commences to press upon the means of subsistence in their respective countries must pour all of its vast tide of human beings into the great valley of the Amazon, and will eventually unite in one living chain of industrial life the waters of the Atlantic with the Pacific.

This country as yet is but a wilderness, but the inexorable laws of civilisation will at no distant day thread the labyrinthian mazes of this immensely fertile valley, and when teeming with industrious life it will pour into the coffers of this Empire untold wealth, thereby giving this portion of the Imperial Government a significance second to no portion of the earth.

The rich natural and agricultural productions of this valley must be poured out to the balance of the world. Upon the banks of each of the tributaries of the mighty Amazon city after city will as by enchantment arise to export the productions of the soil of this favoured country. The valley of the Amazon is yet to exercise a powerful influence on the political destinies of this Empire.

The future destiny of this valley is to be a glorious one; and fortunate the descendants of those who may now obtain a foothold and interest upon this soil. As already indicated the true elements of future greatness lie in the substratum of industry. The valley of the Amazon must have labour to develop its resources. The cities of North America and Europe are crowded with young men seeking employment.

The offices of European Consuls in the United States are crowded with foreigners, who have exhausted their last cent and are seeking for any kind of work.

Let them come to the valley of the Amazon with agricultural implements and obtain a home upon these fertile lands. Those who are lingering around the crowded seaports of poverty and vice, having no chance with others in the great world, should turn their attention to the valley of the Amazon, where a free homestead upon rich lands and with salubrious climate can be obtained.

The prosperity of this country is the future welfare of all civilised nations. This country has everything to hope for; nature has not been unmindful of its most precious gifts to this land.

In the selection of lands, upon which it is my purpose to establish a colony, I will be governed by the advantages offered by the lands at Brigança over those explored. If the lands at Brigança are well watered and rich its accessability will decide me.

The migration to Brazil of energetic and agricultural population from the former Confederate States of North America is still going on, and may produce hereafter a a most beneficial effect on the destinies of the Empire. On this topic General Hawthorn and Mr. W. T. Moore have addressed some interesting remarks to the Brazilian Minister of Agriculture. The following is the concluding paragraphs of the communication to which I refer:—

The people of the South must emigrate but how, and where to? These are questions that may well engage the earnest attention of every Government that desires to increase the number of its good and loyal citizens. Though there may be a few unworthy persons claiming to be from the late Confederate States who have imposed and forced their lazy carcases and worthless habits upon this kind and liberal Government, we desire to say in the most emphatic and unequivocal terms that the great body of the Southern people are not professional emigrants, who systematically cringe the knee and hypocritically kiss the feet of every monarch that will scatter among them the crumbs of charity; on the contrary, they are the remnants of a gallant race, who, having struggled in vain to save their country from destruction and themselves from slavery, will like Æneas and his Trojan followers gather round them their aged fathers and mothers, their wives, their children, their household gods, and, emigrating to some foreign land, lend their powerful aid in building up the country of their adoption and pushing it forward to a conspicuous place in the front rank of nations.

They will carry with them their statesmen, their orators, and their men of science, and though they may carry little gold and silver, and but a few of this world's goods, yet they will carry with them rich stores of great and active thought, vast mines of unflagging energy and industry, immense treasures of practical and scientific knowledge in planting, navigation, commerce, and the fine arts. They will carry with them stout hearts, untarnished honour, and unconquered manhood; but above all, for that Government which shall now extend its liberal hand and relieve them in this their hour of need, they will cherish that unshaken fidelity and loyalty that will uphold and maintain it in its prosperity and rally around and die for it whenever its day of trial and danger comes. They are a race that have won imperishable honours in every walk of life, and upon every field of action that has ever been opened to human enterprise, and wherever they go in large bodies they cannot fail to add wealth to the coffers and prosperity to the land of their adoption.

Having adopted Brazil as our future home, and believing as we do that it is better adapted to the wants of our people than any other country upon earth, we should rejoice to see the good and true people of the South emigrate in masses to this wonderful country. Hence our anxiety that this Government should fully understand the character, the capacities, and the habits of the Southern people. Since we have been in Brazil we have reflected deeply upon this subject, and the result of our observations and reflections is that the people of the late Confederate States, being, as they are, strangers to the language, habits, and customs of this country, cannot be completely prosperous or contented here unless they settle in colonies by themselves, and that too upon a scale sufficiently large to carry on successfully all the various trades and professions, to have their own schools and churches, in short, to relieve them from the necessity of learning a foreign language before obtaining complete success in their agricultural, manufacturing, or mercantile operations. We are also deeply impressed with the belief that in order to a full development of their energies as a people and a successful renewal of those glorious triumphs in every art and science that once rendered them so illustrious, it is necessary they should be left as free and untrammelled in their action as the safety and dignity of an enlightened and liberal Government will admit. We therefore respectfully suggest that (as an inducement for this heroic people to emigrate to Brazil in one vast body, bringing with them their greatest, their wisest, and their best men; bringing with them their household gods, their customs, their manners, their indomitable energy and unflinching courage; but above all, bringing in their bosoms the bright hope that their race is not yet run, but that a brilliant and a glorious future awaits them here) the Government cause to be set apart and reserved for their settlement and use large bodies of the public lands, which may be selected by judicious and intelligent men; that these lands be surveyed as occasion may require, and sold in limited quantities, at fixed uniform rates, to that people alone, or to such as they may desire to settle in their midst; and that they be allowed full and complete religious toleration, as also the full rights of citizenship, whenever they shall take the oath of allegiance to the Government; that each of these colonies, including such as are already established, as well as those that may be established hereafter, be made a congressional, military, and judicial district, which, when it shall have the requisite number of inhabitants, shall be entitled to representatives in the national and provincial assemblies, chosen from among themselves; that so far as possible all their officers placed immediately over them be men speaking their own language, and familiar with their customs and manners; that all professional men among them who shall produce satisfactory evidence of good character and a reputable practice in the land from which they came be permitted to practice their respective professions within the limits of the said colonies, without having to undergo rigorous examinations in a foreign language; in short, that every liberal concession be made that a true and loyal people could ask, or a wise and generous Government could grant.

Your Excellency need not fear the result. Ours is not a race that breeds either traitors or cowards. When we have once plighted our faith, dangers cannot weaken nor bayonets break its clasp. Every liberal concession which a generous prince may grant, or an enlightened people sanction, will but strengthen our loyalty and increase our gratitude. We sincerely trust that your Excellency will live to see the day when Brazil, renovated and strengthened by the infusion of this great Southern element, will assume among the nations of the earth the very first place in prosperity, glory, and power, as she now holds the first in charity and true kindness to a brave but unfortunate people,

That the policy of the Brazilian Government with regard to her territories on the Amazon is in the right direction no one can deny, and it is in striking contrast with the proceedings of the ruler of Paraguay, who could, in the erection of his formidable strongholds, have had no other object in view than that of impeding, if he did not absolutely obstruct, the passage of the River Paraguay. Paraguayan advocates have, indeed, endeavoured to show that the opening of the Amazon by Brazil was solely dictated by self-interested motives, but let the world look at the facts and judge accordingly:

Many years back the Government largely subsidised a steam company to navigate on the Amazon, which it continues to support notwithstanding the pressure of financial difficulties. This company goes on prospering, and adding to its fleet, and will now be still more useful in assisting foreigners to pioneer their way. Thus the country can be explored and settlements made. It is gratifying to hear the climate of the Amazon so favourably spoken of in the reports I have inserted, as at one time it was feared this would be a barrier to successful emigration. The emphatic language of the writers is not to be mistaken, and the Government of Brazil will do well to afford to the active and go-a-head Anglo-Saxon race every possible encouragement in their emigration work.

The city of Para is admirably placed and its trade has largely augmented of late. In fact, it promises ere long to become the emporium of the northern commerce of Brazil as Rio de Janeiro is of the southern, and when we glance over the map, and see the enormous tributaries of the Amazon extending as far as the waters of the great La Plata itself, it is difficult to say what new sources of wealth may not be opened up from the countries through which these rivers flow. There are natural obstructions to be overcome, and tribes of Indians to be encountered, but the strong arm and the willing heart can conquer these difficulties, clearing their pathway through the forests to the fertile plains beyond.

But little is yet known as to the Indian tribes scattered over the immense valley of the Amazon and its tributaries. That they are not numerous, however, is pretty certain, nor can they offer much resistance to the advance of the white man, when once the tide of emigration to that country is fairly set in. It would, of course, be politic to conciliate and make friends of the aborigines, but circumstances do not appear favourable to such an arrangement.

By a recent Rio paper it appears that a lightship is shortly to be placed at the entrance to Para, and that it had been successfully experimented upon outside the port of Santa Cruz in the presence of the Emperor.

Alluding again to Professor Agassiz, I have had the pleasure of perusing his valuable narrative, which, although containing much matter only of interest to naturalists and scientific people, conveys at the same time a wonderful amount of practical information, and from which a pretty correct idea may be formed of the probable or speculative future of the Amazon valley.

THE RIVER AMAZON. 195

The Amazon, I may just observe, flows through the territory of the Empire for a distance of upwards of 500 leagues, and in its course towards the ocean receives no fewer than eighteen affluents of the first magnitude. The names are as follows: From the south, the Xingú, Tapajoz, Madeira, Purus, Coary, Teffé, Myuruá, Hyutuby, and Hyavary; and from the north, the Sary, Perú, Trombetas, Nhamunda, Uatuman, Uruba, Negro, Hyupurá, and Iça. These rivers, from above the falls which exist on the boundaries of the provinces of Pará and Amazonas, are collectively navigable by steamers for 7,351 leagues, not going outside the Imperial territorial limits. In this total, navigation on the Amazon proper figures for 580 leagues; that on the basins of the principal affluents for 5,771 leagues; and that on the lesser tributaries, lakes, and canals for 1,000 leagues.

As I have already remarked the Amazonian network of navigable streams reaches to within a little of the La Plata riverine system. The sources of the Tapajoz, flowing into the Amazon, are only separated by an inconsiderable strip of land from those of the Paraguay, flowing into the River Plate, and were these two rivers connected by artificial means an immense section of the South American Continent would be insulated by ocean and fluvial waters. This great work may probably remain undone for many years to come, but that it will be eventually accomplished I do not at all doubt. The progress of commerce and the development of enterprise in these countries clearly point to the ultimate realisation of this magnificent result.

Before passing to other topics, I will briefly notice another noble river of Brazil—the San Francisco—which traverses the central portion of the Empire, and waters the extensive and important provinces of Minas

Geraes, Bahia, Pernambuco, Alagoas, and Sergipe. The Rio das Velhas, Rio Verde, Rio Grande, and the Paracatu are amongst its tributaries, and are all of them streams which in Europe would be regarded as of very superior size. The San Francisco is notable for its famous falls of Paulo Affonso, which witnesses of both have pronounced to greatly excel those of Niagara in their imposing majesty and grandeur. Above these falls there is an uninterrupted navigation of about 230 leagues, and below to the mouth, nearly 50 leagues, there is not the slightest obstruction to vessels of respectable tonnage.

A large part of the immense basin of the Paraguay, in the River Plate, also belongs to Brazil, in whose territories most of the principal rivers of that system have their origin; and numerous other streams, of more or less consequence, permeate different parts of the Empire on their way to the sea. Several of these are capable of navigation by steamers for at least 100 leagues.

TELEGRAPHIC COMMUNICATION.

The North American Continent has now for some time past been linked to Europe by the electric wire, inaugurating what may almost be termed a new era of civilisation; and the fact of laying the cable will live in history as long as the name of the leviathan ship through whose medium this great result was accomplished.

South America has yet to depend solely upon steam communication, but doubtless the means of magnetic intercourse will soon be supplied. Already a rival company has been formed to lay down a cable from Brest to America under privileges obtained from the French and American Governments, and the great ship, with her gallant commander, Sir James Anderson, is again to be called into requisition. It is very desirable that extra cables should be laid in case of accident to those at present existing.

I had hoped on my arrival home to find a company organised and a cable about to be laid from Falmouth to Portugal and the Azores, for which a concession had been obtained by Messrs. Rumball and Medlicott; but it appears that the stupidity of the Cortes prevented this important line being carried out—important to the world and to Portugal in particular, as it would have rendered that country the great centre of telegraphic communication, not only with her own islands, but also with North and South America, to which it was intended the line should eventually be carried. There would also have been a large and lucrative business between England and Lisbon, in connection with the mail steamers to and from Brazil, which at present is carried on under great disadvantage through Spain. Portugal and Spain are sadly in arrear as regards commercial progress and advancement, and Messrs. Rumball and Medlicott experienced the same fate as the South Eastern of Portugal Railway, which, though the Government had agreed to take it over, on equitable terms, the Cortes refused to ratify the agreement. All Messrs. Rumball and Medlicott required was an alteration in the law which prevented the Government granting concessions for more than twenty years. The concessionaries asked for ninety-nine years, which ought to have been readily granted, seeing the manifest advantage to Portugal of establishing such a facility for communication; but no, these *pés de chumbo* (leaden feet), as they are designated in other parts of the world, would not quicken their pace even to promote the best interests of their country. Sordid motives would also appear to be at the bottom of these acts of repudiation, with which both Spain and Portugal are too familiar.

I think a line might be stretched across the Isthmus of Panama, passing from the West Coast and over the Andes to Buenos Ayres, where a telegraphic cable can easily be laid along the seaboard to Rio de Janeiro. The Argentine Government is now laying down wires from Buenos Ayres to Rosario, whence the Central Argentine Railway carries them on to Cordova, so that a communication with Valparaiso or some port on the West Coast would not be a very formidable work.

Nothing would tend more to consolidate and bind the Argentine provinces together than railways and electric wires. It is true the latter might be exposed to temporary injury, from political agitators and others, but this is no argument against the introduction of so great a civiliser, which even savages soon learn to respect, and look upon with a certain degree of awe. The onward march of civilisation and progress in the Argentine, as well as the Chilian Republic, would most certainly, under every circumstance, greatly tend to secure and keep open an agency so useful to both.

I understand that General Webb, United States Minister at Rio de Janeiro, has lately been authorised to submit an important scheme for the laying of an ocean cable to place Brazil in telegraphic communication with both Europe and North America; and I am glad to learn that there is great probability of something practical resulting from the negotiations in progress in respect to this proposal.

RELIGIOUS INSTITUTIONS.

Spain and Portugal as a matter of course introduced the Roman Catholic religion in their South American conquests. The aborigines, being imbued with a veneration for forms, or imagery of some kind, soon fell under the influence of the priesthood. Volumes have been written on the power and grandeur of the Jesuits, who were assuredly the pioneers of civilisation in South America, and they certainly accomplished what the sword could never have done. Papal and monarchial jealousy led to their expulsion, but many substantial buildings still remain as evidence of their activity and influence. The district called Missions, lying between Paraguay, Brazil, and the Banda Oriental, which has long been a bone of contention between the ruler of Paraguay and the Argentine Republic, abounds with their ancient edifices, mostly in ruins, and Paraguay itself retains to this day many of the characteristics of the Jesuit rule, which was exercised in a despotic manner—half sacerdotal, half military.

Any one visiting South America must be struck with the enormous size of the churches and convents, so utterly out of proportion to what must have been the wants of the population at the period of their erection, and even at this moment many of these buildings are unoccupied, as stated in my notice of the Brazilian city of San Paulo. These churches and convents were endowed with enormous tracts of land, which in process of time have become very valuable, and if appropriated to State purposes would go a long way towards paying off the national debt of Brazil. Some measure of this kind will inevitably be adopted at some future period, as in most instances the property itself is unproductive of any national benefit, nor is it utilised for any national object. The power of the priesthood still predominates and subjects the masses, if not a majority of the enlightened population, to its influence, and little short of a social revolution can wrest from the Church what is no longer required for religious observances, or distributed in any way towards the spread of religious knowledge. Mexico is an instance of the pernicious and fatal effects produced by a dominant priesthood, and although the more liberal views of Brazilians have weakened the priestly trammels in which some other parts of South America are still held, few have come forward to propose divesting the Church of her non-productive property.

The Roman Catholic religion is the religion of the State in Brazil, though all others are tolerated by law and treaties, nor has any difficulty ever arisen in this respect. At the same time it cannot be denied that open attempts at proselytism would be attended with danger. So long as foreign communities carry on their own religious ceremonies quietly and without ostentation all will be well, but too much demonstration might be productive of mischievous results.

As a body it cannot be said the Roman Catholic priesthood of South America is held in much esteem by the laity. Their stronghold is in the subserviency of the more ignorant and narrow-minded of their flock, precisely as we find it all over the world, and even at home.

In the River Plate, owing in a great measure to the scattered nature of the population, the influence of the priesthood has been less felt or exercised than in Brazil, besides which the large introduction of the foreign element in its towns and cities has led to greater freedom of thought and action. Nevertheless the church has large possessions in land, to which the same objections may be urged as in the case of Brazil, and the sooner they are appropriated to national objects the better. Cordova may be termed a city of churches and convents, the greater number of which are useless. A recent writer on Cordova says:—"In telling anything of Cordova it is impossible to omit to speak of her churches: there are over thirty of them, besides the the Cathedral. A description of them and their riches and institutions would make a large book. I have neither the requisite information, inclination, nor the time to go into the details of this painful theme—the Church in Cordova being so manifestly an incubus on the advancement of the country. Immense capitals are locked up in massive buildings and lands, which the clergy will neither sell nor cultivate, and a small army of friars and nuns—unproductive men and women in every sense—is detached from the world to manage these great properties, which yield nothing to the people moral or material." The great Republic of the United States presents a good example to those of South America by permitting free admission of every religion its citizens may choose to adopt without allowing the predominance of any one in particular.

THE AFFLUENTS OF LA PLATA.

Here and there, in the progress of my work, I have casually referred to the Rio de la Plata and its affluents; but the fluvial system which they together constitute is certainly deserving of more than a merely cursory comment. I will, therefore, add to my remarks on the Amazon and its tributaries some more precise observations with respect to the numerous rivers which give access to the fertile regions of Paraguay and furnish the Argentine Confederation with an extensive littoral coast.

The rivers Parana, Uruguay, and Paraguay are, however, now too well known to necessitate any very minute description. The first originates at no great distance from the shores of the Atlantic in that part of the table land of Brazil which divides the watershed of the Amazon from the watershed of the River Plate. Its most distant branch is the Rio Grande, which it receives at the confluence of the latter with the Paranahyba; and after an interrupted course of about 1,000 miles it finally effects a junction with the Paraguay, its largest affluent. Thence its huge volume of water, further augmented by the Uruguay, rolls to the ocean, forming that wide fresh water sea known as the estuary of the Plate. The Parana runs for nearly 900 miles within the limits of the Argentine Republic, and of this distance quite 750 are navigable throughout the whole year for sailing vessels and steamers of 300 tons burden. It begins to rise owing to intertropical rains towards the end of December, and this continues up to the close of April. Below its confluence with the Paraguay the average rise is eleven to twelve feet. The only tributary the Parana receives between its confluence with the Paraguay and its absorption in the estuary of the La Plata is the Rio Salado, a river of great length, and having its source in the Andine regions of the Argentine Confederation.

The Paraguay, like the Parana, has its origin in Brazilian territory. After passing through the Estrecho of Sao Francisco, (lat. 20° S.) it flows southwards, dividing the Republic of Paraguay from the Gran Chaco; a few miles below Asuncion, at a point called Angostura, the channel is narrowed by rocks, and the current becomes very rapid in consequence, taking a bend west by south until it mingles with the Parana. The Paraguay is navigable by large craft, and steamers have for some years ascended to Asuncion and Matto Grosso. The Paraguay receives the Pilcomayo, a very large stream of over 1,000 miles, and which, taking its rise near the city of Chuquisaca, in Bolivia, traverses a vast portion of that Republic, finally issuing from the Chaco wilderness at a point a little above Asuncion. Of course the Paraguay is augmented by numerous tributaries previous to its junction with the Pilcomayo, but these need not be specially mentioned. The Araguarmini empties itself into it at Oliva, and further down is the mouth of the Vermejo, a very considerable river, the navigation of which opens to commerce a territory of almost unrivalled fertility, and affords an easy access to Bolivia, in which State, like the Pilcomayo, it has its sources. Efforts have been made to facilitate the navigation of this fluvial highway, in connection with which the name of Sor. Arce is deserving of special allusion. This gentleman was the first to traverse the entire length of this previously unexplored river, his first descent having been effected in 1856. He followed its windings on a raft for a distance of 1,200 miles, penetrating in his course dense forests, and braving exposure to the rays of a tropical sun, not to speak of the danger incurred from wild beasts, and the yet more formidable Indian savages. The Vermejo will yet prove of incalculable advantage in coveying to the ocean the valuable products of the Argentine and Bolivian interior.

The Uruguay and the Parana partially enclose the Provinces of Entre Rios and Corrientes, and the former is only navigable from the sea as far as Salto, where rapids and falls occur; but above this point its waters are adapted to small steamers and sailing craft. Its source is in Brazil. On its banks are situated the towns of San Borja, Salto, Pysandu, Concepcion, Fray Bentos, and Soriano. It passes through a well wooded and picturesque country. Up to Salto it is constantly navigated by steamers trading between that place and the lower communities, especially Buenos Ayres and Monte Video.

THE REPUBLIC OF PARAGUAY.

The long and sanguinary conflict which the despotic ruler of this country has been enabled, from various causes, to maintain against the allied arms of Brazil and the other Platine States has naturally excited considerable curiosity in Europe to know something of its past history, people, and form of government.

In order to arrive at a correct judgment in respect of this singular people, and of their political and social condition, it is absolutely necessary to go back to the time when the Jesuits exercised so potential an influence in the River Plate, as in other parts of South America where the members of this remarkable order were permitted to carry out their questionable designs for the religious subjection and social domination of the aboriginal inhabitants.

The Jesuits first arrived in Paraguay at the beginning of the 17th century, when they obtained from Spain the concession of a vast territory of their own choosing, traversed by the Parana and Uruguay rivers, and capable of growing a great variety of products, including the sugar cane, indigo, cotton, tropical fruits of every description, and almost every kind of edible root and vegetable. The forests contained woods of the most valuable character, and the region in question also possessed great mineral wealth. The Fathers, having established themselves in their conceded territory, forthwith set about devising schemes for its population by civilised, or, at least, subjected Indians. The means adopted were characteristic. Azara describes the ingenius, if not very ingenuous, system adopted for this purpose. Having failed in their attempts to subdue the wilder Indian tribes, the Fathers soon directed their efforts to the reduction of the Guaranis, who were of a milder and more tractable temperament. By great industry, and by dint of patience, a small community was formed, over whom the Jesuits possessed the most entire control, and whose members were used for the reduction of savages in much the same fashion as the fowler uses his "call-birds" for the capture of others. The following is a brief description of the method usually adopted:—

They sent to a savage community some small presents by two Indians speaking the same language, and who had been chosen in their oldest communities. They repeated these embassies and presents at different times, the messengers always stating that they were sent by a Jesuit who loved them tenderly, who desired to come and live in their midst, and to procure for them other objects of greater value, including herds of cows, in order that they might have food to eat without exposing themselves to fatigue. The Indians accepted these offers, and the Jesuit started with what he had promised, accompanied by a considerable number of Indians selected from amongst those of their early redacciones. These Indians remained with the Jesuit, as they were needed to build a house for the curate and to take care of the cows. These were very soon destroyed, for the Indians only thought of eating them. The savages asked for more cows and they were brought by additional Indians chosen like the first; and the whole of them remained on the spot, under the pretext of building a church and other edifices, and of cultivating maize, the yucca root, &c., for the Jesuit and for all the others. Food, the affability of the priest, the good conduct of the Indians who had brought the cattle, festivals and music, the absence of every appearance of subjection, attracted to this settlement all the savage Indians in the neighbourhood. When the priest saw that his selected Indians greatly exceeded the savages in numbers, he caused the latter to be surrounded on a determined day by his people, and mildly told them, in a few words, that it was not just their brethren should work for them, that it was therefore necessary they should cultivate the earth and learn trades, and that the women should spin. A few appeared dissatisfied, but they perceived the superiority of the Indians of the curate, and as the latter was careful to caress some and punish others with moderation, while exercising a surveillance over all for a time, the new mission was at length entirely and successfully formed.

The internal government of the Jesuits was quite as peculiar as the proceedings by which they widened their influence and brought the outlaying savage populations under control. From the Indians an unquestioning and absolute submission was exacted, and the hours and the nature of their labours were fixed without appeal by their clerical masters. M. Quentin, in his very interesting work, translated from the French by Mr. Dunlop, thus depicts the interior life in these *redaccions*, the name given to their establishments by the Jesuits themselves:—

The Indians knew no other authority than that of the Father. The Father fed and clothed them, and promised the joys of Paradise as the reward of their submission and assiduity in labour. They lived in common, they worked in common, they prayed in common, under the direction of the Father, who was the representative of God. The Indian laboured, but nothing belonged to him individually; everything was the property of the whole community. The Father distributed amongst the different families the things necessary for their sustenance, and the remainder was carefully stored and guarded in immense warehouses. The Indians had nothing to do with the traffic; the Father it was who sold in distant markets the precious woods cut in the forests, the Paraguayan tea, the tobacco, and the hides: he it was who brought back fine garments, the most beautiful of which were given to the most docile and submissive, and returned with implements of agriculture, looms for the weaving of cotton, and splendid stuffs for the adornment of the chapel on holidays, when work was suspended and the bells sent forth jubilant peals. Those days were days of high festival in the rodaccion. The Fathers of the neighbouring missions assembled. They invested themselves in copes resplendent with gold; children, clothed in white robes, carried censers, which they waved to and fro; and the whole population, in good order, and to the sound of music, slowly advanced, singing canticles as they went under the shade of the orange trees which fringed their path.

The Indians were, it will be seen, entirely deprived of liberty. They were not allowed to do anything of their own motion. They could engage in no private pursuits, and there was, therefore, wanting every stimulus to individual elevation. A dead level was created, above which none rose save by grace and selection of the priests themselves. But in return for their confiscated freedom of action, the Indians were relieved of all care for the morrow; and otherwise the Jesuit Fathers, it must be confessed, were at pains to make despotism sweet and not bitter. The labour tasks imposed were in no sort onerous, and, as Azara remarks, they were amused "by a great number of balls, fêtes, and tournaments," on which occasions the actors were invariably clothed in the most costly and magnificent vestments to be had in Europe. To the aspiring, cultured, exalted spirit slavery in a gilded cage would be simply intolerable; but in the case of the Guarani Indians it was very different. They were slaves, and they were perfectly contented with their slavery.

The Fathers were very careful to prevent their neophytes from acquiring the Spanish language; only a few, who occupied certain subordinate offices, were trusted with this knowledge, for the Fathers were well aware that the only basis on which their system could possibly rest secure was that of universal ignorance. Every channel of information or of communication was in consequence rigorously closed and barricaded by the institution of the most exclusive regulations. Education was summed up in the oral teaching (they were not taught to read or write) of certain church prayers and the ten commandments; and the time not monopolised by labour, or in the childish games provided for their relaxation, was devoted to exercises of piety and worship according to the pompous ritual of the Romish Church.

When, therefore, for reasons and under circumstances which I will not now stay to particularise, the Jesuits were expelled from the River Plate, and were compelled to abandon their missions, the pretentious fabric they had raised, possessing in itself no sustaining power, collapsed almost immediately. The withdrawal of the Fathers was an inexorable call to their former disciples to self-thought and self-action. They were, however, unequal to the demands of the situation; everything fell into disorder, and "villages in ruins, fields untilled, yerbales destroyed, at once demonstrate the grandeur and the fragility of the work undertaken by the learned ambition of the Jesuits." But the labours of the Fathers were far from fruitless. They had sedulously cultivated amongst the Guarani populations of Paraguay sentiments of obedience and fanaticism, and, incapable of managing their own affairs, they have always reposed their destinies in the hands of some authority, invested with the power, as with the title, of *El Supremo*.

The history of this people, since the expulsion of the Jesuits, is, therefore, that of a succession of tyrannies. When all the neighbouring countries were engaged in a bloody war for the attainment of their independence no throb for liberty disturbed the popular heart of

Paraguay. The Metropolitan supremacy was exposed to no tumultuous assault, and was subverted only when its official guardians betrayed their trust. The nation allowed itself to pass from one master to another, just like a herd of cattle, without protest and without the manifestation of any special interest, but to the new authority as to the old they rendered the same homage of unreasoning and unreflecting obedience. It is true that some forms of popular ratification were given, but only given because they were asked.

I cannot pause to specify the intrigues which resulted in placing Francia in the seat of power. Suffice it to say that in 1817 this terrible man caused himself to be proclaimed Supreme and Perpetual Dictator, and never surely did tyrant exercise absolute rule with a more ruthless and cruel rigour. Even the humblest ceased to find safety in their obscurity. For the most trifling reasons men and women were thrown into prisons and there tortured often to the death. Espionage was general; mutual confidence was destroyed; the members of society "moved as in a desert," scarcely daring to address their dearest friends lest some thoughtless word might be reported to their detriment.

Francia lived in the most complete seclusion:—

He was as unapproachable as a divinity. Hidden in the recesses of his palace, nobody could penetrate to his presence. He only went out in the evening, and his progress was marked by a solitude. At the moment he quitted his palace the clock of the Cathedral sounded, and all the inhabitants, seized with affright, hastily retreated within doors. If one of them, by chance too late, was encountered by the *cortège* of the Dictator, he cast himself upon his knees, with his face to the earth, never daring to contemplate the features of *El Supremo*, and awaiting the chastisement he had incurred in an agony of fear. Sometimes he was carried to prison; more frequently he was let off with a few blows with the flat of a sabre, heartily applied by the soldiers of the escort.

Under such a Government neither agricultural nor trading industry could do other than languish, and the country was cut off from all commercial communication with the outer world.

The following extract will show how the Dictator was in the habit of accomplishing his ends:—

Only a few stuffs and clumsy implements were with difficulty produced in the country. But, in times of urgent necessity, the Dictator knew how to improvise workmen and teach them those arts of which they were ignorant. The means he employed are worthy of notice. He required belts for his soldiers: no one could make them. "Having prepared a gallows, he threatened to hang thereon a shoemaker who had failed to fashion the belts according to his desire. By this process blacksmiths were converted into locksmiths, armourers, and cutlers, shoemakers into saddlers, goldsmiths into founders, and masons into architects. That their zeal might not be permitted to cool, he condemned a blacksmith to penal servitude who had badly constructed the sight-piece of a cannon. Everything was done by rule. The citizens were divested of all power of initiation. If they became proprietors, even their goods were subject to the arbitrary caprices of the Dictator. Under pretext of embellishing the capital, Francia "pulled down several hundred houses without compensating the owners, or troubling himself as to their fate or that of their families. Each was compelled to demolish his own house, and if he lacked the means, convicts were employed to do the work, and afterwards carried away what they thought proper."

On the 19th of September, 1840, Francia died. But unhappily his death did not prove the dawn of freedom for the Paraguayans. After a brief interregnum Don Carlos Lopez, a lawyer, finally took up the sceptre of his terrible predecessor, and wielded it with a hand equally relentless. He professed, it is true, to rule in conformity with the constitution of 1844, if this name can be given to an act which merely legalised despotism; but if any difference existed between the position of Lopez and Francia, it was simply that the iron rod of the latter was gilded and painted in the grasp of the former.

Without repudiating the exclusive policy of Francia, Lopez the elder permitted some partial commerce with foreign nations. But this licence was hampered by the most absurd restrictions, and he continued to exhibit the greatest dislike for foreigners, upon whom extreme barbarities were inflicted. If the isolation of the state was a little relaxed it was because the "trading" interests of the Dictator would else have suffered:—

The modifications effected in the commercial and economic system were of such a nature as to secure for the State a monopoly in the majority of mercantile transactions. Paraguay was and is a great firm under the management of the President. Lopez authorised the people to work in the yerbales, but it was necessary to ask and obtain a licence. The yerba thus produced was purchased by the State, which exported it on its own account. The Government paid for it five piastres per arroba, and resold it for fifteen in the interior, and for so much as forty piastres to export. In consequence of the monopoly in the sale of this important product, an exorbitant price was maintained, which enabled the Brazilians to give a great development to its production in the province of Parana. The yerba there grown, though of inferior quality, nevertheless found an immense consumption in the Plate, on account of its more moderate price. The utilisation of the forests of Paraguay was also permitted; but the State imposed a duty of 20 per cent.; and as the value was fixed by itself, this pretended liberty of commerce in timber was simply a device to extort money, and ruin the individuals who might engage in it.

With regard to the raising of cattle and the commerce in hides, the State possessed farms and tanneries, and did not allow private persons to offer any serious competition. The State could, in addition, command labourers without payment; for the citizens were still subject, as under the colonial administration, to be pressed into the public service. At every requisition of authority they are bound to work without receiving either reward or nourishment; and it was by means of these *auxilios* that roads have been made and repaired, churches built, and both the fortress of Humaita and the arsenal of Villa Rica erected. The *Guardias Auxiliares*—to-day soldiers, to morrow labourers—are employed in the cultivation of the lands of the State. These soldiers carry the posts, gather the maté harvest, and fell timber; but receive no remuneration, being only fed like the rest of the army. These labourers cost so little, that, thanks to them, the State defies all private competition in the produce of its yerbales, forests, and farms.

One thing Don Carlos Lopez did not leave out of sight. He felt his Government was an anomaly and a menace to civilisation and political freedom in the surrounding States, and any day even his so patient subjects might find their bonds too galling for longer endurance. He, therefore, developed the military strength of the Dictatorship, and raised the fortress of Humaita on the banks of the Paraguay in such a position as to render the country all but impregnable to external assault.

At the end of a long reign Lopez I. died, and his dominion went by testament to his son,—Don Francisco Solano—as Vice-President. M. Quentin gives the following account of the proceedings adopted by the present ruler of Paraguay to secure the position he has used to bring ruin upon his unfortunate country:—

Don Carlos Antonio Lopez died on the 10th of September, 1862. On the very same day Don Francisco Solano Lopez assembled the bishop, the supreme judge, and the principal functionaries, and in their presence opened the sealed envelope which contained the testament of his father. In virtue of the law of 1856 Don Francisco Solano Lopez was designated Vice-President, and in that capacity he convoked the Extraordinary Congress.

As under such circumstances it is well to neglect nothing, young Lopez prudently confided the command of the army to his brother, and one of his uncles was already at the head of the clergy. Thus all the avenues to power were guarded.

The Congress assembled under the presidency of Don Solano Lopez. The result of the vote was certain. Every precaution had been well taken. They were about to proceed to the ballot, when a deputy, named Varela, commenced speaking. He began by eulogising General Lopez, and assuring him of his personal esteem and sympathy, reminded Congress of the express terms of the Act of Independence—Paraguay shall never become the patrimony of a family, and concluded with these words :—" I have the most profound respect for General Lopez, but I have sworn to obey the laws of my country. I hesitate between my affection and my conscience" The moment was a critical one. An unexpected opposition manifested itself, and drew its force from the law, for the first time invoked in the heart of a Congress. Lopez tremblingly witnessed this episode, but retained his coolness and self-possession. He made a sign to Father Roman, the Bishop of Asuncion, who of right formed part of the Congress. The prelate approached Varela, who humbly fell on his knees in the midst of the assembly, and the bishop, placing his hands upon his head, said with a loud voice— "*Ego te absolvo;* thou art released from thy oath; this is not the case for its observance (*no es este el caso de observarlo*)." Varela rose with delight, and cried, " Then I will be the first to give my vote to his Excellency General Lopez!" It need not be stated that the President obtained unanimity, and that the people welcomed his new master with transport. The Lopez dynasty was founded.

Lopez II., thus firmly seated in his place of supremacy, adhered to the traditions of his father. His government has been equally despotic, and the same policy of isolation and monopoly has been persistently observed. Public opinion has no existence, and the only paper published in Paraguay is the official organ, edited by the Dictator himself. The commerce and industry of the people—their toil, their means, their blood—are at the uncontrolled disposal of their tyrant. And how this authority has been exercised we all know. Inflamed by ambition, and desirous to extend his power beyond the limits of Paraguay, the greater part of his reign—I use the word advisedly—has been devoted to the steady accumulation of military and naval stores, the organisation of an army out of all proportion to the number of inhabitants, and the erection of strong fortresses on the riverine passages to the interior. For what purpose? Let his acts of gratuitous invasion tell; let the story of the present war with Brazil and her allies testify. I have already placed the facts with respect to this struggle before my readers, and I feel sure they will concur with me that the real object of Lopez was to bring the whole of the River Plate under the terror of a Guarani-Indian subjection. Happily this calamity has not occurred, but it has only been avoided by a prodigious outflow of blood and treasure.

BRAZILIAN CURRENCY.

Like most new countries achieving their independence and establishing constitutional government under circumstances of difficulty, internal and external, Brazil has been subject to vicissitudes in her monetary circulation, and has been affected by occasional aberrations from the great truths of economical science in the emission of paper money. The law of 1866 has, however, corrected the errors previously committed, and when the restoration of peace shall afford the present President of the Council and Minister of Finance, who, when holding the same offices in 1853, evinced both the capacity and determination to place the financial condition of the Empire on a sound foundation, the Viscount Itaborahy will, no doubt, achieve for his country even a greater financial reform than that which secured for him in Brazil a reputation not dissimilar from that of Sir Robert Peel in England.

The Brazilian standard of value is the gold oitava of 22 carats, of the value of four milreis, the par value of each milreis being by law 27d. sterling. The ancient mercantile par of the exchange of the milreis was in sterling 60d. After the arrival of King Dom Joao VI. in Brazil the exchange on England gradually rose, until in 1814 it reached 96d. This rise was owing to the increase of its commerce, consequent to the freer commercial legislation which was then first introduced and to the depreciation of English irredeemable paper money consequent on Mr. Pitt's Bank Restriction Act. The war which the Argentines plunged the Empire into immediately after their independence to deprive it of its Cis-Platine province produced, however, great financial embarassments, and they were increased by the mismanagement of the paper circulation by the then Bank of Brazil, which King Dom Joao VI. had founded, by attempts at revolution in the northern provinces, by the intervention of the Emperor Dom Pedro I. in the affairs of Portugal, by his abdication of the Brazilian crown in 1831, and by serious and prolonged domestic troubles. The consequence was in 1833 the reduction of the ancient par to 43½d. the milreis. From 1831 to 1840 distracted regencies governed Brazil. During one of the regencies a civil war broke out in the great province of the Rio Grande do Sul, which only terminated in 1845, thanks then to the efforts and capacity of Count (now Marquis) de Caxias, who is at this hour as heroically fighting, in his old age, the battles of Brazil in Paraguay with equal success. Then followed other provincial and political difficulties of less importance, but all reacting on the financial position of the Empire. So that again in 1846 the par of the milreis had to be lowered to 27d., at which it has since been preserved. And it is to the credit of the Empire, its Government, Legislature, and people, that subsequently, neither the great financial and banking crisis of 1864, nor the pressure of the war with Paraguay, which has continued from 1865 to the present time, has produced any propositions for its further reduction. The maintenance of the par of the milreis at 27d. is now the established fundamental policy of Brazil. This policy is made especially and emphatically manifest in the financial measures of Viscount Itaborahy, who is once more Prime Minister and Finance Minister of the Empire, with the prospect, it may be hoped, of as long an administration as that which distinguished his Government from 1848 to 1853, during which period he governed so greatly to the advantage of the nation, terminating the slave trade, and introducing a financial system, the departure from and disregard of which in 1857 undid the good which he then accomplished.

The free trade legislation of England in 1845 opened the consumption of this country to Brazilian sugar, one of the great productions of Brazil, and the Revolution of 1848 in France was followed by the partial admission to France of Brazilian coffee, then the largest item of the agriculture of the Empire. Under these influences an immense impetus was given to the productive capacity of Brazil. The firm and enlightened Government of Viscount Itaborahy gave the Empire concurrently a period of domestic repose, of which the planters made the most. Political passions subsiding agriculture made huge strides. The termination of the African slave trade gradually relieving agriculture from debts and embarrassments, introduced better systems of cultivation, largely increased production, augmented commerce, released for better purposes a great amount of capital engaged in that abominable traffic, stimulated honest improvements of every sort and kind, and the exchange on England rose to 28$\frac{1}{4}$d. the milreis. At this time Treasury notes were the only paper money in circulation, and their amount was so insufficient for business purposes that coin became more abundant than paper money, to the inconvenience of trade and society in so vast an empire.

The necessity of a convertible paper money became apparent and it was generally demanded. The result was the enactment, on the proposition of Viscount Itaborahy, of the law of the 5th of July, 1853. Under it the Bank of Brazil was established as a bank of issue to a limited extent; other banks were merged in that great institution; branches of it were established in the larger provinces, with similarly restricted powers of issue in circumjacent districts; the privilege of issue was confined to this one establishment, and Brazil was provided, as England now is, with one great bank issuing convertible paper in connection with, yet to a large extent independent of, the State, and the Executive Government had virtually no authority or power to found other banks of issue. Thus unity of banking was established so far as paper money was concerned, and to the immense advantage of the country. An easy, cheap, and convenient paper currency was provided, always convertible into coin, yet preferable for the ordinary purposes of life to coin; and the provinces and the metropolis were equally well supplied with this currency. The consequences were still further progress in the Empire, the Treasury was relieved from the trouble of regulating the currency, the revenue and trade increased, and an impetus was given to activity throughout the Empire. For all this Brazil had to thank the good sense and statesmanship of Viscount Itaborahy.

The Viscount's Cabinet terminated in 1853 in the midst of the improvement it had created. The progress thus produced by wise and scientific legislation unfortunately rendered a powerful section of the country impatient for further progress and misled succeeding Governments into a policy of a very different kind, whence mainly have flowed the subsequent financial misfortunes of the country. From the substantial but slow benefits of sound legislation, Senhor Souza Franco, a successor of Viscount Itaborahy in the Ministry of the Treasury, was led into the evils of unsound banking. He became enamoured of the then American system of free banking, as it was termed, and in 1857, misinterpreting the real meaning of the law of 1853, established plurality of banks of emission. Banking societies were then empowered to issue their own notes convertible by law, it is true, on presentation into coin, but without any corresponding security wherewith to furnish gold for their payment on presentation. The Government sanctioned no fewer than six banks of emission, two in Rio de Janeiro and four in the provinces, and assigned to each districts within which the right of paper issue might by means of branches be further extended. In the same spirit the Government sanctioned the establishment of joint stock companies and anonymous societies for all kinds of purposes throughout the Empire. The right thus assumed by Government was superabundantly exercised. Speculation spread apace in all directions, and fictitious prosperity for a moment took the place of real progress; shares and pecuniary responsibility, far beyond the means of those who assumed them, became the order of the day; long credit and increased discount aggravated the evil; gold began to leave the Empire rapidly, the rate of exchange to fall heavily, and in 1859 pecuniary anarchy was the consequence of this policy.

Senhor Souza Franco had to retreat before this result, and he was succeeded by Senhor Torres Homem, who soon found in the Chambers a spirit opposed to those wiser measures he recommended which he was unable to overcome during his short tenure of office. Then came Senhor Ferraz at the Treasury; he was more fortunate in remedying the mischief thus caused. The Empire and the General Assembly had recovered from their delusions. So, on 22nd August, 1860, a new law of banking, &c., was enacted. Its principles were the resumption of cash payments by the banks of emission and the withdrawal of all power from the Executive Government to sanction powers of emission or of anonymous societies, reserving such power for the Imperial Legislature. By this law the Bank of Brazil was prohibited from further emission until it had resumed payment of its notes in gold, the power of emission was reduced and fixed, and no banks can now be established except by legislative authority.

Immense as was the mischief caused by the measures of 1857, the law of 1860 to a considerable extent corrected it. The two banks of emission at Rio de Janeiro resigned the privileges they had acquired; within two years the Bank of Brazil resumed payment of its notes in cash; the Bank of Pernambuco withdrew its notes from circulation; and the currency of the Empire had undergone substantial improvement when—in September, 1864, suddenly a great "crisis" burst on Rio de Janeiro, immediately the consequence of adverse European influences, but substantially the result of unscrupulous and indefensible mismanagement of discount and private bankers in that capital.

Their establishments were in the enjoyment of great credit. Their chiefs were men of mercantile activity and public spirit, living *en evidence*, pushing business, giving facilities to everybody, and dealing with money as if possessed of boundless capital of their own.

Their means for this pecuniary profusion was, however, chiefly derived from money deposited with them, for longer or shorter periods, or "at call," sometimes in large, but more frequently in small sums, on which they allowed interest of, say, 8 per cent. Thus they became possessed of a greater part of the floating and uninvested capital of Rio de Janeiro. Receiving money in this way freely and largely, from the poorer public chiefly, it was the duty of these bankers to place it out at higher rates of interest, but on ample security always, and easily convertible into cash. By such business they would have reaped substantial profits for themselves, have assisted honest commerce, and have provided effectually for their depositors. A run upon one of these houses in September, 1864, after the arrival of bad financial news from Europe, resulted in its closing its doors on its depositors. This stoppage alarmed the creditors of the other houses, and they followed suit by demanding back their deposits. With the same effect —the closing of doors and stoppage—until five of these bankers suspended payment with deposits of £5,655,000.

Investigation into their affairs showed how reckless had been their management, how disregardful of every rule of deposit banking. The funds entrusted to them had been invested in houses, advanced on mortgages, lent to planters on bills renewable; and thus Rio de Janeiro was by their misconduct involved in unexpected ruin. The Government had to interfere with the payment of bills of exchange, to direct the administration of their insolvent estates. The Bank of Brazil was involved in large advances to these houses and unable to assist the community at the moment when assistance was most needed. The consequence was a suspension of its cash payments.

This crisis once more raised the question of the currency and of banking, and led, after a prolonged discussion, to further legislation in 1866.

By the beginning of 1865 the paper circulation of the Empire reached the enormous sum in sterling of £11,025,000, of which, however, only £3,150,000 were notes of the Government having general circulation throughout the country. For the balance of £7,785,000, the circulation of which was limited to defined districts in which the issuing banks were situate, the public, had no adequate security. The natural consequence was disarrangement in the internal exchanges and general disturbance of the money market. To remedy it Government proposed a radical reform of the Bank of Brazil, and its separation in two departments,—one of issue, the other of banking. The discussions on this question continued through the legislative sessions of 1865 and 1866. And during these discussions the adverse situation was illustrated by further decline in the foreign exchanges and the augmentation of the non-Government paper in circulation to £9,225,000, to which it had swollen in May, 1866.

In the session of that year the difficulties of this state of affairs were brought under the consideration of a Committee of the Senate, of which Viscount Itaborahy was the most eminent member, and to which a remedial measure of a radical character was referred for examination. The result of its deliberations was the expression of an opinion that the Bank of Brazil, having in two years doubled its circulation, could no longer accomplish the essential objects of its existence. Thus sentence of death was passed on that institution by the statesman who had formed it, and legislation became inevitable after such a condemnation.

Accordingly, on the 12th of September, 1866, a measure became law which enabled the Government to abolish the contract under which the Bank of Brazil existed. The principal provisions of this law were: 1. The cessation of the bank's privilege of emission. 2. The division of the bank into two departments—one for banking purposes only, the other for mortgage loans, in order to effect a gradual liquidation of the securities given by the agricultural classes, and so to form the commencement of the operations of the law of September, 1864. 3. The sale of the bank's stock of bullion, which amounted to £2,925,000 and the application of the proceeds to a proportionate withdrawal of its notes from circulation. 4. The annual contraction of its remaining paper circulation. 5. The payment to the bank for the State notes it used in accordance with its primitive contract, in withdrawning from circulation about £1,237,500, by the substitution of bank notes by State notes, and the discharge of an insignificant amount of treasury bonds cashed by the bank. 6. The issue in payment of floating debt, and those treasury bonds of State notes, to the amount of notes withdrawn by the bank.

Thus the Government were supplied with coin for remittances to the army and navy engaged with war in Paraguay, and the Bank of Brazil was reduced to a mercantile association. So it now remains, only a small and scarce portion of its notes having a forced circulation, and that small portion is being greatly reduced.

Thus, too, the exclusive functions of providing for the circulating medium were restored to the State, instead of being confided to a bank on which were at times painfully and mischievously exercised the exigencies of internal credit, and the reaction in Brazil of those crises in Europe and the United States, that affected the Brazilian Empire while its currency was in so unsound a condition with great violence.

In 1867, the increasing pecuniary requirements of the war compelled the General Assembly to vote the Government a credit of fifty thousand contos (£5,625,000) which have in great part been used by the Government. But, inserted in the law which authorised the issue, is a provision that on the termination of the war, the legislature will fix in the budget of each year the necessary amount to be applied to the withdrawal of this addition to the State notes.

It was not, however, only by further emissions of State notes that the General Assembly in 1867 made provision for the extraordinary expenditure of the Government. In that session old taxes were increased, new sources of taxation opened up, and the whole system of taxation was re-organised in a more rational and scientific way, greatly to the increase of the general revenue of the Empire. So much so that in the session of 1868 the budget for 1869-70 showed under the influence of greatly enlarged receipts, and of economies effected in the various departments of the State, an important surplus.

And while thus placing the paper circulation on the more solid basis of national security, important reforms were effected in the same session of 1867 in the coinage of the Empire.

Owing to the fineness of the silver coinage a fall in the foreign exchanges was immediately followed by the exportation of silver from Brazil to the great inconvenience of petty commerce. So in September, 1867, for the silver coinage of Brazil was adopted, in respect of the coins of two milreis (4s. 6d.) and milreis (2s. 3d.) the fineness and weight introduced by the International Convention between France and other countries. And the Government substituted for the old copper coinage bronze pieces of twenty reis ($\frac{1}{2}$d.) and ten reis ($\frac{1}{4}$d) of a similar alloy to that of our present bronze coinage—viz., ninety-five parts of copper, four of tin, and one of zinc. So that the Brazilian coinage consists of gold pieces (of twenty and ten milreis of 917 milliomes,) legal tender for any amount—that is, of 27d. per milreis, and of these silver and copper pieces for tokens. In addition, English sovereigns and half-sovereigns are also legal tenders for any amount in Brazil.

On the change of Ministry in July, 1868, which led to the formation of the Cabinet over which Viscount Itaborahy now presides, the Chamber of Deputies, by an unexpected and sudden combination of forces previously adverse to each other, came to a resolution which left the newly formed Cabinet no alternative but an appeal at once to the nation, and that without the Chamber making full financial provision for the conduct of the war. Left in this position by no fault of its own, the Cabinet in September, 1868, had no alternative but the adoption of financial operations on its own responsibility. But they have fortunately met with the full approval of the country, and will, no doubt, be sanctioned by the result of the now impending general election of deputies.

These measures were of an alternative character. First of all they consisted of a decree authorising a further issue of State notes to the amount of 40,000 contos, viz., £4,500,000. But this decree was followed by another empowering the Treasury to raise a domestic gold loan of 30,000 contos, £3,335,000. The former decree was, however, only intended to support the credit of the Government, in the event of the failure of the loan authorised by the latter decree, and as it has been successful, a further issue of State notes will, it may be anticipated, be averted to any considerable amount.

In explanation of these measures it is necessary to state that the pressure of the war expenditure going on since April, 1865, had led, under the previous Cabinet of Senhor Zacharias, to the creation of a large floating debt, represented by Treasury Bonds, issued for various short periods. There is always in Rio de Janeiro a large amount of loanable capital seeking interest on temporary investment, which it had found previously to the crisis of 1864 in the deposits of private bankers' establishments. This loanable capital deprived of such resource after the crisis of that year found better and safe temporary shelter in Treasury Bonds. And obtaining money in this way to carry on the war, the preceding Cabinet was able to avoid new permanent operations for supplying the means for its necessities. The wants of the Government so supplied, however, deprived commerce of part of its legitimate supplies of money and made the situation of the Treasury precarious and hazardous. The extent, too, of temporary resources of this kind had obviously reached their limit. It was, therefore, partly to extinguish a large amount of this floating debt, and so to relieve the Treasury from any embarrassment that might arise from failure in the renewal of Treasury Bonds when at maturity, and partly to provide for the exigencies of the war, that the Government in September, 1868, resorted to the internal loan of 30,000 contos, £3,335,000, issued at ninety per cent., in bonds bearing six per cent. interest payable in gold, redeemable in thirty-three years by purchase when under par, and drawing when at or above par, in which last case payment to be made in gold. This loan was so favourably received that applications for it were received in Rio only to the extent of 105,000 contos, and it quickly rose to a premium of seven per cent.

Again, then, complete success has attended the financial policy of ViscountItaborahy, and the Treasury has been provided with the means of discharging a large amount of floating debt and of prosecuting the war.

In spite of the provisions adopted by the legislation, and of the concurrent necessary activity of Brazilian commerce, the exchanges in London after the crisis of 1864, though high in reference to the over issue of inconvertible paper, had fallen, and in February, 1868, declined, as if in panic, to 14d. This fall was partly due to the remittances to England of bills for purchasing gold and honouring the Government commitments on this side, and still more to the large orders from the Plate for operations in exchange, and purchases of bullion here caused by the financial crisis of Monte Video.

This decline in the rate of exchange on London was, however, brief. Thanks principally to the financial measures just described, and to the improving prospects of the war, the rate has again risen, and is still rising.

Such, in necessarily brief and rough outlines, is the history of the circulating medium of the Brazilian Empire.

Everything, it will be seen, conduces to the conviction that with the close of the war and expenditure there will be a certainty of maintaining the standard of 1846, so solemnly reproduced in the laws of 1853, 1860, and 1867, and in the internal loan of 1868, and that the foreign exchange will once more rise, in the interests of commerce and of all domestic industries to above the legal level so fixed in 1846. When this has been accomplished it will be recognised, and be due to an intelligent and prudent administration of the finances, to the prodigious development of the external commerce and to the inexhaustible resources of the great American monarchy.*

---

* In the preparation of this chapter we are indebted to several important and valuable Brazilian works—"Systema Financial do Brazil," by Conselheiro C. B. de Oliveira; the Report on the Circulating Medium of the Empire, made in 1859-60, by a Commission presided over by Conselheiro Almeida Areas, now Brazilian Minister in London; the Report on the Crisis of 1864, by a Commission presided over by the late Conselheiro Silva Ferraz (Baron de Uruguayana); the *Relatorios*, from 1865 downwards, of the Ministers of Finance, and the Annals of the Senate and Chamber of Deputies for the same period.

ARGENTINE FINANCES.

A NOTICE of this extensive and rising country would be incomplete without some allusion to its financial condition, and in order to illustrate this more clearly I must revert to the year 1824, when the first loan of a million sterling was raised in London, to assist the young republic in meeting the expenses incurred during the War of Independence. That the money thus obtained was more or less squandered, and did not find its way into legitimate channels, is probable enough; nevertheless the liability was always admitted by the existing Governments, although interest had ceased to be paid on the loan for upwards of twenty years and the original stock was almost worthless.

At the period I allude to the revenue and resources of the country were small, and during the reign of Rozas they were entirely under his private direction, and the national means spent according to his will. In fact, what is now known as the Argentine Republic had no existence until after the downfall of Rozas in 1852, Buenos Ayres up to that period exercising sovereign control. A heavy internal debt, represented by paper money, had also generally reduced the value of the dollar (originally worth about four shillings) to two pence, and there appeared little chance of the English bondholders ever obtaining again the money lent in 1824, through the agency of Messrs. Baring Brothers and Co.

But on the downfall of Rozas, a new era dawned upon the republic. Many illustrious citizens, who had been obliged to expatriate themselves in order to save their lives, returned to Buenos Ayres, and the principles of constitutional government were again infused into the body politic, subject, however, to many vicissitudes, which, for a a time, retarded internal progress, and prevented the real resources of the country from being profitably utilised. So soon as these difficulties were overcome the question of its indebtedness forced itself upon the Executive and Legislative powers, who wisely decided that their first great financial effort should be to come to some understanding with their English creditors.

At the same time a movement was set on foot by the bondholders themselves, and a Committee was formed in London, under the auspices of Messrs. Baring Brothers and Co., comprising some of the largest bondholders. Negotiations were entered into with the Buenos Ayres Government, who evinced every disposition to meet the matter fairly; and eventually, in the year 1857, an arrangement was come to by which the original debt in full, with its accumulated interest, was consolidated, and interest agreed to be paid thereon; and this arrangement has been most faithfully adhered to up to the present hour. The decree in which this honourable recognition of a great principle is contained is dated the 12th December, 1857, and is signed by the Governor Filipe Llavallol and Norberto de la Riestra the then Minister of Finance. I insert a copy of the document itself:—

MINISTRY OF FINANCE.

Buenos Ayres, Nov. 20th, 1857.

The Government of the State of Buenos Ayres, in virtue of the authorisation conferred upon it by the law of the 28th of October last, has made the following arrangement with Mr. George E. White, representative of Messrs. Baring Brothers and Co., agents of the loan contracted in London in 1824 for settlement of the said debt, viz.:—

Art. 1st.—To meet the payment of the interest upon the original bonds the Government of Buenos Ayres engages to remit to the Loan in London in

  1857 the sum of £36,000
  1858   48,000
  1859   60,000

And from and after 1860, inclusive, besides the above-mentioned sum of £60,000, it will also remit annually the sum of £5,000 as a redemption fund. This sum, together with the interest of the shares redeemed, or that may be redeemed, shall be employed, one half each six months, in the purchase or redemption of the new bonds of this class till the whole of them have been redeemed. The funds corresponding to the stipulated remittances shall be placed in London, one half before the 30th of June, and the other half before the 31st of December in each year.

Art. 2nd.—The sums appropriated to the redemption shall be employed by the agents of the London Loan in the purchase of bonds in the market at the current price so long as that is less than par; but should the price of the bonds exceed par, the funds to be redeemed by the redemption fund shall be determined by lot, in presence of the principal agent or representative of the State of Buenos Ayres existing in London.

The bonds drawn by lot shall be published in the *Gazette*, or two of the London journals, stating the day on which payment will be made at par, and from which date they will cease to bear interest.

The bonds purchased or redeemed by the redemption fund, with their corresponding future dividends of interest, shall be cancelled in presence of the principal agent or representative of the State of Buenos Ayres in London, and immediately deposited in the Bank of England, publishing their numbers in the *Gazette*, or in two of the principal London journals.

Art. 3rd.—The holders of the original bonds shall receive a new list of debentures for their future dividends, with a copy annexed to it of the two preceding articles, beginning with the debenture for the dividend that falls due on the 12th of January, 1861.

Art. 4th.—For the interest due upon the original bonds up to this date, and for those that fall due to the end of 1858, amounting to the sum of £1,641,000, the Government of Buenos Ayres shall emit new bonds to bear interest at the following rates, viz :—

Art. 5th.—From 1861 to 1865 inclusive, one per cent. per annum. From 1866 to 1870 inclusive, two per cent., and from and after 1871, three per cent. The first half-yearly dividend upon these new bonds shall fall due on the 12th July, 1871, and subsequently on the 12th January and 12th July of each year, on which days the half-yearly instalments or dividends due shall be paid in London. All the guarantees accorded to the original bonds shall be extensive to these new bonds.

Art. 6th.—The Government of Buenos Ayres engages to remit to the agents of the loan in London the funds necessary for meeting the payment of the interest assigned to these new bonds, and moreover, from and after 1871, the sum of £8,205, or, say the 200th part of the total amount of the said bonds, as a redemption fund for them. This sum together with the interest of the bonds that have been redeemed shall be employed in equal proportion every six months in the purchase or redemption of these new bonds, till the whole of them have been redeemed. Accordingly the sums that must be remitted to meet the interest and redemption fund shall be as follows, viz., from 1861 to 1865 inclusive, £24,615, annually; from 1866 to 1870 inclusive, £41,025; and from and after 1871, the sum of £47,435; the Government engaging to place these funds in London, one-half before the 30th June, and the other half before the 31st December of each year. The Government reserves to itself the right of employing in the redemption of these new bonds, over and above the sum stipulated, any further sums the Legislature may appropriate to this purpose.

Art. 7th.—The sums applicable to the redemption fund, as also the others that may be destined to this purpose, shall be employed by the agents of the loan in London, to the purchase of these new bonds in the market, at the current price, always that this is less than par; but in case the price of these bonds should come to exceed par, the bonds that are to be redeemed shall be determined by lot, and those that are drawn by lot, as also those purchased in the market shall be published in the journals, paid and cancelled on the respective debentures in the manner and form established in the second Article in respect to the six per cent. bonds.

Art. 8th.—The new bonds shall be denominated Three Per Cent. Buenos Ayrean Bonds, shall be signed in the name of the State, by the Minister of Finance in Buenos Ayres, and shall be emitted through the medium of Messrs. Baring Brothers and Co., of London, by whom they shall be countersigned.

Art. 9th.—The payments stipulated in the present convention are specially assigned upon the products of the rents of the public lands of the State, excepting those belonging to the Municipalities, and in case of deficiency this shall be made up from the general rents of the State, or from the special resources created by the Legislature for the purpose.

The conduct of Buenos Ayres statesmen in respect to the obligations referred to was fully appreciated in this country, and the bonds gradually rose up to par value, holding even during the great monetary crisis a good position; nor must it be lost sight of that, although the original debt was incurred for the benefit of the entire Confederation, yet the Province of Buenos Ayres alone took upon itself the sole responsibility; and, up to the present confederation with the other Argentine provinces, always paid the interest out of its provincial resources.

Subsequent to the settlement of the English debt, what is known as the National Government was formed, and the internal debt of the entire provinces has been consolidated into a national stock, bearing interest at 6 per cent., which is punctually paid, and the stock, from being worth 30 to 40 a few years back, has latterly risen to 55, subject, of course, to fluctuations generally caused by speculation on the Bolsa of Buenos Ayres, where, for a long period, gambling in paper money was the chief business, until a wise measure of Governor Alsina, in establishing an Exchange Office, and fixing a paper value for gold, put a stop to this element of financial and social disturbance.

As already mentioned, there is a provincial revenue and a national revenue, as well as expenditure; that of Buenos Ayres being the most important, from its great commercial wealth. Until recently, the only bonds known here were those of Buenos Ayres. Now we have what are called Argentine bonds, lately issued on the security of the National Government; and in order to show the nature of this latter security, as well as the progressive state of the national revenue, I cannot do better than quote the following figures, issued by their able representative Minister, his Excellency Don Norberto de la Riestra, in a circular dated 1st June last, at the time he was negotiating this important transaction:—

In 1864 the General National Revenue
amounted to . . . . $7,005,328 or £1,401,065
In 1865 it reached . . . . 8,295,071 or 1,659,014
In 1866 . . . . . 9,568,554 or 1,913,711
In 1867 the yield is estimated at 2,600,000
it having produced in the first eight months of the year $8,981,430.
The Revenue estimates for 1868
amount to . . . : . . . 2,647,200
as follows:—
Ordinary Import Duties. . . $7,650,000
Do. Export do. . . 2,070,000
Storage Dues 350,000
Stamps. 160,000
Post Office and Miscellaneous . . 206,000
$10,436,000
Additional Customs' Duties . 2,800,000
$13,236,000 or £2,647,200
The Budget of ordinary expenditure for
1868 amounts to £1,581,649
as follows:—
Ministry of the Interior . . $ 901,079
„ of Foreign Affairs . 99,538

Ministry of Finance	729,491
„ of Justice, &c.	487,940
„ of War and Marine	3,116,593
Service of Public Debt.	2,573,626

$7,908,267 or £1,581,649.

The surplus revenue over ordinary expenditure is applied to defray the extraordinary war expenses.

The above revenue is distinct and independent of the private revenues, both State and Municipal, of the different Provinces of the Republic, which are raised for local purposes.

The Public Debt of the Republic at this time is as follows :—

EXTERNAL.—Old Buenos Ayres Debt (London Loan of 1824) now in charge of the nation, say :—

Original Six per Cent. Stock	£ 905,800
Deferred Three per Cent. do.	1,110,900
Argentine Six per Cent. Loan of 1866	540,000
Total	£2,556,700

INTERNAL.—

Consolidated Six per Cent. Argentine Stock . . . . $12,839,535 or	£2,567,907
Buenos Ayres Public Stock (in paper currency)	596,988
Paraná Debt 1858, including Interest	433,309
Obligations to Foreign Creditors	18,852
Loan from Brazilian Government 1851	228,541
Do. do. do. 1865-66	400,000
Total	£4,245,597

There is besides a floating debt in Treasury Bills to a moderate amount, which is being rapidly cancelled.

I think this statement, combined with the facts I have elsewhere given from personal experience and observation, as to the rapidly extending commerce of the Argentine Confederation, will fully bear out the favourable impression that is now gaining ground in England, and in Europe generally, as to the *bona fide* security presented by Argentine bonds; and I must say that, looking back to the conscientious course pursued by the

Government, no country in the world deserves more to enjoy the confidence of British capitalists.

It will be seen from Senor Riestra's statement that the only foreign debt of the Argentine Republic is that due to English bondholders. Her internal debt is due chiefly to her own citizens, who are safe to be paid both principal and interest; nor has any act of repudiation, or compromise ever stained the character of the Argentine people. The pursuance of this praiseworthy conduct has been followed by the investment of British capital in promoting railways and other industrial enterprises. Indeed, look around in whatever direction we may, it is difficult to find a more pleasing illustration of the maxim, that "honesty is the best policy," than that exhibited by the Argentine Republic.

TOWN AND HARBOUR OF SANTOS.

BEFORE recording the details of my passage home I wish to say a few words more with regard to the rising port of Santos, a notice of which has been accidentally omitted in a former part of my work. Its connection with the San Paulo Railway and the fact of its being the shipping port of the province renders Santos of much future importance. The distance from Rio de Janeiro is about 200 miles, and the navigation is simple enough—in fact, in sight of land the whole way, the sea coast ridge of mountains being conspicuous. The only danger is from the Alcatrazes rocks, which lie some distance to the eastward of Santos, and very ugly customers they are, towering a considerable height above the sea. Steamers can, however, have no difficulty in avoiding them after getting hold of the island of San Sebastian, from the point of which the Santos light becomes visible, and can be seen at a distance of 20 miles, but coasting craft require to keep a good lookout at night. The light is placed on an island of some elevation, covered with trees to the summit, and it has a very picturesque appearance. Rounding a bluff point, you enter at once what appears to be a river channel, though it is an estuary, for Santos is really an island. The passage is winding and the land on each side is covered with shrubby vegetation, the distance up four miles, with deep water for vessels of 1,000 tons. There are some scattered houses on the beach, chiefly used by sea-bathing residents, and on one side is an antiquated looking fort, supposed at one time to have guarded the entrance of the estuary—a specimen of early Portuguese defences; and on the island of Santos are the remains of the old town of San Vincente, the first founded on this part of the coast. The anchorage opposite the town is convenient and well protected; several wharves extend out where vessels lie alongside to discharge and load cargo, and at the Custom House there is an iron pontoon used for the same purpose. At this wharf the steamer I came down in (1,000 tons burden) received a full cargo and sailed within three days, a feat without parallel in any other port in Brazil.

There is some pretty scenery around Santos—on the coast side a range of hills, and opposite to the town, across the estuary, rise the bold mountain ranges covered with verdure. It is a pleasant ride round the base of the hills on the seaside until you come to the town of San Vincente. The railway is laid along a swampy marsh, running parallel and close to the old San Paulo road until it crosses the bridge of Cubitao, which connects the island and the main land. The town itself is long and straggling, containing from 8,000 to 10,000 inhabitants, with some fine warehouses or stores for storing coffee, cotton, or other country produce previous to shipment. At the extremity of the town is the railway station, a commodious building, having wharves, alongside of which vessels can come, and opposite to the station is what looks like a palace, with two wings and a centre, the outside almost entirely lined with ornamental blue Lisbon tiles, and the whole bearing an appearance quite out of keeping with the general features of the place. It is the costly hobby of an old Portuguese merchant, and intended for his own residence, but it progresses very slowly towards completion. The streets are paved with roughish stones, not easy for a novice to walk on, but a great improvement on the sandy clement which formerly characterised primitive Brazilian streets. The class of buildings is generally solid, and there are some good, well stocked shops. There is also a theatre on a very diminutive scale, where I went to see an amusing amateur performance, but the heat was stifling; nevertheless, it was quite full, and some well dressed and sprightly young ladies formed part of the audience, and did not appear to be very much troubled by the not very aromatic flavour of the atmosphere. It was a relief to get into the fresh air for a few minutes between the acts.

Santos is not to be judged by its present status, but by what the railway must make it; and a few years will produce a very great change, further accelerated by the introduction of gas, water, and drainage, which are here much needed, as well as in the City of San Paulo. There is a specialty about the old Brazilian towns that one cannot help being struck with, and they present a striking contrast when railway innovation comes to disturb the slumbrous habits of the people. As a seaport and a rising town Santos is deserving of this additional notice, and, I may observe, its close proximity to the sea renders it exceedingly healthy.

MR. PERKINS ON EMIGRATION.

In the elaborate and interesting report of Mr. William Perkins, who was at the head of a recent Government expedition to El Rey, an old Spanish settlement in the Gran Chaco, occurs the following remarks:—" The northern part of the Province of Santa Fé is justly considered the most important, being so highly favoured by nature; and in truth the Creator has here scattered with a prodigal hand all the elements capable of attracting population and industry. For these reasons it saddens the heart to see these magnificent lands deserted, teeming as they do with natural riches. Mighty rivers and streams cross each other in all directions; first-class timber in the woods to an extent the eye cannot reach; picturesque meadows of rich pasture,—in a word, whatever can be desired for agricultural and industrial pursuits."

Mr. Perkins has been one of the most active and intelligent agents in the cause of emigration to the Argentine Republic and so soon as the land transfers of the Central Argentine Railway are completed the company intend to send him to the United States and to England for the purpose of making arrangements, and to bring out people to occupy their land, a desirable step, which will at once enhance its value and that of the immense tracts by which it is surrounded. The peculiar feature of this railway is the territory attached to the concession, namely, a league on each side of the line, comprising a total of about a million of acres, one half of which is the property of the contractors, the other half belonging to the shareholders, who have, besides, the national guarantee of 7 per cent. on the capital of £1,600,000, which the railway is to cost, or about £6,500 per mile. It is, perhaps, one of the easiest railways in the world to make, the chief expense being the rails and rolling stock, few earthworks or ordinary sleepers being required. As I have before noticed, there is plenty of wood higher up the country, about Villa Nueva, where a large quantity of sleepers of excellent quality were being prepared to complete the line to Cordova.

In Mr. Perkins' report just alluded to are some very graphic descriptions of the riverine facilities, at present so little known or availed of, but it is to be hoped when he revisits those scenes, after utilising his services at home, he will return to see progress already made, and some at least of the lands of the Central Argentine Railway occupied by thriving settlers. It only requires encouragement, and a beginning to be made, which I believe will not long be delayed.

The Argentine Government has come forward to assist the Argentine Railway by an issue of bonds for £300,000, the contractors supplying the remaining £300,000, which, with £1,000,000 in shares when the company was formed, completed the capital. The timely assistance thus rendered by the Government is an earnest of their desire to see this great work accomplished, in which the welfare of the upper provinces is so deeply concerned, as there are no navigable rivers running westward to Cordova, the Parana and the Paraguay tending northward into Paraguay and Matto Grosso. It follows, as a matter of course, that a large portion of the produce of these western provinces will find its way to Cordova and to the railway, amongst them many articles which have never yet been brought down to Rosario or Buenos Ayres, on account of the great cost of transit.

Reverting to Mr. Perkins, his services in the cause of exploration of the country have been very valuable, and few there are better acquainted with the facilities it presents for emigration, when once centres of population are established by this main trunk railway from Rosario to Cordova.

MY VOYAGE HOME.

My visit has been prolonged by unforeseen events, but I am on my way home again, on board the steamer City of Buenos Ayres, commanded by my old friend Captain Peters, also belonging to Tait's Line, which has experienced some of the incidents and drawbacks peculiar to the formation of new companies; but from the spirit manifested by that firm, there is every prospect of the enterprise proving a successful one. The rapid increase of passenger trade to the River Plate is a notable fact that has to be provided for, independent of that to Brazil, which continues to assume larger proportions, and steamers now will get a preference of freight both ways. Two days after the storm at Buenos Ayres, to which I have referred in another place, the vessel was enabled to complete her cargo, and to get under weigh at 9 p.m., on the 19th June, reaching Monte Video at 11 a.m. on the following day. There was a fresh breeze blowing, which rendered boating somewhat hazardous, and prevented our leaving the harbour until 8 a.m. on Sunday, the 21st, when we steamed down the river, passed Maldonada, and after five days we once more entered the bay of Rio de Janeiro, where several men-of-war were at anchor. As we passed the American frigate Guerriere, the band struck up "God save the Queen," in compliment to our captain, who was a friend of the American admiral. Her Majesty's ship Narcissus, with Admiral Ramsay on board, was also lying in the harbour, with the American steamer Kersseage, which terminated the career of the world-famed cruiser, Alabama, in the combat off Cherbourg.

The weather was beautifully fine, clear, and pleasant at Rio, very different from that I had experienced a few months previously, and rendered the two days on shore very agreeable. I had a busy time of it, seeing and taking leave of old friends, but managed to get through, and embarked on Sunday afternoon. We sailed down the harbour, again passing the men-of-war, officers and crews of which were collected on deck, and returned our salutation. Captain Wilson, flag-captain of the Narcissus, lunched on board us, with some of the officers, and a number of other friends of the passengers were on board before we started. We passed the fort at 5 p.m., when they very politely hoisted the number, "Wish you a good voyage." The scenery of the bay looked, if possible, more magnificent than ever, under the influence of the setting sun, the outline of mountains being so clearly and vividly portrayed, and few could leave so grand a scene without a feeling of admiration and regret. Our passengers were a mixed group (including about a dozen children of various ages) of different nationalities, English, Scotch, Irish, Belgian, Dutch, and Germans, so almost all languages were spoken on board. Some English families were returning from a residence of some years in the campos of Buenos Ayres, not very well pleased with the result of their speculation in sheep farming, which has no doubt been a bad one of late, but I could not find from their report that they had undergone any particular hardships, besides which they had other reasons for returning home. As I have before observed, it is a mistake for people to go out to the River Plate to commence sheep farming under the idea they can realise a fortune and retire in a few years. They must make up their minds to rough it, and to persevere as they would have to do at home in a similar occupation.*

We had favourable weather, and crossed the line on the eighth day after leaving Rio, expecting to reach St. Vincent, our only place of call between Rio and Falmouth, on the 10th of July, say thirteen days out, which is pretty fair work for a steamer with only moderate power, and carrying a large cargo. We passed many vessels knocking about in what sailors call the "doldrums"—various winds and calms—which prevail between the north-east and south-east trades, and amused ourselves with exchanging signals with several of them, getting their names, destination, &c. The monotony of a sea voyage is always relieved by incidents of this kind, and making land, the latter generally creating much excitement.

* A life in the camp may not be very agreeable, or such as is experienced on a farm at home. People have to put up with a good deal if they wish to better their condition, and remember that it is not always a matter of choice, but of necessity, which compels them to seek their fortunes in a foreign country. Those who can live comfortably or find suitable occupation at home should remain there. One of the great drawbacks to the success of young Englishmen out in the camp is, I am sorry to say, the terrible propensity to indulgence in the free use of ardent spirits, which soon enfeebles their constitution and often leads to an untimely grave. This a little self-denial would soon enable them to avoid. Several of these melancholy instances occurred during my short stay in the country. The climate isself is sufficiently stimulating without the excitement arising, from the brandy bottle, the use of which, even in towns and cities, is often carried to excess. As a rule, the natives are sober, and set a good example to foreigners in this respect if they would only profit by it.

We got into the harbour of St. Vincent about 8 p.m., on the evening of Saturday, the 11th of July, in time to be visited, and I went on shore to spend the night with Mr. Miller, at his country place up the mountains, about two-and-a-half miles distant from the Consulate. It was dark, of course, but Mr. Miller's son led the way on a pony, and I followed him on another, the ascent being rather steep as we approached the house, which is very nicely perched on ground levelled on a spur of the mountain, and called Arcia from the dark brown colour of the hills. Sleeping at an elevation of 800 feet, was a pleasant change after the rocking motion and closeness of the steamer's cabin, and on looking out of my window early next morning there was a charming view of the little harbour, and the picturesque mountains on all sides of it, wanting only verdure to constitute an agreeable picture. Everything was burnt up from the want of rain, which is expected about this time, when I believe the Island wears quite a cheerful aspect, though for a short time only. After breakfast, we rode down to the Consulate, where I spent a portion of the day, instead of being on board during the delightful operation of coaling, when everything is covered with coal dust. Mr. Miller has a farm on the other side of the island, where he is cultivating vines, fruits, and vegetables, having a supply of water on the spot,—the most difficult of all things to find—and he has by means of a large tank, brought a supply into the town.

I have before alluded to the great advantage presented by St. Vincent as a coaling station, and to the facilities Mr. Miller has provided to carry it on—which he is continually adding to. A steamer can take on board 200 to 300 tons of coal in a few hours, and lately the

Tamer, on her way home from the Cape, took in upwards of 600 tons during daylight. It was Sunday again when we were there (a constant recurrence during the last six months, when I have been so often in and out of ports); but we were coaled and all ready to start by 5 p.m. Unfortunately, some little repairs to the boiler tubes were not completed, and we did not get up steam until 1 a.m. on Monday morning, thus losing several hours. The night was fine, and we soon got again into the open sea, on our way to Falmouth, steaming against a north-east trade. The Zaire, Portuguese mail steamer from Africa, came into St. Vincent on Sunday for a small supply of coal, sailing again in a few hours. The only other vessels were a small paddle wheel steamer, bound to Bahia, intended for the navigation of the bay, and two vessels discharging coal. At times there is quite a little fleet there, and a good many steamers are shortly expected to call with troops on their way back from the Abyssinian expedition.

Four days' hard tugging against a strong north-east trade has diminished our hopes of a tolerably quick passage. During the many passages I have made I do not recollect such strong trades at this season of the year. Our progress has, in consequence, been very slow, not averaging more than 150 miles in the twenty-four hours; and the only amusement, if it can be called such, is to exchange signals with vessels passing us, going along with the wind right aft and all sail set. It is steaming against these north-east trades that generally renders the homeward passage so much longer than the outward one, unless a steamer has great power. Still it is an immense stride over the old days of sailing ships, which generally took fifty or sixty days home from Rio, and often more. The trim of the vessel being rather too much by the head, some cargo has been removed from the fore to the after hold, and the top gallant yards struck, offering less resistance to the wind.

Two more days of trade winds, dead against us, the time being only relieved by passing a large number of sailing ships and exchanging signals with them. It would appear as if they had experienced some detention in crossing the bay, and that a considerable fleet had reached the latitude of Madeira in time to avail of the strong north-east trades between Madeira and St. Vincent. Sunday, 19th July, we passed close to the Island of Madeira, topped with clouds, preventing our seeing more than the outline, and the verdure and cultivation lies on the eastern side; still it is an event that breaks the monotony of a voyage. Before this day week, if all is well, we hope to reach Falmouth. On Thursday, 23rd July, after three days of almost complete calm, with scarcely a ripple or movement on the water at times, looking for a favourable breeze to waft us to Falmouth, this morning our old friend, the persevering north-easter, came on again, right in the middle of the Bay of Biscay, and we were compelled to steam head to wind, with a considerable sea getting up. At this season of the year westerly winds generally prevail in these latitudes, but we have not met with any, nor been able to make any use of our canvas from the latitudes of 10° north. Numerous sailing vessels keep passing us with studding sails set, but there is no help for it. From this date up to the time of our making Falmouth on the morning of Sunday, the 26th, it blew almost a gale, with a nasty rough sea, against which our progress was very slow. We steamed into the harbour on a miserably cold, wet day, but the fields about appeared burnt up for want of moisture, and we learnt that the weather had been exceedingly hot. I did not find the Railway Hotel much improved as regards board and attendance, which is a great pity, as it is a spacious, comfortable house, situated in one of the most picturesque spots in England, and would be very attractive with better management.

APPENDIX.

POSSESSIONS AND PRODUCTS OF THE DIFFERENT PROVINCES OF BRAZIL.

S. Pedro do Rio Grande do Sul (situated between 27° 50' and 33° 45' S. latitude).—Possesses coal mines and other minerals; herva-matte, natural pasture grounds perfectly appropriate to the successful breeding of cattle, mules, horses, and sheep.

Produces wheat, barley, potatoes, grapes, and all the fruits of temperate climates; cotton, and different grains of tropical climates.

Santa Catharina (24° 53' and 27° 50' S. latitude).—Possesses coal mines and a great quantity of iron ores; timber, woods for cabinet work and dye woods; natural pasture for the breeding of cattle, mules, horses, and sheep.

Produces wheat, cotton, tobacco, sugar-cane, coffee, and all the grains of tropical countries.

Parana (between 20' and 27° 20' lat. South).—Possesses diamond and gold mines; herva-matte in great abundance, natural pastures for the breeding of cattle, horses, mules, and sheep.

Produces wheat, oats, barley, hemp, flax, potatoes, grapes, and nearly all the fruits of temperate climates; cotton, tobacco, sugar-cane, coffee, and all the grains of tropical climates.

S. Paulo (between 19° 40' and 25° 40' lat. South).—Possesses mines of iron ore, copper, silver, gold, precious stones, coal; natural pastures for the breeding of cattle, mules, sheep and swine; woods of different sorts.

Produces wheat, flax, grapes, and nearly all the fruits of temperate climates; tea, coffee, and sugar-cane in great abundance; cotton, tobacco, and all the grains of tropical countries.

Rio de Janeiro (Capital of the Empire of Brazil, between 21° 25' and 23° 25' lat. South).—Possesses iron mines, clays for china ware and porcelain; woods and timber of all sorts.

Produces excellent coffee and sugar-cane, tea, cotton, and all the grains of the tropics.

Espirito Santo (between 18° 50' and 21° 20' lat. South).—Possesses gold, iron, and diamond mines; excellent timber and woods for cabinet work; breeds cattle.

Produces coffee, sugar-cane, cotton, and all the grains of the tropics.

Bahia (between 9° 35' and 18° lat. South).—Possesses rich gold, diamond, silver, iron, copper, coal, and marble mines; timber and Brazil wood; breeds cattle.

Produces sugar-cane, coffee, excellent tobacco, cotton, cocoa, clove, and all the grains of the tropics.

Sergipe (between 10° 30' and 11° 40' lat. South).—Possesses gold and diamond mines; marble, crystals, nitron, nitrates of soda salts; iron, slate, salines, precious woods and plants, vanilla.

Produces abundantly sugar-cane, cotton, and all tropical grains.

Alagoas (between 8° 50' and 10° 30' lat. South).—Possesses mines of anthracite, bituminous schist; timber, Brazil wood.

Produces sugar-cane, tobacco, and all tropical grains.

Pernambuco (between 7° 10' and 9° 45' lat. South).—Possesses unexplored mines, timber; Brazil wood, breeds excellent cattle.

Produces very abundantly sugar-cane, cotton, and all tropical products.

Parahyba (between 6° 15' and 7° 50' lat. South).—Possesses gold mines, iron ores, saltpetre; timber and wood for cabinet work, Brazil wood; breeds cattle.

Produces sugar cane, cotton, and all tropical grains.

Rio Grande do Norte (between 4° and 6° 10' lat. South).—Possesses gold and silver mines, abundant Brazil wood, carnaúba, cochineal; breeds cattle.

Produces cotton, sugar-cane, and all tropical grains.

Ceara (between 2° 45' and 7° 10' lat. South).—Possesses mines of gold, silver, lead, iron, antimonium, amianthus, coal, marble, nitron, salines; timber, wood for cabinet work and dyeing, quinine, ipecacuanha, carnaúba; breeds excellent cattle.

Produces coffee, sugar-cane, cotton.

Piauhy (between 2° 40' and 11° 25' lat South).—Breeds much cattle, horses and mules.

Produces all tropical fruits.

Maranhao (between 1° 10' and 7° 30' lat. South).—Possesses gold mines, splendid timber, and other woods of all sorts; breeds cattle.

Produces in great abundance cotton, rice, sugar-cane, and all the other tropical products.

PARA (between 4° lat. North and 8° lat. South).—Possesses in great abundance the indiarubber tree, sarsaparilla, copaiba, vanilla, clove, vegetable ivory, and rich woods of all sorts; breeds cattle and turtles.

Produces cocoa, tobacco, cotton, and sugar-cane.

AMAZONAS (between 4° lat. and 10° lat. South).—Possesses mines of crystals, marble, silver; precious woods of all sorts, the indiarubber tree in great quantity, sarsaparilla, ipecacuanha, cloves; breeds cattle and turtles.

Produces in extraordinary abundance all tropical fruits.

MINAS GERAES (between 14° and 20° lat. South).—Possesses gold mines, diamonds, precious stones, iron; natural prairies, where much cattle and swine are bred.

Produces in abundance cotton, tobacco, coffee, tea, sugar-cane, and all tropical grains.

GOYAZ (between 7° and 20° lat. South).—Possesses mines of gold, iron, diamonds, and crystals; Brazil wood, logwood, and many medicinal plants; breeds cattle, horses, and swine.

Produces sugar-cane, coffee, tobacco, and all tropical grains.

MATTO GROSSO (between 7° and 24° 30' South).—Possesses mines of gold, diamond, iron, and copper; timber and medicinal plants as ipecacuanha; breeds cattle.

Produces coffee, tobacco, and all tropical grains.

BRAZILIAN FINANCES.—LAW OF 1860.

The following are the chief leading provisions of this law, which may be called the Banking Law of Brazil:—

1st. To limit the issues of independent banks to the average of the first six months of 1860 during the suspension of cash payments.

2nd. To limit the issues of the Bank of Brazil and its branches to double its unengaged funds, the Government being empowered to grant their issue to be raised to three times the value of the said disengaged funds, but this only in case they do not exceed the average of its issues since its foundation. All this during the suspension of cash payments.

3rd. To abolish small note issues of the independent banks. The Bank of Brazil to withdraw from circulation its small notes if within six months it did not resume cash payments.

4th. To contract the issue of all banks at the rate from 3 to 12 per cent. if within a year they did not resume cash payments.

5th. To subject for the future banks to the Bankruptcy Law, in case of their not paying their notes in gold.

6th. To appoint an official Government Inspector for each bank.

7th. To limit the dividends of all commercial companies to their net profits on each half-year's operations.

8th. To prohibit the issue of promisory, or other notes to bearer, without authorisation of the Legislature, except cheques on bankers.

9th. To allow to the banks the mutual exchange of their notes received in payment.

10. To submit to the Government's approval all sorts of companies and corporations, after certain formalities for the guarantee of the public.

11th. To make concessions for banks of issue for railways and canals dependent on the Legislature.

12th. To regulate the organisation of savings-banks, friendly societies, and pawnbrokers.

13th. To substitute the copper coins by bronze.

14th. Finally, to facilitate the acquisition of the Railways for the State by exchanging their bonds for Government internal stock of 6 per cent., or for external of $4\frac{1}{2}$, both at par.

Of such efficacious character were the provisions adopted by the Law of 1860 that the foreign exchange, infallible thermometer of the circulating medium, was gradually rising, and from $25\frac{3}{4}$d., where it was at the publication of the said law, it rose to $27\frac{5}{8}$d., that is to say, it went above par, and this was the rate at the time when the financial crisis of 1864 occurred. Accordingly the market price of bullion also went down.

WORKSHOPS OF THE WESTERN RAILWAY OF BUENOS AYRES.

(From the *Buenos Ayres Standard*.)

Buenos Ayres has at last thrown off the mantle of dignified idleness in which she has been so long enveloped, and is taking her place amongst the leading nations of the earth. The days are past when every article for social comfort or consumption had to be imported from abroad. We are creeping along in the right path at last, and Governor Alsina and Emilio Castro are head workmen of Buenos Ayres. They are creating mechanical power in this country, calculated at no very distant date to develop the resources of her natural wealth to such a point that it will enlarge her credit, extend her commerce, and give birth to manufactures.

Happy indeed is it for the interests of this country that so immense a capital has found its way into steam hammers, saws, lathes, and all the mighty elements which mechanical genius has called into the service of man. We are on the right track at last, and people who want to judge of the real progress of this place should visit the workshops of the Western Railway. Within the last few years this grand mart of mechanical industry has sprung into existence. We recollect Buenos Ayres without a railway—still more without a workshop—unless the humble smith's forge may be dubbed by this title; but on last Wednesday it was with agreeable astonishment we witnessed the foundries, shops, forges, warehouses, &c., all in full play, and every man at his post; in fact, the only alloy to our feelings of satisfaction was the utter absence of the youth of the country from these, the finest and best schools for boys and young men. The whole mechanical work going on is in the hands almost exclusively of foreigners, and hardly a single native boy as apprentice for the entire length and breadth of the establishment is to be seen. We trust when the great advantages of these shops are brought properly before the public that we shall see some change in this respect.

At one o'clock a select party attended at the Railway Station in the Parque, to witness the working of some new machinery sent out recently by Mr. Thomas Allen, the Government engineer abroad. We noticed amongst those present, Dr. Rawson, Sres. Gonsalez, Santa Maria, Coghlan, Gowland, Fleming, Aguirre, Velez, Castro, Gutierrez, Dr. Seguel, and several other leading men whose names we forget. A beautiful model locomotive was, with the aid of a small kerosene lamp, set a-going; it worked on a tray, and fairly astonished with the precision of its movements some Cordova friends present. A portable galvanic telegraphic apparatus was next introduced, and one of the operatives in charge showed the working of it, the great merit of which appeared to us to be its extreme simplicity. On the table lay drawings of the new fountains for the Water Works; the "jet d'eau" for the Plaza Victoria is a truly magnificent and useful ornament; it will cost when put up about £1,500, but those for the other Plazas are less expensive.

At the Parque Station they have now a complete set for twelve stations of Morse's Printing Telegraph. Everything has arrived in first-rate order for connecting Rosario with this city. There are over 500 wrought iron posts, with twelve tables. The whole affair will cost, we believe, about £11,000. The manager, or chief electrician, is expected out in the packet; at present M. Ringallé is in charge. Four telegraph clerks have also been engaged in England.

About half-past one we proceeded to the special train in waiting to convey us to the Once Setiembre depots. We noticed that the Bragge roof is completely worn away, but we understand that the new iron and glass roof, from England, has arrived, and will be put up immediately. Every day materials are arriving from abroad, owing to the convenience of having such a practical agent as Mr. Thomas Allen, who, from his lengthened experience on the road, knows precisely what is wanted and what will suit. A large turning table is now coming out, upwards of forty-two feet. It will be the largest in the country; it was made at Birmingham, and will be put up at the Parque Central Station; also a large travelling truck, to carry railway carriages, waggons, &c., from one line to another. We entered Governor Alsina's state coach, being accompanied by the guests, and pushed on for the depots. The coach is elegantly fitted up with every convenience, and we are surprised his Excellency the Governor does not take a trip out twice a week to Chivilcoy or Mercedes.

Arriving at the depots, we first entered the foundry department, and came on a hydraulic press used for taking the wheels off axles; it works up to a pressure of fifty tons; three men work it, and it is one of the most useful machines in the shop, doing in ten minutes the work of ten men for a whole day.

Next we inspected a hydraulic pump for trying the state of boilers to 500 lbs. per square inch, which is constantly in use.

A large planing machine next met the eye. This machine planes up to nine feet, and is used for making points and crossings, or any large planing, and is worked by a boy.

Alongside is a small screw cutting lathe, twelve inch centres. This machine is useful for all kinds of work.

Then we have a small lathe for brass turning, eight inch centres, worked by apprentices.

Further on is a screwing machine, patented by Messrs. Sharpe, Stewart & Co., of Manchester, to screw from $\frac{1}{4}$ to $1\frac{1}{2}$ inches; also worked by a boy.

Another machine, patented by the same firm, called a shaping machine, for all kinds of work; one of the most useful in the shop, and worked by apprentices.

Next comes a break lathe; will turn up to six feet for screw cutting and for all other kind of work; attended to by operatives.

The shaft pump supplies the great tank with water from a huge algibe, throwing up 3,500 gallons 18 feet high. This water is used for washing boilers, &c.

The large wheel lathe, a ponderous machine, turns wheels six feet diameter: this is used to repair wheels, which, being in constant use, require continued attention—worked by an operative.

Then comes a double-faced wheel lathe, turning two wheels at one time; turns up to 4 feet diameter—worked by an operative.

The large stationary engine, the great motive power of the whole shop, drives all the shafts, is 12-horse power, burning about three quarters of a ton of slack and ashes per day—attended by one operative.

The patent silent fan, which is used to supply six blacksmiths' forges, making 2,000 evolutions per minute.

Then comes the monarch of the shop, the steam hammer. Here we witnessed the strokes of this huge machine, at which even Vulcan himself would stare. The noise of this hammer striking on the red hot bars echoed around the whole square. Mr. Daniel Gowland remarked that the first steam hammer he ever saw in South America was in the ill-fated Paraguay.

There are six blacksmiths' forges constantly at work, fed by the steam fan, and always occupied in repairing locomotives, coaches, waggons, &c.

Mr. Manier is the foreman of this shop. Before, however, we leave it, we must notice the casting or blast foundry. Whilst we were present we witnessed the workmen casting old brass into new plates, which latter arrangement realised an immense saving, and redounds to the credit of the indefatigable Emilio Castro, who perceived the great loss in selling old brass and buying new; and last, not least, we must not omit the huge punching machine, very useful in its way, but little used. It punches quarter inch to an inch, and cuts up to three quarter boiler plates.

The repairing shop is large (50 metres by 50), and capable of holding thirty locomotives; we noticed four locomotives under repair. Damaged engines are here turned out as good as new; and, indeed, Mr. John Allen, who is the moving genius of the whole mechanical department, assures us that they can make their own locomotives, so replete with every utensil are the shops; but, of course, it is cheaper to import them. Two damaged engines were landed not long ago, and were about to be sold by auction, but Mr. Allen took them in hand, and now they are in excellent working order. Owing to the great falling off of traffic on the line, there are now only eight engines daily under steam, whereas this time last year they had sixteen; but in this shop all kinds of repairs can be done. Already the shops have built several first and second-class coaches—genuine native industry.

We next pass to the coach and waggon shop, (50 by 12), capable of holding about twelve carriages. Here all the coaches are overhauled, repaired, varnished, and even the upholstery attended to, and coaches built. The only thing which as yet baffles the mechanics are the wheels, which must be imported.

And now we come to the new carpenter's shop, where the new machines sent out by Mr. Allen have been just put up.

The chief attraction is the new machine which, as it does every imaginable kind of work, is called the "General Joiner." None of the gentlemen present could give us the exact name in Spanish for this machine, so we call it the "Nuevo Carpintero General." A facetiously disposed writer might opine that as President Mitre has given to the Republic a new cavalry major, Governor Alsina, not to be outdone, has given his country a new "General," the best and most potent general in the Republic; and we congratulate the Governor on the acquisition of the new "Carpintero General."

We all stood astonished at the work it did, and have not now time to explain its varied powers; it plains, moulds, and saws planks of every size in a few moments; and beside it we noticed the new endless saw; also the jigger saw for pattern making; also the new wood turning lathe, and the large drilling machine, the largest in this country for drilling wheels.

In the yard we noticed sixty pair of extra wheels from the States, but at these depots they have an immense extra supply of everything.

And if we were to stop to detail all we saw in those wondrous workshops it would fill half-a-dozen *Standards*.

The works are a credit to Buenos Ayres, and an honour to the present Administration. We left these busy haunts with the most favourable impressions, well recollecting that but a few years ago this very site was a rude brick-kiln.

Yes, there is vitality, after all, in Buenos Ayres, and if any man doubts it, let him pay a visit on a working day to these shops. The store-rooms, under the charge of Mr. Tucker, are replete with everything, and the wool depots are the grandest and most extensive in the country, capable of holding at one time 100 waggons.

There are sixty-eight mechanics in the workshops constantly employed; 600 men engaged in working the line.

Mr. Emilio Castro, head director; Don Luis Elordi, second in command; Mr. John Allen next; and Mr. Zimmermann head electrician.

SANITARY CHARACTER OF THE ANDINE HEIGHTS.

We have made the following extracts from an article published in the "Revista de Buenos Ayres," on the climates of the Andine Heights, and mountains of Cordova, written by Dr. Scrivener, who has himself resided for many years in those countries. The "Revista de Buenos Ayres" is a most valuable publication, and those who are interested in South America will find much reliable information in it. It contains many curious articles on the history and literature of the country. It has now reached its 13th volume, each book containing 640 pages, 8vo.:—

The sky at the Andine Mountains is pure azure, and the atmosphere bright and clear, and is so very transparent that it enables you to see objects at a distance, making them apparently close at hand, although in reality it would require a journey of several days to reach them.

The climate is fine and healthy, the lightness of the atmosphere produces an exhilerating effect, and an increase of energy and activity. The grandeur and magnificence of the mountains fill the mind with sentiments of veneration and awe.

I have traversed these mountains on many occasions, and am therefore enabled to form an opinion of the salubrity of the climate, as also of that on the route from the Province of Cordova to the banks of the Pacific. All over this vast tract of land, that fatal enemy of man, the tubercular phthisis, so justly feared by the inhabitants of Lima, and Buenos Ayres, is entirely unknown.

During a residence of nearly ten years in different and widely spread districts of the whole country, I never saw nor heard, either directly or indirectly, through my intercourse with others, of the existence of that disease.

Doctor Smith remarks,* "that incipient and tubercular phthisis, usually attended with more or less hemoptisis, is one of the most common pulmonary affections known in Lima and other parts of the coast of Peru.

"Besides, it is a disease almost certainly cured if taken in time, by removing the *coast* patient to the open inland valley of Jauja, which runs from ten to eleven thousand feet above the sea level.

"This fact has been known and acted upon from time immemorial by the native inhabitants and physicians, and I have," observes that physician, "sent patients from the capital to Jauja, in a very advanced state of phthisis, with open ulcerations and well marked caverns on the lungs, and have seen them again after a lapse of a little time, return to their homes free from fever, and with every appearance of the disease being arrested; but in many instances it would, after a protracted residence on the coast, again become necessary to return to the mountains, to prevent a recurrence of the disease."

We thus learn from the preceding extract, that the influence of the atmosphere in the mountains of Peru will remove pulmonary consumption in its first stage, and arrest its progress when far advanced. That such is the fact, I can also myself vouch from my own experience during a residence of sixteen years in that country.

Dr. Jourdant remarks,† "that consumption is very rare in high elevations, which is not to be attributed to the latitude of the place, but to its elevation; that Mexico and Puebla, which are almost free from this disease, are in the same latitude as Vera Cruz, where it prevails; and that the condition of the patient who suffers from consumption is considerably relieved in elevated districts, which he attributes to a less amount of oxygen in the rarified air."

From these facts we can assert with safety, that those who unfortunately suffer from incipient tubercular phthisis, will almost with certainty obtain a cure in the mountainous districts which extend at a higher or lower elevation from the province of Cordova to the valley of Rimac, whilst, on the other hand, those in the later stages of that malady will find it will be arrested, and that their lives will be prolonged for years.

---

* See " Climate of the Swiss Alps and of the Peruvian Andes compared."

† See " Les Altitudes de l'Amerique Tropical au-dessus le niveau des mars au point de vue de la constitution medicale."

It becomes a matter for most serious consideration, whether it would not be well for patients suffering from pulmonary complaints to seek the renovation of their health in these salubrious regions, in preference to the Island of Madeira, Italy, and the South of France, where these diseases are known to originate, and where hundreds have gone to without obtaining any advantages, and many with positively evil results.

"There is something," says Mr. Burkhardt,* "like the sound of a death-knell in the physician's mandate sending the sick patient to those places and scenes where so many fellow-sufferers have preceded him, in vain search for health, and found—a grave."

The invalid will not find this in these healthy districts. In the mountains of Cordova, as well as on the Andino Heights, the patient will find his disease alleviated, and in time removed, (let him come from what quarter of the globe he may) by the hand of Nature. There pulmonary complaints are never known to originate, and there those who suffer from it, on the borders of the Parana and the River Plate, seek and find a permanent cure for their ailments proceeding from all affections of the lungs. "He will not have before his imagination the phantoms of numberless victims, his predecessors in the same hopeless career, to cast the shadow of death upon a being already depressed in mind by disease and loneliness, and pining after the familiar sights and sounds he may perhaps never hear again." There, on the contrary, he will be in the midst of all that is grand—a thousand magnificent objects will excite his attention, and divert his mind from his unhappy malady, on which he will not dwell, but, on the contrary, on well founded hopes of a perfect recovery and a speedy return to his family and friends.

We believe, that when the benefits to be derived from a residence in the climate of these mountains are more generally known in Europe, very many who suffer from pulmonary complaints will visit these regions for a renovation of their health and system.

We would recommend the mountains of Cordova to consumptive patients, in preference to the Andine Heights of Bolivia, as being the nearest to the River Plate, and containing a greater variety of objects to divert the attention and amuse. The facility of transport, the shortness of the passage, combined with a well-founded hope of renovating the health, will be of themselves sufficient reasons for undertaking the journey.

The passage from England can be made in thirty-four days. There are several lines of merchant steamers, from London and Liverpool, as well as the Government vessels from Southampton and Bordeaux, which arrive at Buenos Ayres every month. From this port you can embark in a steamer for the city of Rosario, which is most beautifully situated on the banks of the river Parana, and is the

* See "Syria and the Holy Land."

finest port in the Argentine Confederation, at which you arrive in about twenty-six hours.

From thence you take the Argentine Central Railway, and arrive at the city of Cordova on the same day.

Here commence the serraicias or mountainous districts, which extend to the valley of Rimac, comprising an area of about 1,000 leagues.

We believe that at no very distant time, a public establishment will be founded in the mountains of Cordova for consumptive patients; should this be the case, we can vouch that there would be no lack of visitors willing to support the establishment, and anxious to aid it by their means, in exchange for the benefits they have received there; the natural grandeur and magnificence of the mountain scenery would also contribute, in no small degree, to the attractions of the place, and the benefit of the invalids.

The city of Cordova is situated in a deep valley on the banks of a river, amidst the most beautiful and varied scenery.

Ascending from the city to the mountains, the traveller finds every variety of climate, with a difference of temperature at every additional ascent.

In these varieties of temperature, he will be certain to find one that is suitable to his complaint, and agreeable to himself.

The tops and sides of the mountains are partly covered with trees and shrubs, and the soil in the valley is rich and very fertile, producing Indian corn, wheat, barley, sundry fruits and vegetables, and whatever the husbandman may desire to cultivate. Cattle, horses, mules, with sheep and goats, roam in large herds, on most excellent pasture. Huanacos and other wild animals inhabit the mountains. The wool of the sheep is of a superior quality and highly prized in the European markets.

There are great varieties of trees on the plains, many of which are very lofty, and their branches form an agreeable shade, as well as add to the beauty of the scenery. The timber of these trees is of superior quality, well suited for the construction of houses, and in the manufacture of furniture, &c.

There are mines of gold, silver, copper, and iron; the latter is very abundant and of good quality; there are also marble quarries, and the marble is very fine and of different colours; limestone of an extremely white nature is abundant; in short, there are few spots in the world where nature has lavished such a variety of animals, vegetables, and mineral productions as the province of Cordova.

It must follow, that with all these natural advantages, a country producing every commodity for the subsistence of man, and capable of affording all that tends to the convenience and luxury of life, will become at no distant period the abode of a numerous, industrious and wealthy population.

For a long period the Jesuits held their head-quarters in this province, and they were remarkable for their tact and knowledge in selecting the most healthy and fertile spots for their residences.

They erected in the capital the finest churches in the Argentine Confederation: they acquired large possessions throughout the province, and they also built splendid country mansions, which are models of art, taste, and convenience.

The fine edifices at Santa Catalina, Jesus Maria, and Caraga, are much visited and greatly admired by strangers.

It has been truly remarked by an eminent writer, that the greatest wonder of the age is a locomotive engine; that since its adoption travellers have been multiplied through the facility of transit: and that the greater those facilities, the greater the number of travellers. These facts have become generally known in this Republic, where several railways have already been made, and others are being constructed. The Central Argentine Railway, when completed, will extend from the city of Rosario to Cordova; this will be a great and lasting benefit to the commerce of the country. Cordova is now the grand emporium of the inland provinces; their productions of hides, wool, cotton, indigo, sugar, wine, wheat, tobacco, skins of animals, gold, silver, copper, iron and other valuable productions, are transported thither and conveyed by rail to the port of Rosario and shipped for Buenos Ayres, or direct to Europe. This railway extends 248 miles in length. Passengers have much increased since the opening of this line to Villa Nueva, and will still further increase on its completion to Cordova. In addition to men of business, many will avail themselves of it as a journey of pleasure, to visit the city and its beautiful mountain scenery.

Those who are fond of this kind of scenery will find much to please them. The mineralogist will see minerals, and the botanist plants, to attract their attention. We fully believe that before the lapse of many years strangers from Buenos Ayres, and other provinces, will build cottages in these beautiful and healthy regions, which would only require taste in their erection, and judgment in selecting the sites, to render them all that can be imagined as beautiful and romantic.

BUENOS AYRES AND THE OTHER PROVINCES A FIELD FOR EUROPEAN IMMIGRATION.

The following interesting and reliable statement has been published and circulated under the authority of the Argentine Government:—

The recommendations of the Argentine Republic to Europeans are:—

1. That the climate is as healthy and as favourable to vigour and longevity as that of England, or any other country of Europe.

2. That its cultivable lands are practically of unlimited extent, and require no outlay for clearing.

3. That it contains already, and especially at Buenos Ayres, the Capital, a large and prosperous European population, composed of Italians, French, English, Scotch and Irish, Germans, Portuguese, and others.

4. That the Government is solidly established and perfectly liberal, the aim of all parties being to maintain the financial honour of the country, to preserve peace, and to promote the development of industry and commerce.

5. That, while the State religion is Roman Catholic, complete toleration is upheld, Churches of all denominations being established at Buenos Ayres and other places, where a considerable portion of the settlers are English or German Protestants, or Scotch Presbyterians.

6. That there is fornightly* postal communications with England and the Continent by powerful Mail Steamers from Southampton and Bordeaux.

7. That the commercial policy of the country is in the direction of free trade.

8. That there is a treaty of amity, commerce, and navigation between Great Britain and the Republic, and that foreigners are exempted from compulsory military service or forced loans.

9. That there are a sufficient number of British subjects in the Republic to render a knowledge of the Spanish language non-essential for immigrants, and that this language is capable, during a short residence, of being more easily acquired than any other: likewise, that an English newspaper is regularly published at Buenos Ayres, and also at the city and port of Rosario, and that there is an influential English Bank and other institutions.

10. That the staple productions of the country are such as at all times to command the markets of the world, the principal exports being tallow, hides, and wool, while, during the past year, a trade in preserved meat has been opened up which seems to promise, if sufficient attention be given to establish a scientific process of curing, to assume proportions as sudden and profitable as those of the newly-developed petroleum trade of North America; that there is also a mining district in the interior provinces on the slope of the Andes, which appears, from the operations thus far conducted, to be one of the richest silver regions yet discovered.

11. That the country is being opened up in all directions by English Railway enterprises, one of which, the Rosario and Cordova Line, will be 247 miles in length, and is considered to be ultimately destined to cross the entire country to Chili, and thus to form a highway for the traffic between the Atlantic and the Pacific.

12. That the acquisition of land is easy and its tenure secure, and that additional and extraordinary facilities for settlement are in course

* There is now weekly communication by steamers between Europe and the River Plate.

of introduction by the circumstance of about a million of acres on the sides of their line having been ceded to the Rosario and Cordova (Central Argentine) Railway Company, and of a grant of 10,400 square miles in the fertile province of Cordova having been made to Mr. Etchegaray, which is to be transferred to a London Company.

Finally, it is to be observed, that the debt of the country, foreign and internal, the interest on which is paid with unfailing punctuality, is comparatively small; that it is gradually in course of extinction, and that the six per cent. bonds in the London market range between 90 and 100; that there are no direct taxes; and that the commerce of the country is increasing with such rapidity, that in the Board of Trade Returns of British exports for the past year (1864), it figures for £1,758,058, and stands higher in the list than Chili or Peru, and, as regards European countries, higher than Prussia, Sweden and Norway, Denmark, and many others with which we have an important traffic.

The present population of the Argentine Republic is but about 2,000,000, and immigration may be said to be its only want. This is felt and acknowledged by all classes, and every arrival is therefore warmly welcomed. The tide thither is gradually increasing, and persons best acquainted with the country express a conviction that the growth of Buenos Ayres, which at present is a fine city, with about 200,000 inhabitants, will during the next twenty years rival that which has been witnessed at New York during the like period in the past. In several cases persons of moderate capital have emigrated from Australia and New Zealand to the Argentine Republic, owing to the advantages of its greater proximity to England, and its superior facilities for the acquisition of land.

By far the greater portion of the country consists of rich alluvial plains, constituting what are called the Pampas. The climate is subject to a great difference of temperature in winter and summer, but the changes are gradual and regular. The winter is about as cold as the English November, with white frosts, and ice at sunrise. "Taken as a whole, the Pampas may be said to enjoy as beautiful and as salubrious an atmosphere as the most healthy parts of Greece and Italy, and without being subject to malaria."*

The country is universally celebrated for the abundance of its cattle, horses, sheep, goats, asses, mules, and swine. The number of cattle fifteen years ago was estimated at 12,000,000, and the horses, mules, and asses at more than 4,000,000, and they are supposed since that period to have largely increased.

The salubrity of the climate seems especially beneficial to immigrants from this country, its influence being singularly restorative wherever there is any tendency to bronchial or pulmonary affections. In some districts, such as that of the beautiful city and province of Cordova, these disorders appear to be almost unknown, and as on the completion of the Central Argentine Railway it will be possible

* "Encyclopædia Britannica."

to reach the city of Cordova from London in little more than a month, that place may probably become a sanitarium for Europeans in a majority of the most important cases where change of climate is desirable.

Protection of Immigrants.

An influential Commission, of which Senor Don M. J. Azcuenaga *is President, is formed at Buenos Ayres to assist Immigrants, by whom the following Notice is issued. Similar care is exercised at the Port of Rosario:—*

Notice.—The Committee of Immigration to Immigrants arriving at the Port of Buenos Ayres.

This Committee gives notice to Immigrants who arrive at this port that whaleboats have been engaged by the same to bring them on shore and that a commodious "Asylum" is prepared for them, where they will find lodging and food during the first eight days after their arrival, all gratis; and that in case any sick persons should be amongst them, they will be sent to the hospitals of this city, where they will be attended with the utmost care, likewise gratis; and finally, that this Commission will undertake to procure suitable employment for them, as well in town as in the camp, without any charge.

The present notice is given as a precaution that the Immigrants may not be imposed upon by individuals who go on board with whaleboats, offering to take them on shore, because, besides that those individuals make them pay for landing them, they take them to taverns where they are obliged to spend their money, and, having no means to pay with, they lose their luggage.

The Immigrants are therefore advised in their own interest to disembark in the whaleboats sent by the Committee, and to go direct to the "Asylum," situated in the street Corrientes, No. 8, where they will have nothing to pay.

By order of the Commission,
Buenos Ayres, Nov. 1, 1864. George P. E. Tornquist, Secretary.

The following is a list of the classes of Immigrants most required in Buenos Ayres:—

Occupation.	Monthly Wages with Board.
Farmers	£3 0 0
Gardeners	£3 15 0 to 4 10 0
Farm Servants	£2 5 0 ,, 3 0 0
House Servants, Men	2 5 0
,, Women	£2 0 0 ,, 3 0 0
Cooks, Men	3 0 0 ,, 3 15 0
,, Women	2 5 0 ,, 3 0 0
Boys from 10 to 15 years	0 15 0 ,, 1 5 0
Sempstresses	2 15 0
Milliners	2 15 0
Dressmakers	2 15 0
Laundresses	2 16 0

	Daily Wages without Board.
Bricklayers	6s. 0d.
Joiners	6 6
Blacksmiths	6 6
Shoemakers	7 6
Tailors	6s. 0d. to 9 0
Labourers	4 6
Railway labourers	6 0
Miners	—

NOTE.—*Higher Wages may be calculated upon in the interior Provinces, and Artisans of superior merit will always obtain more than is quoted.*

OBSERVATIONS.

In the rural establishments merely, situated in the suburbs of the capital, thousands of families may engage themselves immediately.

With respect to those Immigrants who may come to establish themselves in the flourishing Colonies of Santa Fé, Baradero, San José, or others actually forming in various parts of the Republic, we do not hesitate to say that, owing to the fertility of the land, they will rapidly acquire a modest fortune.

In summer, Farm Labourers get 6s. to 7s. 6d. per day.

The scarcity of Domestic Servants is notorious—a preference being given to Women.

Sempstresses, Milliners, Dressmakers, and Laundresses, however numerous the arrivals, are certain of employment.

Artisans of all descriptions, and Immigrants, even though of no fixed calling, will get employment to their satisfaction, immediately on landing.

The Railways now employ a large staff, but some thousands of labourers are required for the earthworks that are being pushed forward with the greatest activity.

Immigrants—above all, those with a knowledge of Minerals—will find very lucrative employment in the rich and numerous Mines of San Juan, Mendoza, La Rioja, Catamarca, Jujuy, Cordova, and Salta, which are now being worked with the most satisfactory results.

A fortnightly journal, called *The Brazil and River Plate Mail*, is published in London by BATES, HENDY & Co., 4, Old Jewry, E.C.

STEAM NAVIGATION ON THE RIVER PLATE.

I have been disappointed in getting a statement of the up-river traffic in passengers and merchandise, both of which have assumed very large dimensions; but the following list of steam agents at Buenos Ayres, and the steamers employed, will give some idea of what is doing in this way, as well as the increase that may be looked for when the war in Paraguay is over:—

APPENDIX. 269

Matti and Piera (the leading agents, with a large fleet of steamers.)—The steamer Rio Negro, weekly, for Salto and ports; the steamers Uruguay, for Rosario, Paraná, and Santa Fé, from the Railway Station, Retiro; the steamer Rio Uruguay, for Monte Video; the steamer Rio Negro, for Monte Video; the steamer Lujan, for Gualeguay, Rosario, Paraná, and Santa Fé, from the Railway Station, Retiro. These steamers mostly make weekly passages; the communication with Monte Video is more frequent,

Henry Dowse (one of the oldest steam agents in Buenos Ayres).—The steamer James T. Brady, for Monte Video; the steamer Beauly, for Colonia; national steamer Estrella, from the Tigre, for Rosario, Paraná, Santa Fé, and intermediate ports.

Alvarez and Risso.—For Monte Video, the steamer Villa del Salto, on Mondays, returning early on Thursday mornings; the steamer Rio de la Plata, on Wednesdays, returning early on Saturday mornings. For Salto and ports, the steamer Villa del Salto, on Thursdays, returning early on Monday mornings; for Salto and ports, the steamer Rio de la Plata, on Saturdays, returning early on Wednesday mornings; for Salto and ports, the steamer Salto, twice a month, taking passengers, cargo, and parcels, for all intermediate ports. For Corrientes and Itapiru, the Oriental steamer Tigre, taking passengers, cargo, and parcels; for Bahia Blanca and Patagones, the National steamer Patagones, once a month, taking cargo, passengers, and parcels.

The Steam Company for the Rivers run three screw-steamers, the Taraguay, the Goya, and the Guarani, chiefly with cargo, for Corrientes and Curupaity.

G. T. Paez runs steamers to Gualeguay, to Rosario, and intermediate ports, amongst them the Castor, Pollox (English); national steamers Lucia and Elena, and the Italian steamer Venezia.

Rubio and Foley despatch the British steamer Iaguarete for Corrientes, Itapiru, Curupaity, and ports, and the National steamer Victoria, for La Victoria and Zarate.

The South American Steamboat Company despatch steamers for Humaita, Curupaity, Corrientes, and ports. They also provide steam communication to Monte Video, with cargo and passengers.

At Monte Video there are several steam companies and agencies connected with Buenos Ayres. Monte Video steamers run chiefly up the Uruguay; others going up the Paraná call at Monte Video, and between Monte Video and Buenos Ayres there are now steamers running daily to and from both ports, one or two being powerful American river boats, with splendid accomodation for passengers

The following particulars of up-river distances may be interesting:—

		Miles.	
From Monte Video to Buenos Ayres		106	
Buenos Ayres „ Martin Garcia		33	
Martin Garcia „ Higueritas		30	
			169
Higueritas	to Fray Bentos	60	
Fray Bentos	„ Gualeguaychu	27	
Gualeguaycha	„ Concepcion del Uruguay	33	
Concepcion del Uruguay	„ Paysandú	15	
Paysandú	„ Concordia	90	
Concordia	„ Salto	8	
			228
Buenos Ayres	to San Fernando	18	
San Fernando	„ Las Palmas	12	
Las Palmas	„ Zarate	36	
Zarate	„ San Pedro	55	
San Pedro	„ Obligado	6	
Obligado	„ Los Hermanos	12	
Los Hermanos	„ San Nicolas	32	
San Nicolas	„ San Piedras	8	
San Piedras	„ Rosario	31	
Rosario	„ San Lorenzo	18	
San Lorenzo	„ Diamanto	54	
Diamanto	„ Santa Fé	36	
Santa Fé	„ Paraná	10	
Paraná	„ La Paz	102	
La Paz	„ Esquinao	72	
Esquinao	„ Goya	73	
Goya	„ Bella Vista	53	
Bella Vista	„ Corrientes	87	
The Branch Line	„ Gualeguay	20	
			735
From Buenos Ayres to Bahia Blanca and Patagones			840
From Colonia to Cape St. Maria			200

SHIPPING MOVEMENTS.

MOVEMENT OF SHIPPING (SAILING AND STEAM) TO AND FROM BRAZIL AND THE RIVER PLATE DURING THE YEAR 1867, TAKEN FROM THE BOARD OF TRADE RETURNS:—

	INWARDS.	SHIPS.	TONNAGE.
English	Brazil	477	188,643
	Monte Video	73	23,067
	Buenos Ayres	44	19,237

		Ships.	Tonnage.
Foreign	Brazil	139	29,174
	Monte Video	39	10,153
	Buenos Ayres	32	8,968

Total English and Foreign:—

	Ships	Tonnage
Brazil	616	275,562
Monte Video	112	123,597
Buenos Ayres	76	64,348

OUTWARDS.

		Ships	Tonnage
English	Brazil	493	195,487
	Monte Video	163	79,453
	Buenos Ayres	142	46,462
Foreign	Brazil	291	80,082
	Monte Video	111	44,144
	Buenos Ayres	62	16,886

Total English and Foreign:—

	Ships	Tonnage
Brazil	784	275,569
Monte Video	274	124,597
Buenos Ayres	204	64,348

ADVERTISEMENTS.

OUTFITS
FOR SOUTH AMERICA.

E. J. MONNERY AND SON,
165, FENCHURCH STREET,
LONDON,

Hosiers, Shirt Makers, Tailors, and General Outfitters.

MONNERY'S FLAX CLOTH CLOTHES
For Bush Shooting.

MONNERY'S WATERPROOF PONCHO AND GROUND SHEET COMBINED,
Made Specially for the Climate.

E. J. M. & Son, from their many years' experience in the Colonial Outfitting Trade, are enabled to offer to the intending Settler many useful suggestions as to the proper articles of clothing, &c., required for their voyage to and residence in South America or any of the Colonies.

CABIN FURNITURE AND SEA BEDDING.
Monnery's Patent Portable Cooking Stove.

TENTS OF ALL DESCRIPTIONS.

Illustrated Price List Free on Application.

E. J. MONNERY & SON,
165, Fenchurch Street,
LONDON.

ADVERTISEMENTS.

London and Brazilian Bank, Limited.

CAPITAL £1,940,000, { In 15,000 Shares of £100 Each } £1,500,000
{ In 22,000 Shares of £20 Each } 440,000
£1,940,000

Issued and paid-up Capital............ { 13,000, at £45 } £585,000
{ 22,000 ,, £7 10s., } 165,000
750,000

HEAD OFFICE, 2, OLD BROAD STREET, LONDON, E.C.

Directors.

JOHN WHITE CATER, Esq., CHAIRMAN.
EDWARD JOHNSTON, Esq., DEPUTY-CHAIRMAN.

JAMES ALEXANDER, Esq.	ADOLPHUS KLOCKMANN, Esq.
PHILIP CHARLES CAVAN, Esq.	EDWARD MOON, Esq.,
PASCOE CHARLES GLYN, Esq.	WILLIAM FREER SCHOLFIELD, Esq.

Bankers.

London— { BANK OF ENGLAND.
{ Messrs. GLYN, MILLS, CURRIE & Co.

Paris—Messrs. BISCHOFFSHEIM, GOLDSCHMIDT & Co.

Hamburg—Messrs. J. H. SCHRÖDER & Co.

Branch Banks and Agencies.

Brazil—RIO DE JANEIRO, BAHIA, PERNAMBUCO, RIO GRANDE DO SUL, SANTOS, SAN PAULO, PELOTAS, MARANHAM, CEARA, PARA.

River Plate—BUENOS AYRES, MONTE VIDEO.

Portugal—LISBON, OPORTO,
AMARANTE, BRAGA, COIMBRA, GUIMARAES, VIANNA, VILLA REAL.

THE Directors of this Bank grant Drafts on the Branches and negotiate or collect Bills payable at the above places on the most favourable terms.

They also issue Circular Notes and Letters of Credit for the use of travellers to all parts of the world.

They undertake the Agency of parties connected with Brazil and Portugal, make Investments in the Public Funds, and other British and Foreign Securities, and receive Dividends and Interest free of charge to constituents.

They also receive Money on Deposit at rates of Interest varying according to the length of time for which the Deposit is made.

Current Accounts opened at the Head Office and Branches, Interest being allowed thereon.

For further particulars apply at the Bank, 2, Old Broad Street. Office hours 10 to 4; Saturdays, 10 to 2.

By Order of the Board,

JOHN BEATON, *Secretary.*

ADVERTISEMENTS.

LIVERPOOL, BRAZIL & RIVER PLATE MAIL STEAMERS,

UNDER POSTAL CONTRACT WITH THE GOVERNMENT OF BRAZIL.

* The Steamer of the 20th of each month is under contract with the Postmaster General, and carries Her Majesty's Mails.

Fixed Dates of Departure from Liverpool.

On the **2nd** of every month (Brazilian Post Office Packet) for
BAHIA, RIO DE JANEIRO, AND SANTOS,
(*via* Lisbon). If the 2nd be Sunday, then on the 3rd.

An Intermediate Steamer on or about the **10th**, the precise date being fixed and announced in the previous month.

On the **20th** (British Mail Steamer*) for
RIO DE JANEIRO, MONTE VIDEO, AND BUENOS AYRES (Direct).
If the 20th be Monday, then on the 21st.

On the **30th** for
MONTE VIDEO AND BUENOS AYRES
(direct). If the 30th be Sunday, then on the 31st.

Conditions as per Circulars.

The Steamers of the Line have superior accommodation for Passengers, and carry Surgeons and Stewardesses.

For terms of Freight or Passage, and plans of Cabins, apply to

LAMPORT & HOLT,
21, WATER STREET, LIVERPOOL.

ADVERTISEMENTS.

MEDLOCK & BAILEY'S PATENT
BISULPHITE OF LIME,

For the Preservation of Meat, Fish, Poultry, Game, and all other Animal Substances in Temperate or Tropical Climates, and on Board Ship.

By the use of this valuable Preparation fresh meat can be had throughout a voyage, however long, thus avoiding the expense and losses incidental to the conveyance of live stock on board. No steamer or passenger ship should be without it, as it will enable Captains to lay in provisions at foreign ports, wherever they are cheap and good, relieving them of the necessity of providing for the voyage home. It imparts no flavour to the meat, nor does it lessen its nutritive value, while it prevents scurvy, and destroys contagion wherever it is used.—For further particulars see Descriptive Pamphlet, sent post free for seven stamps.

SOLE MANUFACTURERS.
Messrs. WILLIAM BAILEY and SON, Horseley Fields Chemical Works, Wolverhampton; and 17, Lawrence Pountney Hill, London, E.C.

Price 3s. 6d. per Gallon, packages included. Licenses from One Guinea per annum.

Extract from a Letter received from Sir JAMES MATHESON, Bart., M.P., dated 20th July, 1866, enclosing a further order.

"Sir James Matheson is glad to tell Messrs. William Bailey and Son that their Bisulphite of Lime answered perfectly in carrying the carcases of a deer and calf from Stornoway to London, *quite fresh*, being on the journey and voyage four days during the very hot days of June ; besides enabling the venison and veal to be kept 12 days after arrival by using the Bisulphite according to directions."

THOMAS J. HUTCHINSON, Esq., F.R.G.S., F.A S.L. &c., &c., Her Britannic Majesty's Consul for Rosario, Rio de la Plata, writes—

" When at Monte Video I had the pleasure of tasting at breakfast a small piece of beef prepared by the Bisulphite of Lime, sent out to the Plate. It was given to me by Mr. Prange. The preservation of that meat was perfect, and it was the first piece of real juicy beef that I had tasted for the last seven years."

Dr. STONE, Health Officer, Trinidad, writes—

"I have found your Bisulphite of Lime of great value as a means of preserving meat."

The Governor of the City Poor House, Edinburgh,

Is "very highly pleased with the results obtained from the use of your Bisulphite."

Extract from the Analytical Report of WENTWORTH L. SCOTT, Esq., F.C.S., &c.

"The safest, simplest, and most effective means for the 'preservation of animal substances that has yet been brought before the public."

Mr. J. W. SALISBURY, Meat Salesman, of Newgate Market, London, writes to the Patentees—
"It is *a most valuable thing* for butchers."

Mr. GEORGE BLACKMAN, Butcher, of Newport Market, London, writes—
"I find Medlock and Bailey's Patent Preserving Liquid invaluable."

Mr. GEORGE SCARLIT, Butcher, of Notting Hill, London, writes—
"I believe there is nothing to be compared with your Bisulphite."

Mr. ALEXANDER MCALLISTER, Fish and Game Salesman, of Glasgow, states—
"By your Patent Process I have succeeded quite beyond my most sanguine expectations."

THOMAS SUTTON, Esq., B.A., of Rédon, France, writes 27th August, 1868—
"At last I have tried your Bisulphite of Lime, and I find it a grand success. We dined yesterday off a leg of mutton which I had preserved, and found it delicious—undistinguishable from fresh meat, no flavour of the Preservative—rich red gravy—no loss of weight—every word is true that you say in your Pamphlet."

Messrs. HOFER and SCHWABE, of Berlin, in a letter dated 17th September, 1868, write of our Preservative in the following terms :—

"We have much pleasure in informing you to-day that our success with meat as well as beer has been complete beyond expectation."

ADVERTISEMENTS.

THE "TRAVELLER'S KITCHEN"

Stores Heat from 8 to 30 hours, according to Size, so that **A Hot Meal may be Had Miles Away from any Fire.**

S. W. SILVER & Co.,

Sole Licensees and Manufacturers of the

"PATENT NORWEGIAN COOKING APPARATUS AND REFRIGERATOR."

FOUR PRIZE MEDALS AWARDED AT THE PARIS EXHIBITION, 1867.

To the isolating principle is due the heat retaining power of this portable and inexpensive apparatus adapted for use in EVERY DAY LIFE, THE SICK ROOM, and for TRAVELLERS. For Cooking Purposes, by placing the saucepan on an ordinary fire for six minutes after boiling up, sufficient caloric can be collected; the food, preserves, &c., may remain without any attention whatever from eight to thirty hours, according to size of apparatus beyond the usual time allowed, with advantage as regards QUANTITY, QUALITY, and ECONOMY of fuel and labour; all this time the food will remain smoking hot and cannot be over-cooked.

"In connection with the Exhibition, let me call attention to what appears really a valuable invention—the economy of fuel, the hundred applications of such an admirable plan of sparing and saving time and heat. For campaigning what could be better? In the moor, in yachting, in fact, in all cases where the processes of cooking are wasteful and troublesome—above all, in the cottages of the poor—these Norwegian boxes promise to prove of great utility."—*Times.*

"An Invention of particular interest. By employing this Apparatus the essentials of good boiling and stewing are secured, and wastefulness counteracted."—*Pall Mall Gazette.*

"This capital invention is most simple. For travelling it will prove invaluable."—*Land and Water.*

"It cooks and keeps food hot when carried about on a pack-saddle or in a cart."—*Broad Arrow.*

2, 3, & 4, Bishopsgate Within, and 66, & 67, Cornhill, LONDON, E.C.

WORKS, CANAL CUT, LIMEHOUSE, E.

ROYAL MAIL STEAM PACKET COMPANY.—The Steam Ships of this Company carrying H.M. MAILS, and PASSENGERS, GOODS, etc., are despatched from Southampton as follows :—

2nd of each Month for WEST INDIES,	9th of each Month for BRAZIL and RIVER PLATE Routes, viz. :—	17th of each Month for WEST INDIES,
CUBA AND MEXICO,		GREY TOWN,
SANTA MARTHA,		COLON (Aspinwall),
CARTHAGENA,	LISBON,	PANAMA,
COLON (Aspinwall),	ST. VINCENT,	CENTRAL AMERICA,
PANAMA,	(Cape de Verd),	SOUTH PACIFIC,
CENTRAL AMERICA,	PERNAMBUCO,	ACAPULCO,
SOUTH & NORTH PACIFIC,	BAHIA,	MANZANILLO,
SAN FRANCISCO,	RIO DE JANEIRO,	SAN FRANCISCO,
NEW ZEALAND,	MONTE VIDEO,	BRITISH COLUMBIA,
SYDNEY,	BUENOS AYRES.	JAPAN,
MELBOURNE.		CHINA.

RETURN TICKETS, available for Six or Twelve Months according to destination, at a fare and a half.

For particulars of the reduced fares, the abatement in favour of families, and the rates of freight, apply to the Secretary,

J. M. LLOYD, 55, Moorgate-street, London, E.C.

ADVERTISEMENTS.

SADDLES AND HARNESS.

GEORGE SMITH,

WHOLESALE AND RETAIL

SADDLE, HARNESS, AND WHIP MANUFACTURER,

151, STRAND (Next door to Somerset House) LONDON,

HAS ALWAYS ON HAND A LARGE ASSORTMENT OF

SADDLES, BRIDLES, WHIPS, AND HARNESS,

Suitable for all parts of SOUTH AMERICA.

For Town or Camp use, and at very MODERATE CHARGES.

THE SADDLES ARE GUARANTEED TO FIT THE HORSES.

ALL SORTS OF

SPANISH AND MEXICAN SPURS, BITS, BRIDLE & SPUR FURNITURE,

AT MODERATE CHARGES.

G. C. & R. W. FOX & CO.,

FALMOUTH,

IMPERIAL BRAZILIAN VICE-CONSULATE, &c., &c.

MERCHANTS AND SHIP AGENTS.

AGENCY OF

THE LONDON, BELGIUM, BRAZIL, AND RIVER PLATE ROYAL MAIL STEAMSHIP COMPANY, LIMITED,

Whose magnificent Steamers the

CITY OF RIO DE JANEIRO,	CITY OF LIMERICK,
CITY OF BRUSSELS,	CITY OF BUENOS AYRES,

Call at Falmouth on outward and homeward voyages to embark and land passengers, mails, specie, &c.

Letters and Telegrams for Europe and South America have prompt attention.

ORDERS DELIVERED TO VESSELS OFF PORT.

GOOD DOCK ACCOMMODATION, including WHARVES where Vessels discharge Afloat, EXTENSIVE WAREHOUSES, and TWO LARGE GRAVING DOCKS.

ADVERTISEMENTS.

LONDON, BRAZIL, AND RIVER PLATE.

THE LONDON, BELGIUM, BRAZIL, AND RIVER PLATE ROYAL MAIL STEAM SHIP COMPANY'S (Limited) SCREW STEAMERS.

City of Brussels, .	1427 Tons,	250 Horse Power.	
City of Buenos Ayres,	1314 ...	250	...
City of Limerick, .	1450 ...	250	...
City of Rio de Janeiro,	1597 ...	300	...

Are appointed to leave LONDON on 28th, ANTWERP on 1st and FALMOUTH on 3rd of every Month, and will receive Goods until Two days previously.

These Steamers have unusually fine accommodation for Cabin Passengers, at the following Rates, including all necessaries, namely—

Chief Cabin to Rio de Janeiro, £30, to River Plate, £35.
Second do. to Rio de Janeiro or River Plate, £30.

On application to the Brokers, a few Third Class Passengers can be taken to Rio de Janeiro, £14, and to River Plate, £16.

WINES, SPIRITS, AND BEER CAN BE OBTAINED ON BOARD ON REASONABLE TERMS.

EACH STEAMER CARRIES A SURGEON AND STEWARDESS.

Orders will be granted, on payment of passage money, for Railway Tickets from Paddington to Falmouth at 35s. First Class, and 20s. Second Class.

For Freight or Passage apply to the Brokers of the Company,
ALEX. HOWDEN & CO.,
19, BIRCHIN LANE, LONDON, E.C.

ADVERTISEMENTS.

Just Published, 8vo., Cloth Extra, Price 21s.,

EXCHANGE TABLES,

TO CONVERT THE MONEY OF
BRAZIL, THE RIVER PLATE PORTS, CHILI, PERU, CALIFORNIA, AND LISBON, (Milreis and Reis, Dollars and Reals, Dollars and Cents,) INTO BRITISH CURRENCY, AND VICE VERSA, At All Rates of Exchange that Can be Required, varying by eighths of a Penny. By JOHN and CHARLES GARRATT. London: EFFINGHAM WILSON, ROYAL EXCHANGE. Liverpool: WEBB, HUNT, and RIDINGS.

OPINIONS OF THE PRESS.

Mr. Effingham Wilson has published a useful volume of Exchange Tables, to Convert the Money of Brazil, the River Plate Ports, Chili, Peru, California, and Lisbon into British Currency, and *vice versa*. The Authors are Messrs. John and Charles Garrat. Such Tables are invaluable to a Merchant, if correct, and its correctness can only be tested by buying the book and giving it a trial.—*Morning Star.*

The Title of this book speaks for the Contents, which are exceedingly valuable to Mercantile Men. The Tables have been compiled with great care, and the whole are published in a most compact form.—*Liverpool Albion.*

Some very useful "Exchange Tables," prepared by Messrs. John and Charles Garratt have just been published by Mr. Wilson, of the Royal Exchange, the object being to show at a glance the equivalent in British currency of the monies of Brazil, the River Plate Ports, Chili, Peru, California, and Lisbon, and *vice versa*. The rates of exchange progress by eighths of a penny, and are wide enough in their range to meet all fluctuations.—*Daily News.*

This very accurate and exceedingly well-arranged work by Messrs. John and Charles Garratt is one which no person having business relations with the places named can afford to do without. By a tabular arrangement, the method of which it would be difficult to convey in words, the conversion of Milreis, Dollars, Reals, &c., into Sterling Money of the Realm, and the reverse method are reduced into a process of the simplest character. As an adjunct to the ordinary assisting tables of the counting house the volume of Exchange Tables before us is indispensible. If in commerce to save time is a chief desire, the Messrs. Garratt are to be congratulated on their contribution to this end. Indeed every facility afforded to the operations of business is in reality a public boon.—*Liverpool Daily Post.*

The arrangement of these Tables is very clear, and the variations for which calculations are given are both correct—progressing by eighths of a penny—and of more than sufficient range for all practical purposes, beginning, for instance, with Milreis at 15d. p. Milreis and going as high as 29¼d. The introduction and some explanatory matter are in Spanish and Portuguese as well as English, which is used exclusively in the body of the Tables.—*Economist.*

W. T. HOLLAND,

SOUTH WALES POTTERY,

LLANELLY,

CARMARTHENSHIRE,

MANUFACTURER OF BLUE-AND-WHITE EARTHENWARE; Table, Tea, Toilet, &c., in various Colours and Patterns of Printed Earthenware, also Painted, Sponged, Edged, Dipped, and White Ware of good quality for Exportation; goods made light for duties on weight. Shapes and Patterns suitable for various markets. Established 14 years.

CRATES SHIPPED AND PUT FREE ON BOARD AT LLANELLY, or Consigned (at Moderate Rates of Carriage) for Shipment at other ports in South Wales, London, or Liverpool.

SHIPPER OF SOUTH WALES COALS, IRON, TIN PLATES, LEAD, COPPER, YELLOW METAL SHEATHING, &c., at Current Prices. Vessels Chartered, and Shipments made of Earthenware, &c., to best advantage, direct from Llanelly; facilities afforded to Customers, as far as practicable, to make cheap and paying Shipments from Llanelly, the charges on shipping at this port being light, and the articles named can be supplied from Llanelly or its immediate vicinity.

BATES, HENDY, & CO.'S

LIST of FOREIGN and COLONIAL BOOKS, PAMPHLETS,

&c., &c.

Forwarded on receipt of Post Office Order or Stamps.

THE RIVER PLATE (South America) as a FIELD for EMIGRATION: Its Geography, Climate, Agricultural Capabilities, and the Facilities Afforded for Permanent Setlement. WITH IMPORTANT AND USEFUL MAPS. Price 1s. 1d. post free. "I have carefully examined this little book, and am happy to be able to state that the information it contains regarding my country is sound and correct."—*His Excellency N. de la Riestra.*

BRAZIL AS A FIELD FOR EMIGRATION: Its Geography, Climate, Agricultural Capabilities, & the Facilities Afforded for Permanent Settlement. Price 7d. post free.

AN ACCOUNT OF PARAGUAY: Its History, Its People. and Its Government from the French of M. Ch. Quentine. Price 1s. 2d. post free.

ELEVEN DAYS' JOURNEY IN THE PROVINCE OF SAO PAULO, with the Americans, Drs.Gaston and Shaw, and Major Mereweather. By J. J. AUBERTIN, Esq. Price 7d. post free.

BRAZIL AND RIVER PLATE MAIL, AND SOUTH AMERICAN JOURNAL. Published on the 7th and 21st of each month Price Sixpence. Annual Subscription, 14s. when sent to any place where the Postage does not exceed One Penny per issue. Payable in advance. This important Journal is the only Paper published in England devoted to the interests of South America, and is an established authority upon all matters connected therewith. It circulates most extensively throughout Great Britain, as well as in all parts of Brazil, the River Plate, Uruguay, Chili, and Peru.

BRAZIL AND THE RIVER PLATE in 1868. Showing the progress of those countries since 1853. By William Hadfield. With Map and Engraving, price 11s. post free.

THE RIVER PLATE HANDBOOK, GUIDE, DIRECTORY, AND ALMANAC for 1869; comprising the City and Province of Buenos Ayres, the other Argentine Provinces, Monte Video, &c., &c. Price 3s. 9d. post free.

UP THE RIVERS AND THROUGH SOME TERRITORIES of the RIO DE LA PLATA DISTRICTS In SOUTH AMERICA. By THOMAS J. HUTCHINSON, F.R.G.S., F.R.S.L. F.E.S., F.A.S.L., H.B.M. Consul for Rosario, &c., &c., &c. Price 7d. post free.

VENEZUELA; or SKETCHES OF LIFE IN A SOUTH AMERICAN REPUBLIC, with the HISTORY OF THE LOAN of 1864. By EDWARD B. EASTWICK, C.B., F.R.S. Commissioner of the Venezuelan Loan of 1864. Price 16s. 10d. post free.

MAP OF SOUTH AMERICA (LIBRARY), Constructed by A. Keith Johnstone, L.D. F.R.S.E., F.R.G.S. Scale 83 miles to an inch. Price £3 13s. 6d. post free.

LARGE COLOURED MAP OF SOUTH AMERICA; Embracing an enlarged scale of Galapagas Islands, Valparaiso Bay, and a Map of Rio Janeiro and adjoining Country, and of the Rio de La Plata. Mounted on Canvas, in Cloth Case. Price 11s. post free.

THE SOUTH AMERICAN MISSIONARY MAGAZINE. Published on the 1st of January, March, May, July, September, and November. Illustrated, and printed in large clear type. 8vo. Price 2d. post free 3d., or 1s. 6d. per annum, including postage.

MAP OF SOUTH AMERICA: Compact, handsomely coloured, mounted on Canvas, in Cloth Case. Price 3s. 9d. post free.

MAP OF SOUTH AMERICA: Coloured and mounted in a neat Cover. Price 1s. 1d. post free.

MAP OF CENTRAL AMERICA, (BAILY'S). SHEET 7s. 10d. post free, Case 10s. 4d. post free.

MAP OF CENTRAL AMERICA, (Sonnenstern's). Size 42 inches by 39 inches. Four Sheets, Plain, 20s.; Coloured, 25s.; Case 32s. 6d.; Roller, Varnished, 36s.

MAP OF THE REPUBLIC OF MEXICO. By the Brigadier-General Pedro Garcia Conde. Engraved from the Original Survey made by order of the Mexican Government. Size, 52 inches by 40 inches. Sheets. 10s. 6d. Mounted, in Case, 18s.

LIST OF FOREIGN & COLONIAL BOOKS, PAMPHLETS, &c.—(Continued).

MAP OF THE ARGENTINE REPUBLIC; COLOURED, Showing the Regions of the River Plate, &c., and the Railways open for Traffic. Price 4d. post free.

THE COMMERCIAL AND CONSTITUTIONAL LAWS OF BRAZIL. (Now first translated from the Portuguese). By THOMAS SPENCE, Barrister and Brazilian Jurist. Price 7s. 9d. post free.

THE STATES OF THE RIVER PLATE; Their Industries and Commerce, Sheep-Farming, Sheep-Breeding, Cattle-Feeding, and Meat-Preserving, the Employment of Capital, Land and Stock and their Values, Labour and Its Remuneration. By Wilfred Latham, Buenos Ayres. In 1 vol., 8vo., price 12s. 6d. post free.

TRAVELS IN BRAZIL AND BUENOS AYRES, by Mr. HINCHCLIFF. In one vol., post 8vo., with Coloured Maps and Illustrations in Chromo-lithography. Price, 13s.

SOUTH AMERICAN SKETCHES; Or, a visit to Rio de Janeiro, the Organ Mountains, La Plata, and the Parana. By Thomas W. Hinchcliff, M.A., F.R.G.S., Price 12s. 6d.

BUENOS AYRES AND ARGENTINE GLEANINGS; With Extracts from a Diary of Salado Exploration, 1862 and 1863. By T. J. Hutchinson, F.R.G.S., H.B.M.'s, Consul for Rosario; with Maps, Illustrations, and Statistical Tables. Demy 8vo., cloth, price 16s. 6d. post free.

THE PARANA, with INCIDENTS of the PARAGUAYAN WAR, and SOUTH AMERICAN RECOLLECTIONS from 1861 to 1868. By THOMAS J. HUTCHINSON, F.R.G.S., &c.; Consul for Rosario; Author of "Niger-Tshadde-Binue Exploration;" "Impressions of Western Africa;" "Ten Years' Wanderings among the Ethiopians;" "Buenos Ayres and Argentine Gleanings, &c., &c. Price 21s.; post free 21s. 10d.

A LONG VACATION IN THE ARGENTINE ALPS; or where to settle in the River Plate States. By H. C. R. JOHNSON. With Map, price 10s.

MEXICO AND THE MEXICANS. Landscapes and Popular Sketches. By C. Sartorious, Edited by Dr. Gaspy. With Steel Engravings. Price 16s.

BRAZIL AND LA PLATA; the Personal Record of a Cruise. By C. S. Stewart, A.M., U.S.N. Illustrated. Crown 8vo., cloth, 7s.

BRAZIL AND THE BRAZILIANS. By the Rev. J. A. Fletcher and the Rev. D. P. Kidder. 1 vol. 8vo., with 150 Illustrations; an enlarged edition, 19s.; post free 19s. 9d.

BRAZIL: Its Cities and Provinces. By W. Scully. Price 7s. 6d.

JOURNEYS IN BRAZIL. By AGAZY, Post free 22s.

LIMA; Or Sketches of the Capital of Peru. Historical, Statistical, Administrative, Commercial, and Moral. By Manuel A. Fuentes. Price 21s.

CALIFORNIA and Its RESOURCES: a work for the Merchant, the Capitalist, and the Emigrant. By Ernest Seyd. Price 9s. 6d.

THE REPUBLIC OF URUGUAY, Monte Video, GEOGRAPHICAL, SOCIAL and POLITICAL, to which is appended LIFE IN THE RIVER PLATE A MANUAL OF EMIGRATION, with four Maps and Plans, and very numerous Illustrations. Price 1s. 1d. post free.

COLLOQUIAL PORTUGUESE: or, The Words and Phrases of Every-day Life, compiled from Dictation and Conversation for the Use of English Tourists and Visitors in Portugal, the Brazils, Madeira, and the Azores, with a Brief Collection of Epistolary Phrases, by the Rev. A. J. D. D'ORSEY, B.D. Price 3s. 6d., post free 3s. 8d.

GRAMMAR OF PORTUGUESE AND ENGLISH. EXHIBITING in a series of Exercises in double translation the IDIOMATIC STRUCTURE of both languages, as now written and spoken, adapted to OLLENDORF's System. Price 7s.; post free 7s. 6d.

A NEW POCKET DICTIONARY of the PORTUGUESE and ENGLISH LANGUAGES in two parts viz., PORTUGUESE and ENGLISH—ENGLISH and PORTUGUESE; abridged from VIEYRA's DICTIONARY. Price 10s., complete in two vols. Post free 10s. 6d.

THE ASIATIC, published every Saturday morning (a third edition being posted to subscribers in the East on Friday evenings), contains all the news having relation to matters transpiring in this country in any way connected with the East, and also correspondents letters from India, Ceylon, &c., &c. Price 7d. post free, when the postage does not exceed one penny per issue.

STEAM NAVIGATION DIRECT TO Australia and New Zealand, via The Cape of Good Hope. By W. LONG WEST, a New Zealand Colonist. Price 7d. post free.

HINTS TO INTENDING SHEEP-FARMERS IN NEW ZEALAND. By F. A. WELD, Esq., of Flaxbourn, New Zealand, with an Appendix, containing an epitome of the Land Regulations of the different Provinces. Price 9d. post free.

LIST OF FOREIGN & COLONIAL BOOKS, PAMPHLETS, &c.—(*Continued*).

A SHORT SYNOPTICAL VIEW OF THE "NEW ZEALAND OF TO-DAY," offered to those who are seeking Occupations, Employments, Investments, or New Careers, &c., &c., &c. By C. F. HURSTHOUSE. Price 7d. post free.

THE NEW ZEALAND HANDBOOK; or, Guide to the "Britain of the South," with Practical Information and Advice for all orders of Emigrants, from the "Capitalist" to the "Working Man." With Two Coloured Maps. Price 1s. 2d. post free.

NEW ZEALAND IN 1867, Considered as A FIELD FOR INVESTMENT OF CAPITAL. By W. LONG WREY, of the Province of Nelson. Price 1s. 1d. post free.
"Gives much information concerning the physical features and resources of the three islands. . . . We heartily commend it to all who are interested in our colonies."—*Field*.
"A clear straightforward line of argument is adopted throughout by the author"—*Era*.
"Will be found a most serviceable guide."—*Observer*.

NEW ZEALAND AS IT WAS AND AS IT IS, with Coloured Map. By ROBERT BATEMAN PAUL, M.A., late Archdeacon of Nelson. Price 7d. post free.

NEW ZEALAND THE "BRITAIN OF THE SOUTH." By CHARLES HURSTHOUSE. With an Appendix on the native War in New Zealand, and our future Native Policy. A new and cheaper Edition, thoroughly revised and corrected to the present time, 1 vol. post 8vo. with Maps. Price 15s. 6d. post free.

VOICES FROM NEW ZEALAND: Being a compilation of authentic letters from Emigrants who have located in New Zealand since 1863; also a series of questions answered. By S. BRAME. Price 7d. post free.

STANFORD'S MAP OF NEW ZEALAND, Coloured, in Blue Cloth Case. Price 9s. 9d. post free.

STANFORD'S MAP of NEW ZEALAND. Size, 17 by 14 inches, compiled from the most recent Documents. Price full coloured, 3s. 9d. post free.

LIFE'S WORK AS IT IS; Or The Emigrant's Home in Australia, by a colonist. This is a very unique and interesting book, and contains some very practical hints to Emigrants. Handsomely bound in Red Cloth, price 3s. 8d. post free.

TWELVE YEARS IN CANTERBURY, NEW ZEALAND, with visits to the other Provinces, and Reminiscences of the Route Home. Through Australia, &c. (from a Lady's Journal). Price, handsomely bound in stiff blue cloth cover, 3s. 8d. post free.

THE GREAT WEST; Travellers' Miners' and Emigrants' Guide and Handbook to the Western, North Western, and Pacific States, and Territories, with a Map of the BEST ROUTES to the GOLD AND SILVER MINES, and complete Tables of distances across the American Continent, by C. H. Hall. Price 1s. 2d. post free.

CANADA IN 1868, As a field for Emigration. A handy book for settlers. Price 7d. post free.

CANADA IN 1864: A Handbook for Settlers, by Henry T. Newton Cheshire, late R.N., author of "Recollection of a Five Years' Residence in Norway." Strongly bound in Cloth, price 2s. 8d. post free.

THE CAPE COLONY IN 1868. A Handbook for intending Settlers. Price 7d. post free.

THE SOUTH AFRICAN GOLD FIELDS. A narrative of discovery, together with a description of the Gold Fields, and of the best routes to them, accompanied by a Chart. Price 1s. 1d. post free.

BATES, HENDY & CO.'S MERCANTILE HANDBOOK AND DIARY FOR INDIA, CHINA. AND THE COLONIES, for 1869; comprising a Diary and Directory of British Manufacturers, specially adapted for the Use of Merchants Abroad. Price 2s. 4d. post free.

European Summary Editions of all the Foreign and Colonial Newspapers, may be had at BATES, HENDY & CO.'S Offices, on the arrival of the Mails; and also the Magazines that are published abroad.

Advertisements and Subscriptions received for all the Foreign and Colonial Newspapers, Files of which are kept at the Offices of BATES, HENDY & CO., and are open to the inspection of all persons desiring information.

www.ingramcontent.com/pod-product-compliance
Lightning Source LLC
Chambersburg PA
CBHW032053230426
43672CB00009B/1578